THE ONLY WAY TO...
LEARN
ASTROLOGY
VOLUME II

MATH & INTERPRETATION
TECHNIQUES

Also by ACS Publications, Inc.

THE ONLY WAY TO...

LEARN ASTROLOGY

VOLUME II

MATH & INTERPRETATION TECHNIQUES

BY MARION D. MARCH & JOAN McEVERS

International Standard Book Number 0-917086-26-0

Printed in the United States of America

Published by ACS Publications, Inc.
P.O. Box 16430
San Diego, CA 92116-0430

First printing, July, 1981
Second printing, December, 1982
Third printing, October, 1983
Fourth printing, April, 1985

We dedicate this book to our students who urged, cajoled and even pushed us into writing down what we've been "teaching and preaching," for many years.

Contents

Foreword   1
Preface   3

Part I

Lesson 1: General Rules, Abbreviations, Tools Needed   5
Tools Needed to Erect a Horoscope 7   Notes on Longitude and
Latitude 7   Notes on Time 8   Time Zone Map 10   To Convert Standard
Time 11   To Convert Distance Into Time 11

Lesson 2: Formulas for Noon Math West of Greenwich   13
Formula 1: To Find the Houses for an A.M. Birth 13   Formula 2: To Find the
Positions of the Planets 16   Log Table 18   Formula 3: To Correct Planet
Positions 21   Formula 4: To Find the Houses for a PM Birth 25   Formula 5:
When LMT and GMT are both A.M. 27

Lesson 3: Formulas for Noon Math Other Locations   29
Formula 6: Math for East of Greenwich 29   Formula 7: Math for South of the
Equator 32   Formula 8: Quick and Easy Math 35

**Lesson 4: Formulas for Midnight Math and Unknown Birth
Times**   39
Formula 9: Midnight Math - AM Chart 39   Formula 10: Midnight Math -PM
Chart 40   Formula 11: Midnight Math - PM Chart 41   Explanations for
Formulas 9, 10, and 11 42   To find the GMT and Constant Log and Correct
Planets 43   Formula 12: Quick and Easy Math for Midnight 44   If there is
No Birthtime Available? 45   Quiz for Part One - Math 48

Part II

Introduction   53
Steps to Refine Delineation

**Lesson 5: Standouts — Lack of Element, Lack of Quality, Lack of House
Emphasis and Unaspected Planets**   55
The Lack of an Element in the Horoscope 55   The Lack of a Quality in the
Horoscope 60   Lack of House Emphasis 62   The Unaspected Planet 65

**Lesson 6: Standouts Continued — Lack of a Specific Aspect, Configura-
tions and Final Signature**   77
The Lack of Specific Aspects 77   Configurations 83   The Grand
Cross 84   The T-Square 84   The Stellium 87   The Yod 88   The
Grand Trine 89   The Final Signature 91   Sub-Signature 95

Lesson 7: Retrograde Planets   97
Lesson 8: Intercepted Signs and Houses   105
Intercepted Signs 106   Intercepted Houses 108

**Lesson 9: Mutual Reception, Final Dispositor, Chart Ruler, Planet in
High Focus**   111
Final Dispositor and High-Focus Planet 112   The Chart Ruler 114

Lesson 10: Chart Patterns   117
Lesson 11: The Overview of the Chart   125
Lesson 12: Decanates and Dwads   129
Lesson 13: The Lunar Nodes   133

Lesson 14: Delineating The House Cusps **137**

Aries on the House Cusps 138   Taurus on the House Cusps 142   Gemini on the House Cusps 146   Cancer on the House Cusps 149   Leo on the House Cusps 152   Virgo on the House Cusps 156   Libra on the House Cusps 159   Scorpio on the House Cusps 162   Sagittarius on the House Cusps 166   Capricorn on the House Cusps 169   Aquarius on the House Cusps 172   Pisces on the House Cusps 177   How to Delineate the Cusps of the Houses 180

Lesson 15: Aspects to the Ascendant and Midheaven **183**

Quiz for Part Two 203

Part III

Introduction **207**

Steps to Give You Further Insight

Lesson 16: Planets in Oriental Appearance, the Prenatal Eclipse, the Vertex **209**

Planets in Oriental Appearance 209   Eclipses 210   Eclipse Table 211   The Vertex Point 215

Lesson 17: Arabian Parts **217**

Lesson 18: Fixed Stars and Critical Degrees **223**

Fixed Stars 223   Fixed Star Table 225   Critical Degrees 226

Lesson 19: Earth **229**

Using the Position of the Earth in the Natal Horoscope

Lesson 20: Steps to Delineation **231**

Appendix **235**

Horoscope Calculation for Part One Math (Disney) 235 (Fawcett) 237   Anwers to Quiz No. 1 239   Answer to Review Question - Lesson 7 239   Answer to Review Question -Lesson 8 240   Answer to Review Question - Lesson 9 241   Answer to Review Question - Lesson 10 242   Answer to Review Question -Lesson 11 243   Answer to Review Questions - Lesson 12 244   Answer to Review Question - Lesson 13 245   Answer to Review Question - Lesson 14 245   Answer to Review Question - Lesson 15 246   Answers to Quiz - Part Two 247   Answer to Review Question - Lesson 16 247   Lesson 17 -Calculations for Arabian Parts 248   Answers to Review Questions -Lesson 18 249

Meet the Authors **251**

INDEX OF HOROSCOPES (In alphabetical order)

Baker, Howard	72	Keller, Helen	59
Beatrix, Queen	83	Kennedy, John	75
Benny, Jack	57	Kennedy, Ted	73
Blue, Vida	69	Killy, Jean Claude	123
Brando, Marlon	89	Lawrence, T.E.	67
Bruce, Lenny	123	Leary, Timothy	64
Carter, Rosalyn	124	Lindbergh, Charles	78
Chamberlain, Richard	122	Mancini, Herny	121
Chopin, Frederic	115	Mehta, Zubin	122
Cosell, Howard	113	Namath, Joe	121
Dickinson, Emily	82	Nash, Graham	99
Disney, Walt	236	Nash, Ogden	72
Douglas, Mike	67	Nehru, Jawaharial	88
Dylan, Bob	110	Patton, George	86
Eastwood, Clint	80	Picasso, Pablo	87
Fawcett, Farrah	238	Pyle, Ernie	57
Field, Sally	73	Ronstadt, Linda	99
Flynn, Errol	61	Rooney, Mickey	70
Freud, Sigmund	124	Schweitzer, Albert	85
Gabor, Zsa Zsa	92	Sinatra, Frank	75
Gandhi, Mohandas	70	Smith, Robyn	68
Goldwyn, Samuel	64	Stalin, Joseph	92
Hauptmann, Bruno	61	Streisand, Barbra	79
Hearts, Patricia	63	Sutherland, Joan	34
Hesse, Hermann	31	Toscanini, Arturo	63
Hitler, Adolf	59	Van Gogh, Vincent	66
Hutton, Barbara	66	Welles, Orson	81

We wish to acknowledge the invaluable help of LOIS RODDEN, who with her diligent research for good birth data has enabled all of us to work with more accurate horoscopes.

In accordance with her system we have labeled all horoscope data as:
A - accurate data
B - biographies or autobiographies
C - caution, no source of origin
DD - dirty data, more than one time/date/place

Foreword

Astrology, like every other systematic body of knowledge, should be taught by the teacher and learned by the student in a logical and systematic way. While there are many astrology books available on the market today, few indeed could be termed textbooks in the sense that they could be used in the manner that our schools and universities use them upon which to build a systematic course outline. Fewer still provide homework assignments and test quizzes. This series of volumes fills this need remarkably well.

Over the years, I have had the opportunity to observe the authors of this book in action, to observe their classes, and to see for myself how rapidly their students gain mastery over the astrological material presented in this series of books. I know that their method of presenting this material works because I have taught their students myself. In my own classes, the March-McEvers students are truly stand-outs and superior students. They are easier to teach because they have been fully grounded in, and have mastered, these basics. The material presented in this series of volumes is their secret of successful teaching—not necessarily the basic material which can be found in many other books, but the method, manner and the sequence in which it is taught. Their true secret is the way in which they involve the student in the learning process. It is not enough for the student to listen and take notes. There must be a personal involvement, through thoughtful homework assignments and quizzes if the knowledge presented is to be truly learned and understood.

Particularly outstanding in this volume are the lessons covering "Aspects to the Ascendant and Midheaven" and "Delineating the House Cusps". These descriptions are unique in the sense that the material is fresh and new, based upon the authors' personal observations of real people in the process of living out their horoscopes. While practically every teacher of basic Astrology has his or her own special system for teaching the mathematics of chart erection, the method presented here can be adapted easily to any system of teaching this vital part of basic astrology. I am also particularly impressed by the way in which the authors have placed the various components of chart delineation in their proper perspective—their way of putting first things first.

Sir Isaac Newton said: "To be able to say, he (or she) was my student, to be able to support the weight of even one student who stands on your shoulders, and is able to see perhaps a bit farther than you, ought to be the goal of every teacher." Marion March and Joan McEvers have gladly accepted this burden, and in so doing, have truly given us a superior textbook series in astrology from which all can learn and profit.

Robert Carl Jansky
Van Nuys, California

Preface

In Volume One of *The Only Way to...Learn Astrology* we incorporated the basics of Astrology—the signs of the zodiac, the planets, the houses, the aspects and the interrelationship of the principles involved. We taught you how to interpret a natal horoscope by using keywords and key phrases only as they apply to the horoscope in question, and by using judgment and discrimination in your choice. In this second volume we give you additional tools for chart delineation. This book is divided into three parts:

Part I   Provides the mathematical tools to calculate or erect the horoscope.

Part II   Provides tools to refine your interpretive ability—additional information that enables you to find some of the less obvious areas in the horoscope.

Part III   Provides tools to gain further insight, but in a more psychological or subconscious way, by showing you some of the sensitive points in each chart.

The teaching in this book is on a basic level, and follows our Aquarius Workshops teaching outline. It is again in the form of lessons, rather than chapters, and each lesson is based on many years of teaching experience; therefore, we are able to anticipate most of your questions. Also, as we did in Volume One, we have included homework with each lesson. Again speaking from experience, we must warn you that the old Chinese proverb is true: "You see and you forget, you hear and you remember, you write and you understand". Unless you *write the homework*, unless you try out the formulas for yourself—you will forget, and what is worse, you will not understand the basic nature of Astrology and the principles involved in delineation. We have been most fortunate in the percentage of *good* astrologers as a result of our teaching method. However, these good ones got there by doing a great deal of charting between lessons, by copying the notes into their notebooks, by reading and re-reading, trying and re-trying to blend the many different qualities that make up one human being. As you understand the basic nature of each sign, planet, house and aspect, your own logic will guide you. Our explanations, examples, words and phrases are here as guidelines only, never to be used literally. If something does not make sense to you, if you cannot explain it in your own logical terms, don't use it! And we *mean* that.

By the time you have finished this book, you will be ready to delineate any chart in a basic interpretation. You may not be able to determine all of the lesser potentials, characteristics or psychological needs. To do this you have to spend a few years interpreting charts of people who can tell you whether you are right or wrong. But most of all, you have to realize that each individual has his own free will and therefore a choice as to which parts of the horoscope he will use. You must understand this and not be thrown when the individual tells you "Me, career oriented? Heavens no, I'm a homebody!" after you've seen a stellium in his 10th house. You must grasp the meaning and then be able to guide this person in the right direction; that takes time, practice and understanding of human nature or psychological insight. So please do not get discouraged; practice makes the master.

Good luck to you, and may the knowledge of Astrology bring you new insights into yourself and others.

Joan McEvers and Marion March

Lesson 1
General Rules, Abbreviations, Tools Needed

As we have stressed throughout Volume 1 of *The Only Way to...Learn Astrology,* our books are not the run-of-the-mill astrology books. They are textbooks or manuals taken from our years of classroom experience. Therefore, our approach to teaching you the mathematics of erecting a horoscope will also be different. We begin by giving you the full formula, or dummy sheet, for chart casting, and then, step-by-step, we explain the whys, hows, and wherefores.

First there are some basic rules that you must learn, and there are also some tools you will need.

Rule Number 1   In order to erect an accurate natal horoscope, you need the correct time of birth. The most valid source for birthtime information in the United States is the True Certified Copy of your Birth Certificate on file with the State Board of Health in the state of your birth. For directions and guidance in obtaining a copy of this record send your request to the Bureau of Vital Statistics, Board of Health, in the capital city of the state where you were born. Ask for the Birth Registration with the time listed, also called the long form.

If this document fails to indicate the birth time (which frequently happens), then you will have to turn to some other source for this data, a baby book, a birth announcement, the family Bible, or hospital records where available. The personal recollection of family members like "mother thinks it was about six in the morning" is generally not good enough. For even though your mother was certainly there, she was concerned with more pressing matters than watching the clock, and memories of birth dim with passing time. Base your source for the birth time upon a *written record*, whenever possible, even when a search requires persistence, diligence, effort and time, or you may later discover that your mathematical efforts in erecting a horoscope have been for nought. If, after such a search, you are still unable to determine an accurate time of birth, explain to the person that you cannot guarantee an accurate interpretation. This will save you embarassment.

There is an astrological axiom that you should remember: "The accuracy of your interpretation can be no greater than the accuracy of the birthtime, date, and latitude and longitude used to erect the horoscope." Because of the speed of the earth's rotation, a new degree of the zodiac crosses over the Midheaven every four minutes. Some horoscopes are so time sensitive that an error of four minutes in the birth time can change the house or sign position of one or more planets, and thus, the interpretation given.

Use every means at your disposal to get the most accurate birth data possible.

Rule Number 2   The reference books that you will be using have many abbreviations. Memorize them. Here is a list of abbreviations that you will find most frequently:

ST	Standard Time	DST	Daylight Saving Time
EST	Eastern Standard Time	EDT	Eastern Daylight Time
CST	Central Standard Time	CDT	Central Daylight Time
MST	Mountain Standard Time	MDT	Mountain Daylight Time
PST	Pacific Standard Time		
WT	War Time	PDT	Pacific Daylight Time
LMT	Local Mean Time	PM	Prime Meridian
GMT	Greenwich Mean Time	LMTI	Local Mean Time Interval
ST	Sidereal (Star) Time		
PLR	Planet Logarithm	EGMT	Equivalent Greenwich Mean Time, same as LTE
CL	Constant Logarithm or Constant Log		
LTE	Longitude Time Equivalent, same as EGMT	TCST	True Calculated Sidereal Time

Rule Number 3   Memorize the following mathematical equivalents:

60" (seconds)   =   1' (minute)
60' (minutes)   =   1° (degree) or 1 hour
30° (degrees)   =   1 sign
12 signs   =   360° or the entire zodiac and the circumference of the horoscopic wheel

Rule Number 4   Even to the most experienced professional astrologer it is important that all mathematical calculations used in erecting the horoscope be preserved, for a variety of reasons. We highly recommend that as you proceed you do the math on the blank side of the chart form you use. Check and recheck your calculations for possible errors. Other astrologers will judge your professional competence on your ability to accurately erect a natal horoscope. Start right now to develop the habit of checking and rechecking your work. On all horoscope forms, and on the dummy sheet you will shortly be using, develop the habit of filling in *all* of the blanks. They are there for a purpose — use them! *Neatness is imperative!*

Basic Reference Tools Needed to Ereect a Horoscope

1. Ephemeris (pronounded ef-EM-er-is) This is the basic reference book that provides the exact daily position of each planet at a stated time (either Noon or Midnight) for Greenwich, England which is at exactly 0° of longitude. These ephemerides can be purchased for one year, ten-year intervals, and some for hundred-year intervals. Some ephemerides are more accurate than others. For accuracy, one of the newest ephemerides is *The American Ephemeris* published by ACS Publications, Inc. It is available for either noon or midnight. Other reliable ephemeris are: *Simmons 1890-1950, Raphael's* published in one-year editions, the German *Die Deutsche Ephemeride*, and the *Hieratic 1890-1950, 1950-2000*.

2. *American Atlas; U.S. Latitudes and Longitudes, Time Changes and Time Zones* by ACS Publications, Inc.

3. *The International Atlas; World Latitudes, Longitudes, Time Changes and Time Zones* published by ACS Publications, Inc.

4. *Time Changes in the U.S.* are included in *The American Atlas.*

5. *Koch Book of Tables* published by ACS Publications, Inc. There are many different Tables of Houses — all valid and each having its own supporters. We recommend Koch, it follows the Placidus system but bases the intermediate house cusps on geographical location.

Some Notes on Longitude and Latitude

Geographically, the Earth is divided by two imaginary sets of circles. One set of circles uses the Equator as a reference point, running from East to West, and is used to measure distance North or South of the Equator. This is called *Latitude.*

Turn to the map on page 10 and note that there are numbers given in the lefthand borders of the map. These latitude measurements are commonly referred to as *parallels.* Locate the 40th parallel as it extends across the map. Note that Denver, Colorado, is located very close to this line. Therefore, we would describe Denver as being at a latitude of about 40° *North* of the Equator. Philadelphia is also located on this line, and is thus at the same latitude as Denver.

Since both of these places have approximately the same latitude, we must find another way to locate them so as to differentiate one city from the other.

We stated earlier that the Earth is divided by *two* sets of circles. The second set of imaginary circles divides the Earth longitudinally from pole to pole—these are the *Meridians of Longitude.* All places on the same longitude line have noon at the same instant, no matter how far North or South of the Equator they are.

If you look at the map on page 10 you will see numbered lines running from top to bottom. These are the lines of longitude, and the one numbered 0° is the Prime Meridian at Greenwich, England. All places in the world are considered to be East or West of Greenwich, or the 0° (Prime) Meridian.

So, by longitude we designate a geographic location as being East or West of Greenwich, and by latitude we designate a location North or South of the Equator.

When you say that some place is at such and such longitude and latitude, it indicates a certain place beyond all possibility of confusion. Thus, Denver is 104°W59' 39°N45', Philadelphia is at 75°W11' 39°N37', and even though they are both near the same degree of latitude, the longitude distinguishes and locates them as being in two entirely different locations on the Earth's surface.

Some Notes on Time

Time on Earth is based upon the motion of the Earth around the Sun. As earthlings, we like a certain order in our lives and want to know what day it is, what time, what year, what month, and so on. In order to do this, we have to go against the true laws of nature, since the Earth does not move at a constant speed. So, the day does not have exactly 24 hours, and at the end of every four years we have to add an extra day (leap year) to compensate for our irregular motion. This same principle of being practical applies to the time zones or Prime Meridians established on Earth.

The Sun in relationship to the Earth appears to move 60 miles every four minutes. 60 miles equals 1° on the map. Therefore, the Sun's motion is 2° in eight minutes, 5° in 20 minutes, and 15° in 60 minutes, or in 1 hour. For every 15° the Sun is one hour away from the 0° Prime Meridian at Greenwich. Since the Sun rises in the East and sets in the West, if it is noon at Greenwich and we go 30° to the East, it will be 2:00 PM; the Sun has already been there and gone. On the other hand, if we go 60° West of Greenwich, we know that it must be four hours earlier (60 ÷ 15 = 4). The Sun going from East to West has not yet reached this point; therefore, 12 noon at 0° Prime Meridian will be 8:00 AM at 60° West.

To simplify matters, most Prime Meridians are established at intervals of 15° longitude, or one additional hour for each PM. In the United States and Canada, these PM's are subtitled Standard Time. The United States is divided into four time zones, since most of the continental U.S. falls between 65° and 125° West Longitude. (See the map on page 10.) New York City is located at 73°W57' and thus falls in the 75°W PM, or 5 hours earlier (West) than Greenwich.   In fact, the entire State of New York uses the 75°W PM; thus, if it's noon in Greenwich, it is 7:00 AM clock time in all of New York state.   This is called 7:00 AM EST (Eastern Standard Time).   But, in true time (according to the Sun), is it really 7:00 AM EST everywhere in New York State?   Of course not.   It is 7:00 AM only in those towns that are located exactly on the 75°W PM.   New York City at 73°W57' is 1°03' (' = minutes) east of the PM, or that much closer to Greenwich than the 75°W PM.   Therefore, it would actually be later in New York City than the actual PM of 5 hours difference.

To figure this difference exactly you must convert distance (73°W57') into time.   The formula for doing this is: *Multiply by 4 and divide the result by 60.*   Remember, the Sun travels 4 minutes in 60 miles, or 1°.   1° also equals 1 hour or 60 minutes when converted into time from distance.   73 × 4 = 292; 292 divided by 60 is equal to 4 hours and 52 minutes.   57' × 4 = 228; 228 divided by 60 is equal to 3 minutes and 48 seconds.   Your total conversion reads: 4 hr. 55' 48'', or 4' 12'' later than 7:00 AM clock time.   [5 hr. 00' 00'' − 4 hr. 55' 48'' = 4' 12''] To recheck the accuracy of your math, subtract 73°W57' from 75°W00' = 1°03'.   Multiply this by 4, which equals 4' 12'' and you know that you've calculated correctly.

Thus, the LMT (Local Mean Time) for New York City is 7 hr. 04' 12''.   Just remember East of the PM it is later than Greenwich and you have to add the time. West of the PM it is earlier than Greenwich and you have to subtract the time. In the dummy sheet we will show you, step-by-step, how and when to do this; however, you should understand the principle which necessitates this correction.

There is another time problem that needs your careful attention: Daylight Savings Time (also called War Time in times of war). This is an artificial arrangement which needs to be accounted for in chart calculation. The books mentioned on page 7 are extremely helpful in finding out what areas were on War Time or Daylight Savings Time and when. Until 1971, each state and county did pretty much as they pleased about this. In the United States, a federal law was finally adopted to avoid confusion and the entire country now starts DST on the last Sunday in April and goes back to regular ST on the last Sunday in October. From February 9, 1942 until September 30, 1945, the entire U.S. observed War Time. In Western Europe, all countries except Switzerland now observe DST. In 1974 we had an energy crisis and the entire U.S., except for Arizona, Idaho, and Oregon, went on DST on January 6 until October 27. In Illinois and Pennsylvania, the clocks are set to DST, but not in the hospitals. Until very recently (1959 in Illinois), they continued to use Standard Time. Unless you refer to the *American Atlas* or *Time Changes* books, you will have to consult your library or some other official source for accurate information. War Time and Daylight Savings Time set the clock one hour ahead, so you must subtract one hour from the given birth time before you start your calculations.

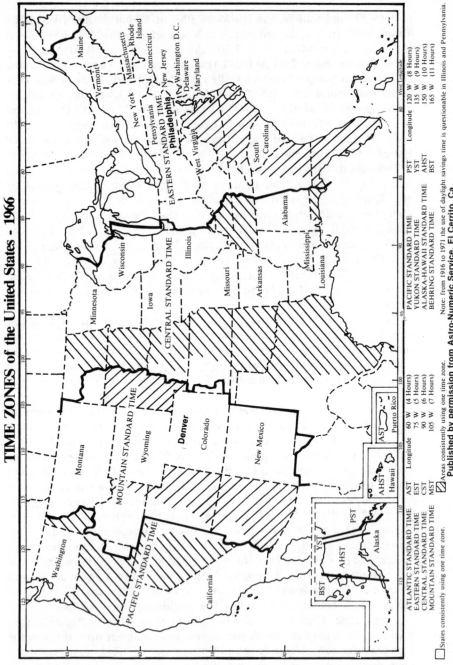

TIME ZONES of the United States - 1966

To Convert Standard Time (based on a Prime Meridian) to Local Mean Time

Local time zones are based on the Prime Meridian. Eastern Standard Time at 75W; Central Standard Time at 90W; Mountain Standard Time at 105W; Pacific Standard Time at 120W.

Los Angeles is on Pacific Standard Time but is located at 118W15 or 1° and 45' East of the Prime Meridian of 120W.

The Sun moves 60 miles or 1° each 4 minutes, thus 1°= 4' and 45' = ¾ ° or 3'. 4'+3' = 7' Meridian Correction which is added, because Los Angeles is located East of the Prime Meridian.

Rule For East of any Prime Meridian *add*. For West of any Prime Meridian *subtract*.

For example: Chicago, Illinois is located at 87W39. The Prime Meridian, is 90°, therefore Chicago is 2° and 21' East of the Prime Meridian. Multiply 2°21' by 4 in order to arrive at the Meridian Correction (also called Local Mean Time-LMT-variation from standard time). 2°× 4 = 8'   21'×4 = 84'' or 1'24''   Add 8' + 1'24'' = 9'24 which is your Meridian Correction and is added to clock time since Chicago is East of the Prime Meridian.

To Convert Distance Into Time or to Convert to Equivalent Greenwich Meantime

To do the EGMT correction for Chicago at 87W39 multiply by 4 and divide by 60.

$$
\begin{array}{ll}
87° & 39' \\
\times 4 & \times 4 \\
348 \div 60 = 5^h\ 48' & 156 \div 60 = 2'36''\ \text{Add these figures} \\
\quad\quad + 2'36'' & \\
5^h\ 50'36''\ \text{is the EGMT for Chicago} &
\end{array}
$$

To do the EGMT correction for San Francisco, California located at 122W26.

$$
\begin{array}{ll}
122° & 26' \\
\times 4 & \times 4 \\
488 \div 60 = 8^h\ 08' & 104 \div 60 = 1'44''\ \text{Add these figures} \\
\quad\quad + 1'44'' & \\
8^h\ 09'44''\ \text{is the EGMT for San Francisco} &
\end{array}
$$

Rule All corrections for West of Greenwich are added. All corrections for East of Greenwich are subtracted.

Much of this work is already done for you in the *American Atlas* but we feel you need to understand the basic principle involved. Also, many people are born in small towns not listed in any of the books.

Sidereal Time (or Star Time)   You will encounter this time term many times in astrology. It is related to the motion of the zodiac—starting at the 0 point of Aries—as LMT is related to the Sun's motion. Since 0 Aries rises and sets faster than the Sun, Sidereal Time is faster than, or ahead of solar time. Most ephemerides list sidereal times for each day, so you will not have to do your own calculating. However, we want you to understand this term when you see it.

Lesson 2
Formulas for Noon Math West of Greenwich

Formula 1: To Find the Houses for an A.M. Birth (using a Noon Ephemeris)

Date: July 12, 1977   Time: 10:30 AM PDT   Place: Los Angeles, CA

Find the longitude and latitude of Los Angeles in the Atlas: 118W15-34N03.
Find the Meridian Correction: +7 minutes. Find the EGMT: +7 hours 53
minutes. Check in Atlas or Time Changes in last column to see if Daylight
Saving Time is observed.

	H.M.S.		
a.	10:30:00	AM	Time of Birth PDT 7/12/1977
b.	− 1:00:00		Subtract 1 hour for Daylight Saving Time
	9:30:00	AM	PST 7/12/1977
c.	+ 7:00		meridian correction (add 7' because L.A. is East of the Standard Meridian)
	9:37:00	AM	LMT (Local Mean Time)
d.	+ 12:00:00		Add 12 hours because this is an AM birth and you must account for time elapsed until noon.
	21:37:00		LMTI (Local Mean Time Interval)
e.	+ 3:36		Add LMTI correction $(21^h37' \div 6 = 3'36'')$
f.	+ 1:19		Add EGMT correction $(7^h53' \div 6 = 1'19'')$
g.	+ 7:17:08		Add Sidereal Time for 7/11/77 (previous day, because this is an AM chart) Found in Ephemeris.
h.	28:58:63		Convert
i.	28:59:03		Because this figure is more than 24 hours, you must subtract 24 hours or 1 sidereal day.
	− 24:00:00		
j.	4:59:03		TCST (True Calculated Sidereal Time)

Open Koch Table of Houses to Sidereal Time closest to this figure (4:59:11) and find the Midheaven or 10th house cusp (16   ). Go down page to proper latitude (34 N is closest) and find the intermediate house cusps. Fill in the wheel (see page 15). The Table of Houses gives the 10th to the 3rd house cusps. The 4th to the 9th are the same degree and minute, but the opposite signs.

If the person is born at 12 AM (midnight) use 0:00:00 AM.

Always check if the Sun falls in the correct house. A person born near noon will have a 9th or 10th house Sun; born early in the morning the Sun should be near the Ascendant, born around midnight will result in a 3rd or 4th house Sun and so on.

Explanation for Formula 1

There are two distinct procedures in erecting a natal (or radix) horoscope. One calculation enables you to find the correct house cusps; the other corrects the planets for the exact time of birth.

Step One On our dummy sheet on page 13, by following steps (a) through (j), you will arrive at the True Calculated Sidereal Time, which will give you the house cusps.

a. Time given for this birth is 10:30 AM PDT, 7/12/77. Check the time table in the *American Atlas* and you will find that Daylight Saving Time is observed.

b. Since July 1977 falls in a DST period, subtract 1 hour. The actual birthtime thus becomes 9:30 AM.

c. Add a 7' correction to the birthtime. You find this by subtracting the EGMT of 7:53 from the Pacific Time Zone of 8:00 (it's in the 3rd column in Dernay's *Longitude and Latitude* book) therefore, the LMT (Local Mean Time) is 9:37 AM.

d. Add 12 hours for AM birth. In using a Noon Ephemeris, the time elapsed until Noon has to be accounted for, so add 12 hours to all AM births. This gives the LMTI (Local Mean Time Interval).

e. Add the LMTI correction. Though the Earth is called round, it is not perfectly shaped. It has a slight bulge, which gives its rotation a wobble and throws off perfect timing. In order to account for this 10" (second) per hour wobble, you must divide the LMTI by 6 hours. The LMTI is 21^h and 37'. Convert into minutes and divide by 6 [1297 ÷ 6 = 216" or 3'36"]. There is a much faster formula. Divide 21 by 6 = 3. Put this figure in the minute column. The remainder of 3 goes in the second column. Then divide 37 by 6 and put those 6 seconds where they belong. Use whichever method is easier for you.

f. Add the EGMT correction. This is the second correction for the Earth's wobble; the correction for the time difference between Los Angeles and Greenwich. Divide the EGMT ($7^h53'$), by 6^h. You have obtained this from the *American Atlas* or the *Longitude & Latitudes* book (column 4) or figured as on page 9. Use the division method given above. The correction is 1' 19".

g. Add the Sidereal Time for July 11, 1977. This is found in the ephemeris. When using a Noon ephemeris, use the Sidereal Time of the previous day for all births that take place before noon.

Date 7/12/77   **Time** 10:30 AM PDT   **Place** Los Angeles, California   **Long.** 118W15   **Lat.** 34N03

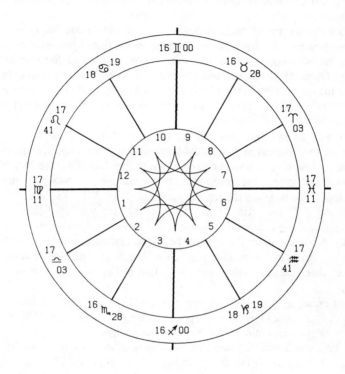

h. Add the four calculations: the LMTI + LMTI correction + EGMT correction + the Sidereal Time and keep in mind that you are dealing with 60 seconds per minute and 60 minutes per hour. Therefore, the total 28 hours, 58 minutes, and 63 seconds must be converted to 28 hours, 59 minutes, and 03 seconds.

i. Since the science of mathematics is very logical, no day has more than 24 hours, so you must subtract 24 hours whenever the final figure exceeds 24.

j. In this way you arrive at the TCST (True Calculated Sidereal Time) of 04:59:03. Open the Table of Houses (we are using Koch) and at the top of the page look for the closest time to the TCST. On page 43 in the lefthand column you will find 4^{h}59'11", which is only 8" in variation from the TCST, and is therefore close enough.

Right beneath the time you will see the letter "M" and 16° Ⅱ. This is the position of the Midheaven and should be placed on your chart. (See the example on page 15.) Now, go down the page to the proper latitude [here 34°N03'], 19 lines down. Always use the closest latitude: for example, 35°N48'; you use 36°N. At the top of the page are the Roman numerals: "XI, XII," the letter "A," and the numerals "II" and "III." These stand for the 11th and 12th house cusps, the Ascendant, and the 2nd and 3rd house cusps. Insert the correct information into the chart. Always look for the signs of the Zodiac and make sure there has been no change of sign in between. (See page 35 of the *Koch Table of Houses* for an example where the Ascendant starts with Leo at the top and then switches to Virgo.)

In our example chart, the 11th house cusp is 18° ♋ 19', the 12th house cusp is 17° ♌ 11', and so on. Only six house positions are given; the others (4th to 9th) are the same degrees and minute but of the opposite sign.

You have now completed Step One. A common question at this point is: "What if the TCST is not close to what is given in the Table of Houses?" Answer: Use the closest one and do not worry about correcting this until you are at the intermediate level and calculating progressions.

Formula 2: To Find the Positions of the Planets

Date: July 12, 1977   Time: 10:30 AM PDT   Place: Los Angeles, CA.

	H.M.S.		
k.	7:53:00		EGMT (Equivalent Greenwich Mean Time) this is found in column 4 of *Dernay's Longitude and Latitude book*, column 3 of the *American Atlas*.
l. +	9:37:00	AM	LMT (Local Mean Time) 7/12/1977-add this
m.	16:90:00		Convert (there are no 90 minutes)
	17:30:00		Because 17:30 is more than 12 (AM or PM) sub-
n. −	12:00:00		tract 12. Since you started with an AM birth your result will be *PM of the same day*. If you subtract 12 hours from a PM birth, it becomes AM of the next day.
o.	5:30:00	PM	GMT (Greenwich Mean Time) 7/12/77

p. Look for the logarithm of this number ($5^h30'$) in the Log Table on page 18. Find the number by looking down in the vertical line marked 5 (hours or degrees) and horizontally across on the line marked 30 (minutes). The resulting figure 6398 is the CL (Constant Log) for this AM chart.

You have determined that if a person is born at 9:30 AM PST in Los Angeles, the time in Greenwich is 5:30 PM of the same day (or 8 hours later).

q. If you are dealing with an AM Greenwich Mean Time, the procedure to find the Constant Log is slightly different. You have to find the *interval* or how many hours and minutes are involved between the actual time and the approaching noon. If the time is 5:30 AM GMT you proceed as follows:

$$
\begin{array}{rl}
11:60 & \text{(noon in hours and minutes, easier than 12:00)} \\
-\ \underline{\ \ 5:30}\ \text{AM} & \text{GMT} \\
6:30 & \textit{Interval}\ \text{(between GMT and approaching noon)}
\end{array}
$$

Look up the logarithm of this number ($6^h30'$) in the Log Table. The resulting figure 5673 is the CL (Constant Log).

Only do this step if you are dealing with an AM Greenwich Mean Time.

Explanation for Formula 2

Step Two   You have erected the wheel and you are now ready to put the planets into the houses. Take your 1977 ephemeris and locate July 12, 1977. There is one problem: the planets are given for their position at noon, Greenwich time. John Doe was born at 9:30 AM PST. How does that relate to noon at Greenwich? On the dummy sheet on page 16, we show you.

k. Take the EGMT (Equivalent Greenwich Mean time) for Los Angeles. This was found in the *American Atlas*, or by the conversion method explained to you on page 9. The EGMT is $7^h53'$.

l. Add the LMT (Local Mean Time), $9^h37'00''$ AM. This was arrived at by adding the meridian correction (c) to the time of birth.

m. $16^h90'00''$ has to be converted to $17^h30'00''$ (90 minutes becomes 1 hour and 30 minutes).

n. $17^h30'$ is past 12 noon, and therefore is 5:30 in the afternoon when you subtract 12 hours.

o. 5:30 PM is the GMT (Greenwich Mean Time). This is the time of birth as converted to Greenwich. John Doe, born at 9:30 AM in Los Angeles, was born at 5:30 PM in Greenwich. Please note the importance of marking the AM or PM position and the date.

p. Look for the logarithm of this number, $5^h30'$ (or $5°30'$), in the Log Table on page 9 of this book. This table saves everyone who is not a math major a lot of calculating. Look across the top where the hours are indicated, and locate the number 5; then, go down the minute column on the page to the line 30, and then find where these two columns intersect. You will find the figure 6398. This is your

Diurnal Logarithms 0 to 7 Hours/Degrees for Each Minute of Time/Arc

HOURS OR DEGREES

	0	1	2	3	4	5	6	7	
M 0	9.9999	1.3802	1.0792	.9031	.7782	.6812	.6021	.5351	0 M
I 1	3.1584	1.3730	1.0756	.9007	.7763	.6798	.6009	.5341	1 I
N 2	2.8573	1.3660	1.0720	.8983	.7745	.6784	.5997	.5331	2 N
U 3	2.6812	1.3590	1.0685	.8959	.7728	.6769	.5985	.5320	3 U
T 4	2.5563	1.3522	1.0649	.8935	.7710	.6755	.5973	.5310	4 T
E									E
S 5	2.4594	1.3454	1.0615	.8912	.7692	.6741	.5961	.5300	5 S
6	2.3802	1.3388	1.0580	.8888	.7674	.6726	.5949	.5290	6
O 7	2.3133	1.3323	1.0546	.8865	.7657	.6712	.5937	.5279	7 O
F 8	2.2553	1.3259	1.0512	.8842	.7639	.6698	.5925	.5269	8 F
9	2.2041	1.3195	1.0478	.8819	.7622	.6684	.5913	.5259	9
T									T
I 10	2.1584	1.3133	1.0444	.8796	.7604	.6670	.5902	.5249	10 I
M 11	2.1170	1.3071	1.0411	.8773	.7587	.6656	.5890	.5239	11 M
E 12	2.0792	1.3010	1.0378	.8751	.7570	.6642	.5878	.5229	12 E
13	2.0444	1.2950	1.0345	.8728	.7552	.6628	.5867	.5219	13
O 14	2.0122	1.2891	1.0313	.8706	.7535	.6614	.5855	.5209	14 O
R									R
15	1.9823	1.2833	1.0280	.8683	.7518	.6601	.5843	.5199	15
A 16	1.9542	1.2775	1.0248	.8661	.7501	.6587	.5832	.5189	16 A
R 17	1.9279	1.2719	1.0216	.8639	.7484	.6573	.5820	.5179	17 R
C 18	1.9031	1.2663	1.0185	.8617	.7467	.6559	.5809	.5169	18 C
19	1.8796	1.2607	1.0153	.8595	.7451	.6546	.5797	.5159	19
20	1.8573	1.2553	1.0122	.8573	.7434	.6532	.5786	.5149	20
21	1.8361	1.2499	1.0091	.8552	.7417	.6519	.5774	.5139	21
22	1.8159	1.2445	1.0061	.8530	.7401	.6505	.5763	.5129	22
23	1.7966	1.2393	1.0030	.8509	.7384	.6492	.5752	.5120	23
24	1.7782	1.2341	1.0000	.8487	.7368	.6478	.5740	.5110	24
25	1.7604	1.2289	0.9970	.8466	.7351	.6465	.5729	.5100	25
26	1.7434	1.2239	0.9940	.8445	.7335	.6451	.5718	.5090	26
27	1.7270	1.2188	0.9910	.8424	.7319	.6438	.5707	.5081	27
28	1.7112	1.2139	0.9881	.8403	.7302	.6425	.5695	.5071	28
29	1.6960	1.2090	0.9852	.8382	.7286	.6412	.5684	.5061	29
30	1.6812	1.2041	0.9823	.8361	.7270	.6398	.5673	.5051	30
31	1.6670	1.1993	0.9794	.8341	.7254	.6385	.5662	.5042	31
32	1.6532	1.1946	0.9765	.8320	.7238	.6372	.5651	.5032	32
33	1.6398	1.1899	0.9737	.8300	.7222	.6359	.5640	.5023	33
34	1.6269	1.1852	0.9708	.8279	.7206	.6346	.5629	.5013	34
35	1.6143	1.1806	0.9680	.8259	.7190	.6333	.5618	.5004	35
36	1.6021	1.1761	0.9652	.8239	.7175	.6320	.5607	.4994	36
37	1.5902	1.1716	0.9625	.8219	.7159	.6307	.5596	.4984	37
38	1.5786	1.1671	0.9597	.8199	.7143	.6294	.5585	.4975	38
39	1.5673	1.1627	0.9570	.8179	.7128	.6282	.5574	.4965	39
40	1.5563	1.1584	0.9542	.8159	.7112	.6269	.5563	.4956	40
41	1.5456	1.1540	0.9515	.8140	.7097	.6256	.5552	.4947	41
42	1.5351	1.1498	0.9488	.8120	.7081	.6243	.5541	.4937	42
43	1.5249	1.1455	0.9462	.8101	.7066	.6231	.5531	.4928	43
44	1.5149	1.1413	0.9435	.8081	.7050	.6218	.5520	.4918	44
45	1.5051	1.1372	0.9409	.8062	.7035	.6205	.5509	.4909	45
46	1.4956	1.1331	0.9383	.8043	.7020	.6193	.5498	.4900	46
47	1.4863	1.1290	0.9356	.8023	.7005	.6180	.5488	.4890	47
48	1.4771	1.1249	0.9331	.8004	.6990	.6168	.5477	.4881	48
49	1.4682	1.1209	0.9305	.7985	.6975	.6155	.5466	.4872	49
50	1.4594	1.1170	0.9279	.7966	.6960	.6143	.5456	.4863	50
51	1.4508	1.1130	0.9254	.7948	.6945	.6131	.5445	.4853	51
52	1.4424	1.1091	0.9228	.7929	.6930	.6118	.5435	.4844	52
53	1.4341	1.1053	0.9203	.7910	.6915	.6106	.5424	.4835	53
54	1.4260	1.1015	0.9178	.7891	.6900	.6094	.5414	.4826	54
55	1.4180	1.0977	0.9153	.7873	.6885	.6081	.5403	.4817	55
56	1.4102	1.0939	0.9128	.7855	.6871	.6069	.5393	.4808	56
57	1.4025	1.0902	0.9104	.7836	.6856	.6057	.5382	.4798	57
58	1.3949	1.0865	0.9079	.7818	.6841	.6045	.5372	.4789	58
59	1.3875	1.0828	0.9055	.7800	.6827	.6033	.5361	.4780	59

Diurnal Logarithms 8 to 15 Hours/Degrees for Each Minute of Time/Arc

HOURS OR DEGREES

	8	9	10	11	12	13	14	15	
M 0	.4771	.4260	.3802	.3388	.3010	.2663	.2341	.2041	0 **M**
I 1	.4762	.4252	.3795	.3382	.3004	.2657	.2336	.2036	1 **I**
N 2	.4753	.4244	.3788	.3375	.2998	.2652	.2331	.2032	2 **N**
U 3	.4744	.4236	.3780	.3368	.2992	.2646	.2325	.2027	3 **U**
T 4	.4735	.4228	.3773	.3362	.2986	.2640	.2320	.2022	4 **T**
E									**E**
S 5	.4726	.4220	.3766	.3355	.2980	.2635	.2315	.2017	5 **S**
6	.4717	.4212	.3759	.3349	.2974	.2629	.2310	.2012	6
O 7	.4708	.4204	.3752	.3342	.2968	.2624	.2305	.2008	7 **O**
F 8	.4699	.4196	.3745	.3336	.2962	.2618	.2300	.2003	8 **F**
9	.4691	.4188	.3737	.3329	.2956	.2613	.2295	.1998	9
T									**T**
I 10	.4682	.4180	.3730	.3323	.2950	.2607	.2289	.1993	10 **I**
M 11	.4673	.4172	.3723	.3316	.2944	.2602	.2284	.1988	11 **M**
E 12	.4664	.4164	.3716	.3310	.2939	.2596	.2279	.1984	12 **E**
13	.4655	.4156	.3709	.3303	.2933	.2591	.2274	.1979	13
O 14	.4646	.4149	.3702	.3297	.2927	.2585	.2269	.1974	14 **O**
R									**R**
15	.4638	.4141	.3695	.3291	.2921	.2580	.2264	.1969	15
A 16	.4629	.4133	.3688	.3284	.2915	.2574	.2259	.1965	16 **A**
R 17	.4620	.4125	.3681	.3278	.2909	.2569	.2254	.1960	17 **R**
C 18	.4611	.4117	.3674	.3271	.2903	.2564	.2249	.1955	18 **C**
19	.4603	.4110	.3667	.3265	.2897	.2558	.2244	.1950	19
20	.4594	.4102	.3660	.3259	.2891	.2553	.2239	.1946	20
21	.4585	.4094	.3653	.3252	.2885	.2547	.2234	.1941	21
22	.4577	.4086	.3646	.3246	.2880	.2542	.2229	.1936	22
23	.4568	.4079	.3639	.3239	.2874	.2536	.2224	.1932	23
24	.4559	.4071	.3632	.3233	.2868	.2531	.2218	.1927	24
25	.4551	.4063	.3625	.3227	.2862	.2526	.2213	.1922	25
26	.4542	.4055	.3618	.3220	.2856	.2520	.2208	.1918	26
27	.4534	.4048	.3611	.3214	.2850	.2515	.2203	.1913	27
28	.4525	.4040	.3604	.3208	.2845	.2510	.2198	.1908	28
29	.4516	.4033	.3597	.3201	.2839	.2504	.2193	.1903	29
30	.4508	.4025	.3590	.3195	.2833	.2499	.2188	.1899	30
31	.4499	.4017	.3583	.3189	.2827	.2493	.2183	.1894	31
32	.4491	.4010	.3576	.3183	.2821	.2488	.2178	.1889	32
33	.4482	.4002	.3570	.3176	.2816	.2483	.2173	.1885	33
34	.4474	.3995	.3563	.3170	.2810	.2477	.2169	.1880	34
35	.4466	.3987	.3556	.3164	.2804	.2472	.2164	.1876	35
36	.4457	.3979	.3549	.3158	.2798	.2467	.2159	.1871	36
37	.4449	.3972	.3542	.3151	.2793	.2461	.2154	.1866	37
38	.4440	.3964	.3535	.3145	.2787	.2456	.2149	.1862	38
39	.4432	.3957	.3529	.3139	.2781	.2451	.2144	.1857	39
40	.4424	.3949	.3522	.3133	.2775	.2445	.2139	.1852	40
41	.4415	.3942	.3515	.3126	.2770	.2440	.2134	.1848	41
42	.4407	.3934	.3508	.3120	.2764	.2435	.2129	.1843	42
43	.4399	.3927	.3502	.3114	.2758	.2430	.2124	.1839	43
44	.4390	.3919	.3495	.3108	.2753	.2424	.2119	.1834	44
45	.4382	.3912	.3488	.3102	.2747	.2419	.2114	.1829	45
46	.4374	.3905	.3481	.3096	.2741	.2414	.2109	.1825	46
47	.4366	.3897	.3475	.3089	.2736	.2409	.2104	.1820	47
48	.4357	.3890	.3468	.3083	.2730	.2403	.2099	.1816	48
49	.4349	.3882	.3461	.3077	.2724	.2398	.2095	.1811	49
50	.4341	.3875	.3454	.3071	.2719	.2393	.2090	.1806	50
51	.4333	.3868	.3448	.3065	.2713	.2388	.2085	.1802	51
52	.4325	.3860	.3441	.3059	.2707	.2382	.2080	.1797	52
53	.4316	.3853	.3434	.3053	.2702	.2377	.2075	.1793	53
54	.4308	.3846	.3428	.3047	.2696	.2372	.2070	.1788	54
55	.4300	.3838	.3421	.3041	.2691	.2367	.2065	.1784	55
56	.4292	.3831	.3415	.3034	.2685	.2362	.2061	.1779	56
57	.4284	.3824	.3408	.3028	.2679	.2356	.2056	.1775	57
58	.4276	.3817	.3401	.3022	.2674	.2351	.2051	.1770	58
59	.4268	.3809	.3395	.3016	.2668	.2346	.2046	.1765	59

Diurnal Logarithms 16 to 23 Hours/Degrees for Each Minute of Time/Arc

HOURS OR DEGREES

		16	17	18	19	20	21	22	23		
M	0	.1761	.1498	.1249	.1015	.0792	.0580	.0378	.0185	0	M
I	1	.1756	.1493	.1245	.1011	.0788	.0576	.0375	.0182	1	I
N	2	.1752	.1489	.1241	.1007	.0785	.0573	.0371	.0179	2	N
U	3	.1747	.1485	.1237	.1003	.0781	.0570	.0368	.0175	3	U
T	4	.1743	.1481	.1233	.0999	.0777	.0566	.0365	.0172	4	T
E											E
S	5	.1738	.1476	.1229	.0996	.0774	.0563	.0361	.0169	5	S
	6	.1734	.1472	.1225	.0992	.0770	.0559	.0358	.0166	6	
O	7	.1729	.1468	.1221	.0988	.0767	.0556	.0355	.0163	7	O
F	8	.1725	.1464	.1217	.0984	.0763	.0552	.0352	.0160	8	F
	9	.1720	.1459	.1213	.0980	.0759	.0549	.0348	.0157	9	
T											T
I	10	.1716	.1455	.1209	.0977	.0756	.0546	.0345	.0153	10	I
M	11	.1711	.1451	.1205	.0973	.0752	.0542	.0342	.0150	11	M
E	12	.1707	.1447	.1201	.0969	.0749	.0539	.0339	.0147	12	E
	13	.1702	.1443	.1197	.0965	.0745	.0535	.0335	.0144	13	
O	14	.1698	.1438	.1193	.0962	.0741	.0532	.0332	.0141	14	O
R											R
	15	.1694	.1434	.1189	.0958	.0738	.0529	.0329	.0138	15	
A	16	.1689	.1430	.1186	.0954	.0734	.0525	.0326	.0135	16	A
R	17	.1685	.1426	.1182	.0950	.0731	.0522	.0322	.0132	17	R
C	18	.1680	.1422	.1178	.0947	.0727	.0518	.0319	.0129	18	C
	19	.1676	.1417	.1174	.0943	.0724	.0515	.0316	.0125	19	
	20	.1671	.1413	.1170	.0939	.0720	.0512	.0313	.0122	20	
	21	.1667	.1409	.1166	.0935	.0716	.0508	.0309	.0119	21	
	22	.1663	.1405	.1162	.0932	.0713	.0505	.0306	.0116	22	
	23	.1658	.1401	.1158	.0928	.0709	.0501	.0303	.0113	23	
	24	.1654	.1397	.1154	.0924	.0706	.0498	.0300	.0110	24	
	25	.1649	.1392	.1150	.0920	.0702	.0495	.0296	.0107	25	
	26	.1645	.1388	.1146	.0917	.0699	.0491	.0293	.0104	26	
	27	.1640	.1384	.1142	.0913	.0695	.0488	.0290	.0101	27	
	28	.1636	.1380	.1138	.0909	.0692	.0484	.0287	.0098	28	
	29	.1632	.1376	.1134	.0905	.0688	.0481	.0284	.0095	29	
	30	.1627	.1372	.1130	.0902	.0685	.0478	.0280	.0091	30	
	31	.1623	.1368	.1126	.0898	.0681	.0474	.0277	.0088	31	
	32	.1619	.1363	.1123	.0894	.0678	.0471	.0274	.0085	32	
	33	.1614	.1359	.1119	.0891	.0674	.0468	.0271	.0082	33	
	34	.1610	.1355	.1115	.0887	.0670	.0464	.0267	.0079	34	
	35	.1605	.1351	.1111	.0883	.0667	.0461	.0264	.0076	35	
	36	.1601	.1347	.1107	.0880	.0663	.0458	.0261	.0073	36	
	37	.1597	.1343	.1103	.0876	.0660	.0454	.0258	.0070	37	
	38	.1592	.1339	.1099	.0872	.0656	.0451	.0255	.0067	38	
	39	.1588	.1335	.1095	.0868	.0653	.0448	.0251	.0064	39	
	40	.1584	.1331	.1091	.0865	.0649	.0444	.0248	.0061	40	
	41	.1579	.1326	.1088	.0861	.0646	.0441	.0245	.0058	41	
	42	.1575	.1322	.1084	.0857	.0642	.0438	.0242	.0055	42	
	43	.1571	.1318	.1080	.0854	.0639	.0434	.0239	.0052	43	
	44	.1566	.1314	.1076	.0850	.0635	.0431	.0235	.0049	44	
	45	.1562	.1310	.1072	.0846	.0632	.0428	.0232	.0045	45	
	46	.1558	.1306	.1068	.0843	.0628	.0424	.0229	.0042	46	
	47	.1553	.1302	.1064	.0839	.0625	.0421	.0226	.0039	47	
	48	.1549	.1298	.1061	.0835	.0621	.0418	.0223	.0036	48	
	49	.1545	.1294	.1057	.0832	.0618	.0414	.0220	.0033	49	
	50	.1540	.1290	.1053	.0828	.0615	.0411	.0216	.0030	50	
	51	.1536	.1286	.1049	.0825	.0611	.0408	.0213	.0027	51	
	52	.1532	.1282	.1045	.0821	.0608	.0404	.0210	.0024	52	
	53	.1528	.1278	.1041	.0817	.0604	.0401	.0207	.0021	53	
	54	.1523	.1274	.1037	.0814	.0601	.0398	.0204	.0018	54	
	55	.1519	.1270	.1034	.0810	.0597	.0394	.0201	.0015	55	
	56	.1515	.1266	.1030	.0806	.0594	.0391	.0197	.0012	56	
	57	.1510	.1261	.1026	.0803	.0590	.0388	.0194	.0009	57	
	58	.1506	.1257	.1022	.0799	.0587	.0384	.0191	.0006	58	
	59	.1502	.1253	.1018	.0795	.0583	.0381	.0188	.0003	59	

Constant Log, or CL. This is the figure necessary to convert the noon planet positions to the actual birthtime positions.

q. If the birth time in Los Angeles had been 9:30 PM and you had added it to the EGMT and then subtracted 12 hours, the GMT would then be 5:30 AM of the *next* day, and you would have to do one more step. You would have to subtract this figure from noon to find how many hours it is from 5:30 AM until noon. This is called the *interval.* Then, you would find the Constant Log for $6^h30'$. Remember, you *do this step only* if the GMT is AM.

```
      H.M.
      07:53    EGMT              17:30
    + 09:30    PM-LMT          − 12:00
      16:90                      05:30    AM GMT
      17:30
```

Formula 3: To Correct Planet Positions

Date: July 12, 1977   Time: 10:30 AM PDT   Place: Los Angeles, CA

Remember 1 sign = 30°, 1 degree = 60', 1 minute = 60''

r. From the Ephemeris take the Moon position for 2 days

day after birth 7/13/77   19° ♊ 07' (convert to subtract)

18°   67'

day of birth 7/12/77   - 7° ♊ 15' subtract to find difference

11°   52' this is the Moon's motion

for 24 hours (from noon 7/12 to noon 7/13).

s. Find this figure (11 °52') in the Log Table. 3059 is the PLR (planetary logarithm).

```
Add the PLR     3059
   to the CL  + 6398   (see p. Formula 2 on page 17)
t.              9457    Look this figure up in the Log Table and
```
convert to degrees and minutes. The nearest figure is 9462 where 2° and 43' intersect. Therefore 9457 = 2 °43' This is how much the Moon has moved from Noon Greenwich, on 7/12 to 5:30 PM GMT.

u. If the GMT is PM (as in our case) Add the calculated amount (2 °43') to the Moon position on birthday.

```
        7/12/77      7° ♊ 15'
                   + 2°   43'
                     9° ♊ 58'  Corrected Moon
```

If the GMT is AM subtract the Moon's motion from the Moon position on approaching noon.

```
    7/13/77   19° ♊ 07' or    18° ♊ 67'
                             - 2°   43'
                               16° ♊ 24'  Corrected Moon
```

Correct all planets the same way using the same CL (Constant Log). Any planet that is retrograde (marked by an Rx in the Ephemeris) is handled by reverse procedure.

Explanation for Formula 3

You are now ready to correct the planet's positions using the CL (Constant Log). We are dealing with a person born at 5:30 PM GMT (Greenwich Mean Time) on July 12, 1977; in other words, past or later than noon on July 12th, but earlier than noon of July 13th. Therefore, to correct the Moon's position, we take the two dates between which the birth time falls. We correct the Moon on the dummy sheet and all the fast-moving planets must be corrected similarly. The Sun, Moon, Venus, Mercury, and Mars are the only planets that move fast enough to necessitate accurate correction. Jupiter, Saturn, Uranus, Neptune and Pluto are taken as given in the ephemeris on the nearest noon.

r. In the ephemeris, find the Moon position for Greenwich Noon on July 13, 1977, and for Noon on July 12, 1977. Find the difference in degrees and minutes from one day to the next. You see that we have to borrow 1° and convert it into minutes to be able to subtract. This is a normal mathematical procedure, but remember you are dealing with minutes, which convert into 60, rather than a simple decimal conversion. The Moon's motion is 11° 52'.

s. Find the result of this process in the Log Table. Locate 11 in the hours column, and 52 minutes in the minutes column; find the point where these two columns intersect and note the number 3059. This is the PLR (Planet Logarithm) for the Moon. Add this figure (PLR) to your CL (See Step p.)

t. The total of these two figures = 9457. Look this figure up in the Log Table by reversing the previous procedure. Find the figure closest (in this case 9462) and convert to degrees and minutes 9462 = 2°43'. This is how far the Moon has traveled from Noon (Greenwich) 7/12 to 5:30 PM.

u. We have determined that the Moon has to be corrected 2°43'. But corrected which way? Our subject was born 5^{h}30' past noon on the 12th of July, or 18^{h}30' before noon on July 13th. Take the closest position and figure from that point. An easy way to remember is by the rule: *If GMT is PM, add the correction to the day of birth. If GMT is AM, subtract the correction from approaching noon.* By applying this rule, we correct the Moon's position to 9°♊58'.

Using the same method, correct the Sun, Mercury, Venus and Mars.

Please note that the planets Uranus and Neptune have an Rx next to their position in the ephemeris. This indicates Retrograde motion. In order not to overlook this retrograde motion, it is important that you always look one line above and one line below to see if the planet is moving forward or backward. As you can see, Uranus on July 12th is at 7°♏42', but on July 13th it is at 7°♏41', therefore moving backwards. At the top of the page in Uranus' column, you see that there is the letter R, indicating this retrograde motion, but since you may not always look at the top of the page, this might otherwise escape your notice. So, always check carefully. We explain retrograde motion more fully in a later lesson in this book.

Date July 12, 1977   **Time** 10:30 *AM PDT*   **Place** Los Angeles, California   **Long.** 118W15   **Lat.** 34N03

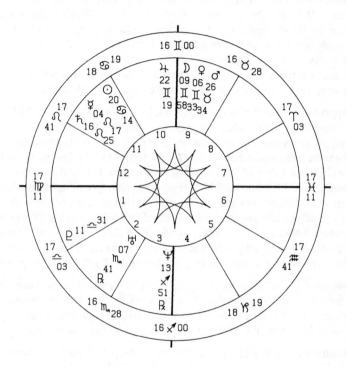

In many ephemerides, the Lunar Nodes are not given daily but only every third day; in some only for the first day of each month. Most Nodes move in a regular fashion, always *backwards,* approximately 03' per day and exactly 10' in 3 days. Since we are calculating for July 12 we are dealing with 4 x 3 days, or 40' less than the position given for July 1st, namely 20°♎16'. Therefore, the corrected nodal position is 19°♎36' for the North Node. The South Node is always directly opposite the North Node, and its position would therefore be 19°♈36'. Some ephemerides use the True Nodes which move irregularly and therefore are listed for each day. More on the Nodes in a later lesson.

You are now ready to insert the planets into the wheel. But before you do, we urge you to take a few safeguards to make sure your calculations are correct.

Safeguard 1   You know that our John Doe is born at 9:37 AM LMT, and if you'll recall the wheel from Volume 1 of "The Only Way to . . . Learn Astrology", you know that each house has a time zone. A 1st house Sun shows a birth time of somewhere between 4:00 and 6:00 AM, the 2nd house anywhere between 2:00 and 4:00 AM, and so on. A person born at 9:30 AM would have the Sun around the 11th house, which covers the time period 8:00 to 10:00 AM. Looking at the wheel you have erected, you see that the cusp of the 11th house is 18°♋19', and you can see that your corrected Sun is 20°♋14'. It falls in the 11th house where it belongs. This is a very good way to check your wheel for accuracy. At times, the Sun may fall just on the other side of the cusp, but reasonably close. This happens when the birth is very far North or South of the Equator.

Safeguard 2   When calculating the GMT (Greenwich Mean Time), keep in mind the time zone you are dealing with. Pacific Time is 8 hours earlier than Greenwich—120°W longitude. The Sun travels 15° each hour, 120 ÷ 15 = 8. Therefore, 9:30 AM plus 8 hours must be 5:30 in the afternoon.

Safeguard 3   When correcting the planets, keep the Greenwich time in mind. 5:30 in the afternoon is nearly 1/4th into the day (24 hours ÷ 6 hours = 1/4). Thus, your corrections should be approximately 1/4th or a bit less, since you are dealing with 5:30 and not 6:00 PM. In the case of the Moon, 2°43' is just a little bit less than 1/4th of 11°52'. If you had come up with a correction of 5°, you would know that your calculations were wrong. In teaching the mathematics of chart erection, we try to stress the *logic* of what you are doing, and why you are doing it. Eyeball everything before you insert the planets; avoid careless mistakes and the resulting embarrassment. We find that if you list the planet's positions in the aspectarian on your chart, before you actually insert their position in the chart itself, it helps to see how many planets go into each house—so that you can allow proper room for them.

Safeguard 4   When dealing with any births involving 12:00 noon or 12:00 midnight, use 00:00:00; i.e., born at 12:10 PM, use 00:10 PM — born at 12:25 AM, use 00:25 AM. You will discover any mistakes made in this area when the Sun falls in the wrong house.

Insert the planets into the wheel. See our sample chart on page 23.

The finished chart should not only be correct, but it should also represent a visual picture. For example, the Sun is at 20 ° ♋ 14', and it is in the 11th house but very close to the cusp of the 10th. Be sure to place it close to this cusp, not in the middle of the 11th house. Pluto is at 11 °♎ 31' in the 1st house, but close to the cusp of the 2nd house. Place it there. For delineating, these visual placements are of great help. Take your time, be accurate, and be neat in placing the planets into the chart.

On the next few pages we give the formulas for doing PM charts, charts for locations South of the Equator, and charts for locations East of Greenwich. Since the principle involved is always the same, no extensive explanations are needed. We urge you to not only read the text, but also to do these examples yourself, to follow along with your own ephemeris and Table of Houses. Only by actually doing the math will you master it and gain proficiency in doing your own charts.

Review Question: Calculate and erect the horoscope for Walt Disney. He was born December 5, 1901, at 12:30 AM CST, in Chicago, Illinois [87 °W37' 41 °N53']. For the correct math, and his actual chart, please refer to the Appendix, pages 235-236.

Formula 4: To Find the Houses for a PM Birth using a Noon Ephemeris

Date: July 12, 1977   Time: 4:13 PM PDT   Place: Los Angeles, CA

Find the longitude and latitude of Los Angeles in the *American Atlas* = 118W15   34N03
Find the Meridian correction = +7 minutes
Find the EGMT = +7 hours 53 minutes
Check to see if Daylight Saving time is observed.

	H.M.S.		
	4:13:00	PM	Time of birth - 7/12/77 PDT
	− 1:00:00		Subtract 1 hour for Daylight Saving time
	3:13:00	PM	PST - 7/12/77
	+ 7:00		Meridian correction (add 7' because L.A. in EAST of the Standard Meridian)
	3:20:00	PM	LMT (Local Mean Time) 7/12/77
	+ 0:33		add LMT correction ($3^h20'$ $6^h = 0'33''$)
	+ 1:19		add EGMT correction ($7^h53'$ $6^h = 1'19''$)
	+ 7:21:04		add Sidereal Time for 7/12/77 (day of birth)
	10:42:56		TCST (True Calculated Sidereal Time)

Open Koch Table of Houses to Sidereal Time closest to this figure (10:42:24) and find Midheaven or 10th house cusp (9 ♍). Go down page to proper latitude (34N) and find Ascendant and intermediate house cusps. See completed chart on page 26.

Sometimes due to the latitude and the inequality in the shape of the earth, it appears that a sign is intercepted between the cusps of two houses. If this occurs, you will have the same sign appearing on successive house cusps on either side of the chart. This will be explained further in Lesson 8.

If a person is born at 12 PM (noon) use 0:00:00 PM

Review Question: Calculate and erect the horoscope for Farrah Fawcett. She was born on February 2, 1947, at 3:10 PM CST, in Corpus Christi, Texas. For the correct math and copy of her horoscope, please refer to the Appendix, pages 237-238.

Date July 12, 1977   **Time** 4:13 *PM PDT*   **Place** Los Angeles, California   **Long.** 118W15   **Lat.** 34N03

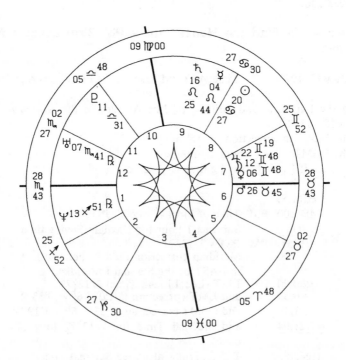

Formula 5: When LMT and GMT are both A.M.

When the LMT is AM and GMT is also AM, the planet correction is handled a little differently and the best way for you to understand is by illustration.

Date: July 12, 1977   Time: 1:15 AM PDT   Place: Los Angeles, CA
118W15 34N03 Mer. Corr. +7' EGMT $7^h53'$

	H.M.S.		
	1:15:00	AM	Time of Birth PDT 7/12/77
	−1:00:00		Subtract 1 hour for Daylight Saving Time
	0:15:00	AM	PST 7/12/77
	+7:00		Meridian Correction for Los Angeles
	0:22:00	AM	LMT (Local Mean Time)
	+12:00:00		Add 12 hours for AM birth
	12:22:00		LMTI
	+2:04		Add LMTI correction ($12^h22'$ ÷ 6^h = 2'04")
	+1:19		Add EGMT correction ($7^h53'$ ÷ 6^h = 1'19")
	+7:17:08		Add Sidereal Time for 7/11/77 (previous day)
	19:42:31		TCST (True Calculated Sidereal Time)

Proceed to set up wheel as on page 15. Closest time is $19^h43'33"$ = MC of 24 ♑.

	H.M.S.		
	7:53:00		EGMT for Los Angeles
	+0:22:00	AM	Add LMT of 7/12/77
	7:75:00		Convert
	8:15:00	AM	GMT (remains AM of the same day) 7/12/77

Because this is AM you must SUBTRACT this from noon to find the INTERVAL

	11:60	
	−8:15	
	3:45	Find this in Log Table 3°45' = CL 8062

In correcting planets, use planet position *on day of birth* (7/12/77) and for *day before birth* (7/11/77) because GMT is *before noon* in Greenwich on the day of birth, or between the noon of 7/11 and 7/12.

Moon position 7/12/77	7° ♊ 15'	
Moon position 7/11/77	− 25° ♉ 27'	
	11° 48'	= PLR 3083
	+ CL 8062	
	1.1145	= 1°51'

Since this is an AM GMT, the 1°51' will be subtracted from the Moon on the day of birth 7/12/77.

7°♊15'
-1° 51'
5°♊24' CORRECTED MOON for 1:15 AM birth time

The daily motion of the Moon varies from 11° 48' to 15° 10'. The daily motion of the Sun varies from 0° 57' to 1° 01'. If you have more or less motion than this within 24 hours, you have made an error in your calculations.

Lesson 3
Formulas For Noon Math Other Locations

Formula 6: Math for East of Greenwich

Hermann Hesse, born July 2, 1877 in Calw (Wuerttemberg) Germany at 7:00 PM 8E03 48N01 Meridian Correction = 27'48" EGMT = $-0^h32'12''$. No Daylight Savings or War Time in effect.

	H.M.S.		
	7:00:00	PM	7/2/1877
	$-27:48$		Mer. Corr. for 8E03
	6:32:12	PM	LMTI (Local Mean Time Interval)
	$+1:05$		LMTI correction ($6^h32' \div 6 = 1'05''$)
	6:33:17		
	$-0:05$		EGMT corr. (Subtract for East of Greenwich) ($0^h32'' \div 6 = 0'05''$)
	6:33:12		
	$+6:42:31$		Sidereal Time for 7/2/1877
	13:15:43		TCST (True Calculated Sidereal Time) Find this in Table of Houses and set up wheel.

	H.M.S.		
	6:32:12	PM	LMT 7/2/1877
	$-0:32:12$		EGMT (subtract)
	6:00:00	PM	GMT 7/2/1877

CL (CONSTANT LOG) for 6°00 = 6021

Since the GMT is 6 PM or 6 hours past noon of July 2, use planets for July 3 and July 2.

	Sun	Moon	Mercury	Venus	Mars
7/3	11 ♋ 35	7 ♈ 20	23 ♊ 56	27 ♋ 07	12 ♓ 02
7/2	− 10 ♋ 38	− 25 ♓ 15	− 22 ♊ 15	− 25 ♋ 54	− 11 ♓ 39
	57	12 05	1 41	1 13	23
PLR	1.4025	.2980	1.1540	1.2959	1.7966
CL	+ 6021	+ 6021	+ 6021	+ 6021	+ 6021
	2.0046	9001	1.7561	1.8971	2.3987
	= 14'	3° 01'	25'	18'	6'
7/2	10 ♋ 38	25 ♓ 15	22 ♊ 15	25 ♋ 54	11 ♓ 39
	+ 14	+ 3 01	+ 25	+ 18	+ 6
	10 ♋ 52	28 ♓ 16	22 ♊ 40	26 ♋ 12	11 ♓ 45

Since this is a PM GMT (6 hours after the noon of July 2) corrections are added to planets on July 2nd.

Explanation for Formula 6

Calculations for Locations East of Greenwich   By now you should have practiced chart erection and be familiar with most of the terms.

As you can see, the formula for East of Greenwich locations does not differ much from the ones you have done for West of Greenwich locations, and the AM and PM variation stays exactly the same. The only change is in the 10'' correction necessary to correct for the Earth's wobble.

If you will refer back to page 8, "A Note About Time," you may recall that anytime you move to the west of the Prime Meridian in Greenwich, the 0° point, it is earlier because the Sun has not yet reached that point in its east-to-west movement. Therefore, when we live west of Greenwich and convert to Greenwich Mean Time (GMT), we must add. Thus, when compensating for the wobble in taking the 10'' EGMT correction. We *add* it.

When we are born East of Greenwich, the Sun has already been there. It is later in the day to the east of Greenwich than at Greenwich, and when we convert to GMT we must *subtract* in order to arrive at the correct time. If we subtract the EGMT (Equivalent Greenwich Mean Time), obviously we also have to subtract the EGMT 10'' correction.

As you can see on the dummy sheet, for East of Greenwich, that's exactly what we have done. We take the time of birth, correct it by subtracting the meridian correction in order to find the Local Mean Time, add the 10'' LMTI correction, and then total it in order to subtract the EGMT correction. To this sum we now add the Sidereal Time. The sum gives us our True Calculated Sidereal Time.

To recap, East of Greenwich is handled exactly as all other chart formulas, *except* that the EGMT corrections are *subtracted,* instead of added.

Name Hermann Hesse
Date July 2, 1877
Time 6:30 PM LMT
Place Calw (Wuerttemberg) Germany
Long. 8E03
Lat. 48N01

Source
His own notes

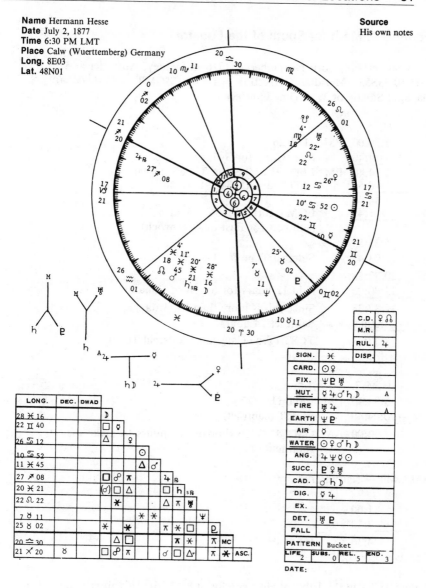

LONG.	DEC.	DWAD
28 ♓ 16		
22 ♊ 40		
26 ♋ 12		
10 ♋ 52		
11 ♓ 45		
27 ♐ 08		
20 ♓ 21		
22 ♌ 22		
7 ♉ 11		
25 ♉ 02		
20 ♎ 30		
21 ♓ 20		

	C.D.	♀ ☊
	M.R.	
	RUL.	♃
SIGN. ♓	DISP.	
CARD. ☉ ♀		
FIX. ♆ ♇ ♅		
MUT. ☿ ♃ ♂ ♄ ☽		A
FIRE ♅ ♃		A
EARTH ♆ ♇		
AIR ☿		
WATER ☉ ♀ ♂ ♄ ☽		
ANG. ♃ ♆ ☿ ☉		
SUCC. ♇ ♀ ♅		
CAD. ♂ ♄ ☽		
DIG. ☿ ♃		
EX.		
DET. ♅ ♇		
FALL		
PATTERN Bucket		
LIFE 2	SUBS. 0	REL. 5	END. 3

DATE:

Formula 7: Math for South of the Equator

Joan Sutherland, born November 7, 1926 in Sydney, Australia at 5:30 PM
151E10 33S55   Meridian Correction = +4'40'' EGMT = −10^{h}04'40''. No
Daylight Saving or War Time in effect.

H.M.S.		
5:30:00	PM	11/7/26
+4:40		Mer. Corr. for Sydney
5:34:40	PM	LMTI (Local Mean Time Interval
+0:56		LMTI corr. (5^{h}34' ÷ 6 = 0'56'')
5:34:96		
−1:41		EGMT corr. (10^{h}04' ÷ 6 = 1'41'')
		(subtract for East of Greenwich)
5:33:55		
+15:03:43		Sidereal Time for 11/7/26
20:37:38		
+12:00:00		Add 12 hours for South of Equator
32:37:38		Since this is more than 24 (1 day)
−24:00:00		Subtract 24 hours
8:37:38		TCST (True Calculated Sidereal Time)

H.M.S.		
5:34:40	PM	LMT 11/7/27
−10:04:40		EGMT (subtract)
7:30:00	AM	GMT 11/7/26 (borrow 12 hours to make the subtraction)

AM GMT − find interval:

11:60	
−7:30	
4:30	Interval

Constant Log 7270

Find TCST in the Table of Houses (closest 8:37:36). This gives a midheaven
of 7 ♌. Reverse this for South Latitude to 7 ♒. Find the other cusps for 34N
and reverse.

Since this is an AM GMT or 4 hours 30 minutes before the noon of
November 7, use planets for November 7th and 6th. Then subtract the
corrections from the planets on approaching noon (November 7). Be sure to
reverse the procedure for Mars which is retrograde in motion.

	Sun	Moon	Mercury	Venus	Mars Rx	
11/7	14 ♏ 19	6 ♐ 30	7 ♐ 23	10 ♏ 51	10 ♉ 30	11/6
11/6	– 13 ♏ 19	– 23 ♏ 42	– 6 ♐ 29	– 9 ♏ 35	– 10 ♉ 08	11/7
	1 00	12 28	54	1 16	22	
PLR	1.3802	2730	1.4260	1.2775	1.8159	
CL	+ 7270	+ 7270	+ 7270	+ 7270	+ 7270	
	2.1072	1.0000	2.1530	2.0045	2.5429	
	= 11'	2°24'	= 10'	= 15'	= 4'	
11/7	14 ♏ 19	6 ♐ 30	7 ♐ 23	10 ♏ 51	10 ♉ 08	
	– 11	– 2 24	– 10	– 15	+ 4	
	14 ♏ 08	4 ♐ 06	7 ♐ 13	10 ♏ 36	10 ♉ 12	

Explanation for Formula 7

Calculations for Locations South of the Equator The basic math formula for making these calculations is exactly the same as the one you have practiced. In our example, we have used Australia, which happens also to be East of Greenwich so we subtract the 10" EGMT correction as we previously explained in the prior East of Greenwich example. The only actual difference is that at the end, before we find the TCST (True Calculated Sidereal Time), we shall add 12 hours.

The reason for doing this is obvious — the sidereal time in all ephemerides is calculated by starting at the 0 point at the time of the Spring Equinox, which falls somewhere around March 22nd of each year. But south of the Equator, when it is spring in the northern latitudes, it is fall to the south of the Equator. We have to bring the Sidereal Time in line by adding 12 hours (or reversing Aries to Libra).

You can quickly check to see that you have done this calculation correctly by noting if the Sun falls into the proper house by time zone. Joan Sutherland, for example, was born between 4:00 and 6:00 PM, so we know that the Sun should fall into her 7th house.

There is one important change to be noted, which really is not a change in the calculations but rather a change in reading the Table of Houses. In the Koch Table of Houses (and most others on the market), the Latitudes are always given for North of the Equator. In order to find the South position, you have to reverse the chart. In our example, on Page 68 of the Koch Table of Houses, we find the TCST of 8^h 37' 36" (very close to our actual TCST of 8^h 37' 38"). The Midheaven or northernmost point indicated is 7° Leo. But we are dealing with a location South of the Equator, so it would be the southernmost point, or the cusp of the 4th house which would have 7° Leo on it. Therefore, the Midheaven should have on its cusp the opposite sign and degree, or 7° Aquarius.

As you go down Page 68 to find the 33° S55', we go to the nearest point, or 34 - but not South, which is not listed in our tables; the table lists 34°N. Again, we are dealing with opposite points. The 12th house cusp would be the opposite, or 6th house. The 6th house would have 4°♎15' on the cusp; the 12th house would read 4°♈15' and so on throughout the chart.

Name Joan Sutherland
Date November 7, 1926
Time 5:30 PM
Place Sydney, Australia
Long. 151E10
Lat. 33S55

Source
Robert Jansky

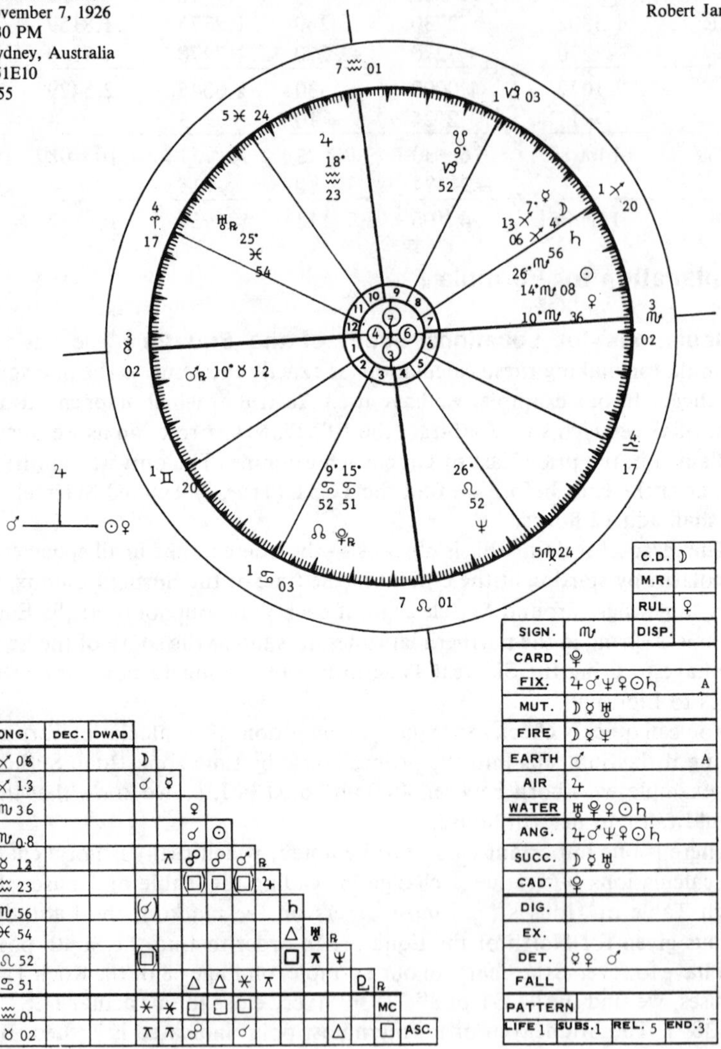

LONG.	DEC.	DWAD												
4 ♐ 06			☽											
7 ♐ 13			☌	☿										
10 ♏ 36					♀									
14 ♏ 08					☌	☉								
10 ♉ 12				⚻	☍	☍	♂ R							
18 ♒ 23					(□)	□	(□)	♃						
26 ♏ 56			(☌)						♄					
25 ♓ 54									△	♅ R				
26 ♌ 52			(□)						□	⚻	♆			
15 ♋ 51					△	△	⚹	⚻				♇ R		
7 ♒ 01			⚹	⚹	□	□	□						MC	
3 ♉ 02			⚻	⚻	☍		☌				△		□	ASC.

		C.D.	☽
		M.R.	
		RUL.	♀
SIGN.	♏	DISP.	
CARD.	♇		
FIX.	♃♂♆♀☉♄		A
MUT.	☽☿♅		
FIRE	☽☿♆		
EARTH	♂		A
AIR	♃		
WATER	♅♇♀☉♄		
ANG.	♃♂♆♀☉♄		
SUCC.	☽☿♅		
CAD.	♇		
DIG.			
EX.			
DET.	☿♀ ♂		
FALL			
PATTERN			
LIFE 1	SUBS. 1	REL. 5	END. 3

DATE:

Formula 8: Quick and Easy Math

Born July 12, 1977   Time: 10:30 AM PDT   in Los Angeles, CA.
118W15 34N03   EGMT: 7:53:00

	H.M.S.	
	10:30:00	AM PDT 7/12/77
	− 1:00:00	(subtract for Daylight Saving Time)
	9:30:00	AM PST 7/12/77
	+ 8:00:00	(add the time zone - see map on page 10 - for Los Angeles, Pacific Zone = 8 hrs.)
	17:30:00	This is the GMT (subtract 12 if over 12) = GMT 5:30 PM 7/12/77
	+ 12:00:00	(add 12 hours because this is an AM birth)
	29:30:00	This is used to obtain the Constant Log (if over 24 hours, subtract 24) = 5°30 CL 6399
	+ 4:55	10" correction (29^{h}30' ÷ 6 = 4^{h}55')
	+ 7:17:08	add ST (Sidereal Time) for day before, since this is AM birth or 7/11/77
	36:51:63	
	− 7:53:00	subtract EGMT for Los Angeles (if EGMT is EAST, you must add)
	28:58:63	
	28:59:03	convert 63"
	− 24:00:00	if over 24 hours, subtract 24
	4:59:00	TCST (True Calculated Sidereal Time) Look this up in Table of Houses for 34N and set up wheel.

To correct planets, take position on birthday and day after; find difference and get PLR (Planetary logarithm) from log table; add the CL to the PLR; look this figure up in log table and add this figure to the planet on the birthday.

Example:

$$\begin{array}{rl}
\text{Sun } 7/13/77 & 20°\, \mathfrak{S}\, 58' \\
7/12/77 & -\ 20°\, \mathfrak{S}\, 01' \\
\hline
& 57' \qquad = 1.4025 \text{ PLR} \\
& \qquad\quad +\ 6399 \text{ CL} \\
& \qquad \overline{2.0424 = 13'}
\end{array}$$

$$\begin{array}{rl}
\text{Sun } 7/12/77 & 20°\, \mathfrak{S}\, 01' \\
& +\quad\ 13' \\
\hline
\text{Corr. Sun} & 20°\, \mathfrak{S}\, 14'
\end{array}$$

Moon 7/13/77	19°♊07'		
7/12/77	− 7°♊15'		
	11° 52'	= 3059	PLR
		+ 6399	CL
		9458 =	2° 43'

Moon 7/12/77	7°♊15'
	+2° 43'
Corr. Moon	9°♊58'

With this System you always *ADD Corrections.*

Rule If the birth time is AM and after adding the Time Zone the GMT is PM you take the birthday and the day after and add to the birthday, as the example above.

If the birth time is PM and after adding the Time Zone the GMT is PM you take the birthday and the day after and add to the birthday, as the example above.

If the birth time is AM and after adding the Time Zone the GMT is still AM you must use the planets of the birthday and the DAY BEFORE, but you still ADD the corrections.

The same holds true if the birth time is later PM but becomes early AM GMT after adding the Time Zone.

Example:

H.M.S.		
0:15:00	AM	7/12/77
+8:00:00		Pacific Time Zone
8:15:00	AM	GMT 7/12/77 (This figure did not pass noon)
+12:00:00		add 12 hours for AM birth
20:15:00		This is your Constant Log = *CL 0738*
+3:23		10'' correction
+7:17:08		ST 7/11/77 (previous day for AM birth)
27:35:31		
−7:53:00		Los Angeles EGMT
19:42:31		TCST

To correct planets:

Moon 7/12/77	7°♊15'		
Moon 7/11/77	− 25°♉27'		
	11° 48'	= 3083	PLR
		+ 0738	CL
		3821 =	9°57'

Moon 7/11/77   25° ♉ 27'
                  + 9°   57'
                  ─────────────
                  34°   84'
Corr. Moon   5° ♊ 24'

This quick and easy math should be used only after you have familiarized yourself with formulas 1 through 7 and thoroughly understand the reasons for doing what you are doing. The ease of this formula is that you never have to worry about whether you add or subtract. You always add. Always. The only thinking you need to do concerns the dates to use. But if you keep the rules in mind: PM GMT use the birth day and the day after, AM GMT use the birthday and day before, it all becomes very easy.

If you look at Formula 1, you will note that we arrive at the same TCST with either system when the birthtime is 10:30 AM PDT 7/12/77.

In Formula 3 you will see that the Moon correction (r through u) results in a corrected Moon of 9° ♊ 58' regardless of which system you use.

Formula 5 shows you that both systems come up with the same TCST and planet correction when the person is born at 1:15 AM PDT (or 0:15 AM PST).

Since the easy math does everything in one step, it is very important to clearly mark your GMT and your Constant Log, since both will be used for many other purposes as you advance in your astrological studies.

All other rules and regulations are as shown in any of the other formulas. The Time Zone when the birthplace is EAST of Greenwich, is subtracted (step 1) and the EGMT is added (last step) just the reverse as the WEST of Greenwich procedure shown in our examples.

For SOUTH of the Equator, add 12 hours as one additional last step, exactly as shown in Formula 7. Be sure to study how to read the Table of Houses for South of the Equator as we explain in Formula 7.

To facilitate matters for you, we have added a Standard Time Zone map on page 10.

Lesson 4
Formulas for Midnight Math and Unknown Birth Times

Formula 9

On the next few pages, we will explain how to use a Midnight ephemeris, should you prefer that method. The principle and the results are, of course, the same; it is a question of personal preference (or which ephemeris you happen to have).

Midnight Math · AM Chart

Date: July 12, 1977   Time: 10:30 AM PDT   Place: Los Angeles, CA
118W15   34N03   Mer. Corr. + 7'   EGMT + $7^h53'$

To find House Cusps:

H.M.S.		AM 7/12/77 PDT
10:30:00		
− 1:00:00		Daylight Saving
9:30:00	AM	7/12/77 PST
+ 7:00		Meridian Correction
9:37:00	AM	LMTI
+ 1:36		LMTI corr. ($9^h37'$ ÷ 6 = 1'36")
+ 1:19		EGMT corr. ($7^h53'$ ÷ 6 = 1'19")
+ 19:19:06		Sidereal Time for 7/12/77
28:58:61		convert
28:59:01		More than 24 hrs. (1 day)
24:00:00		subtract 24
4:59:01		TCST (True Calculated Sidereal Time)

To find GMT and CL:

H.M.S.		
7:53:00		EGMT for L.A.
+ 9:37:00	AM	LMT 7/12/77
16:90:00		convert
17:30:00	AM	(does not exist -
− 12:00:00		subtract 12 hours)
5:30:00	PM	GMT 7/12/77

To find Interval: 11:60 (Midnight in hours and
              − 5:30 minutes)
              6:30 Interval

Constant Log 5673
To Correct planetary positions:

Moon 7/13/77	13°♊10'
7/12/77	− 1° 20'
	11°♊50'

PLR	= 3071
CL	+ 5673
	8744 = 3°12'
Moon 7/13/77	13°♊10'
	− 3° 12'
Corr. Moon	9°♊58'

Rule   If GMT is PM subtract correction from approaching midnight.
    Correct all the other planets using the same Constant Log and the same rule.

Formula 10: Midnight Math - PM Chart

Date: July 12, 1977   Time: 4:13 PM PDT   Place: Los Angeles, CA
118W15 34N03 Mer. Corr. + 7' EGMT + $7^h53'$

To find House Cusps:

H.M.S.		
4:13:00	PM	PDT - 7/12/77
− 1:00:00		Daylight Saving
3.13:00	PM	PST - 7/12/77
+ 7:00		Meridian Correction
3:20:00	PM	LMT 7/12/77
+ 12:00:00		for PM birth (time elapsed from previous midnight)
15:20:00		LMTI
+ 2:33		LMTI corr. ($15^h20'÷6 = 2'33''$)
+ 1:19		EGMT corr. ($7^h53'÷6 = 1'19''$)
+ 19:19:06		Sidereal Time for 7/12/77
34:42:58		More than 24 hrs. (1 day)
24:00:00		subtract 24 hours
10:42:58		TCST (True Calculated Sidereal Time)

To find GMT and CL:

H.M.S.	
7:53:00	EGMT for L.A.
+ 3:20:00	PM LMT 7/12/77
10:73:00	Convert
11:13:00	PM GMT 7/12/77

To find Interval	11:60 (Midnight in hours and
Subtract GMT	− 11:13 minutes)
	0:47 Interval

Constant Log 1:48:63

To correct Planet Positions:

Moon 7/13/77	13° ♊11'
Moon 7/12/77	− 1° ♊21'
	11° 50'

PLR	= 3071
CL	+ 1.4863
	1.7934 = 23'

Moon 7/13/77	13° ♊11'
	− 23'
Corr. Moon	12° ♊48'

Rule   If GMT is PM subtract correction from approaching midnight.
Correct all the other planets using the same Constant Log and the same rule.

Formula 11: Midnight Math - PM Chart

Date: July 12, 1977   Time: 6:15 PM PDT   Place: Los Angeles, CA
118W15 34N03   Mer. Corr. +7'   EGMT +7^{h}53'

To find House Cusps:

H.M. S.		
6:15:00	PM	PDT 7/12/77
− 1:00:00		Daylight Saving
5:15:00	PM	PST 7/12/77
+ 7:00		Meridian Correction
5:22:00	PM	LMT
+ 12:00:00		for PM birth (time elapsed from prev. mid.)
17:22:00		LMTI
+ 2:54		LMTI corr. (17^{h}22' ÷ 6 = 2'54")
+ 1:19		EGMT corr. (7^{h}53 ÷ 6 = 1'19")
+ 19:19:06		Sidereal Time 7/12/77
36:44:79		Convert
36:45:19		More than 24 hrs. (1 day)
− 24:00:00		subtract 24 hours
12:45:19		TCST (True Calculated Sidereal Time)

To find GMT and CL:

```
H.M.S.
7:53:00        EGMT for L.A.
+ 5:22:00  PM  LMT 7/12/77
12:75:00       Convert
13:15:00  PM   (does not exist)
- 12:00:00     subtract 12 hours
1:15:00  AM    GMT 7/13/77 or the next day
```

Constant Log 1.2833

To Correct Planet Positions:

```
Moon 7/14/77      25° Ⅱ 05'
     7/13/77    - 13° Ⅱ·10'
                  11°   55'
         PLR    = 3041
          CL    + 1.2833
                  1.5874    = 37'
Moon 7/13/77      13° Ⅱ 10'
                +     37'
   Corr. Moon     13° Ⅱ 47'
```

Rule   If GMT is AM, add correction to planet position on approaching midnight. Please note - the 2 midnights involved are 7/14 and 7/13.

Correct all the other planets using the same Constant Log and the same rule.

Explanation for Formulas 9, 10, and 11

The Rationale for the Midnight Math   If you have practiced erecting a chart with a NOON ephemeris, as we have shown you with many different examples, understanding the principle as it applies to MIDNIGHT ephemerides should be very easy. In showing you the Midnight formulas, we have purposely used again 10:30 AM and 4:13 PM in Los Angeles so that you can see that the final result is exactly the same (a 2'' difference which will certainly not change anything). And, of course, it makes no difference in correcting the planets either.

Look at Formula No. 1, Page 13, for an AM birth west of Greenwich—and then compare it to the calculations for the same birth data that were calculated using a Midnight Ephemeris. (We have used "Die Deutsche Ephemeride", 1971-1980, but any Midnight Ephemeris will do). We must still subtract one hour for DST. We must still add the meridian correction to achieve the correct local mean time. But, here there is a change. In an AM birth, using a Noon ephemeris, we need to account for the time elapsed until noon. Using a Midnight ephemeris, we need not do that. We just make the LMT and EGMT corrections, and then add the Sidereal Time (for the actual day of birth - not the day before). That is the second change, based of course on the same principle. Please note that the Sidereal Time in the Noon ephemeris reads 07:17:08 for July 11th and 7:21:04 for July 12th (found in the PM chart sample on page 25). The Sidereal Time in the Midnight ephemeris reads 19:19:06. This accounts for the 12 hours we had to add on in the Noon Math. In other words, in any Midnight ephemeris, the day starts at one second after midnight, whereas in a Noon ephemeris, the day begins 1 second after noon.

Now, reverse the procedure. You are dealing with someone born in the afternoon, like our sample chart on page 40—Formula 10. We still have to subtract the one hour for DST and add the meridian correction for Los Angeles, but now we are dealing with a birth that occurred after 12 noon, yet our day starts at midnight, so we have to add 12 hours to account for the time elapsed from midnight to noon. The rest of the procedure is exactly the same, but we take the Sidereal Time of the actual day of birth, because the 4:13 PM time still falls between midnight of the 12th and midnight of the 13th. In doing the AM chart for an AM birth with a Noon ephemeris, the birth in the morning was before noon on the actual day of birth. (The native was born at 9:30 AM PST, July 12, the ephemeris day begins only at noon on that date, so we took the day before, July 11).

Recap: When working with a Midnight ephemeris, use the addition of 12 hours only for a person born after noon. Always use the Sidereal Time for the actual day of birth.

To find the GMT and Constant Log and Correct Planets

In our Formula 9 - AM Midnight Math - you will note that regardless of which method you use, the GMT remains the same, namely 5:30, and the interval from which we figure the Constant Log is the same, namely 5673. (Please refer to Formula 2, page 17). The difference is in the position of the planets, which of course are different at noon than they would be at midnight. The most obvious change is noted in the Moon's position because it is the fastest-moving of all the planets. The position for midnight, July 13, is 13° ♊ 10', and for midnight July 12, is 01° ♊ 20' (we use these two midnights since the GMT of 5:30 PM falls between them). Follow the log conversion and you will see that the actual time difference to 5:30 PM is 3°12'.

At 5:30 PM, you are closer to the midnight of the 13th of July than the midnight of the 12th of July, so naturally you subtract the 3°12' from the 13th - and your corrected Moon is 9° ♊ 58'. If you'll now check our Formula 3 on Page 21, you will see that the Moon correction done with a Noon ephemeris produces the same result: 9° ♊ 58'.

The planetary correction in Formula 10 is the same as the one just explained. We still have a PM GMT and subtract the difference from the midnight of July 13th. If you look at the chart we calculated for you, based on our Formula 4 for PM Math, Page 25, you will note that the Moon is at 12° ♊ 48', just as it is for the Midnight Math.

The planetary correction for our Formula 11 shows a change. The person in question was born at 5:15 PM PST, and by the time we convert this to GMT we find ourselves at 1:15 AM of the next day - July 13th. This brings us closer to the midnight of the 13th than the midnight of the 14th, so we add the time difference of 37' to the 13th.

Recap: Always think of which midnight you are closest to and adjust accordingly.

Formula 12: Quick and Easy Math for Midnight

Born: July 12, 1977   Time: 10:30 AM   PDT in Los Angeles, CA
118W15 34N03 EGMT 7:53:00

```
        H.M.S.
     10:30:00  AM  PDT 7/12/77
    – 1:00:00      Daylight Saving
      9:30:00  AM  PST 7/12/77
    + 8:00:00      Pacific Time Zone
     17:30:00      This is your CL 1372 and GMT (17:30 hrs.)
                   5:30 PM GMT 7/12/77
      + 2:55       10" correction (17:30 ÷ 6 = 2:55)
    + 19:19:06     ST 7/12/77
     39:51:61
    – 7:53:00      EGMT for Los Angeles
     28:58:61
   – 24:00:00
      4:58:61      convert
      4:59:01      TCST
```

To correct planets, take position on birthday and day after.

```
    Sun 7/13/77      20°♋30'
        7/12/77    – 19°♋33'
                        57'      = 1.4025 PLR
                                 + 1372 CL
                                  1.5397 = 41'
    Sun 7/12/77      19°♋33'
                   +     41'
                     19° 74'     convert
       corr. Sun     20°♋14'


    Moon 7/13/77     13°♊11'
         7/12/77   –  1°♊21'
                     11° 50'     = 3071 PLR
                                 + 1372 CL
                                  4443 = 8°  37'

    Moon 7/12/77      1°♊21'
                   +  8°  37'
       corr. Moon     9°♊48'
```

If you look at Formula 9, midnight math - AM chart, you will see the same birthtime and birthdate, the same result for the True Calculated Sidereal Time and the corrected planets, only the steps to get there are slightly different.

Born July 12, 1977   Time: 4:13 PM   PDT in Los Angeles, CA
118W15 34N03   EGMT 7:53:00

```
        H.M.S.
      4:13:00  PM   PDT 4/12/77
    − 1:00:00       Daylight Saving
      3:13:00  PM   PST 7/12/77
    + 8:00:00       Pacific Time Zone
     11:13:00  PM   GMT 7/12/77
   + 12:00:00       to get past midnight
     23:13:00       This is your CL 0144
       + 3:52       10'' corr. (23:13 ÷ 6 = 3:52
   + 19:19:06       ST for 7/12/77
     42:35:58
    − 7:53:00       EGMT for Los Angeles
     34:42:58
   − 24:00:00
     10:42:58       TCST
```

Take planets for 7/13 and 7/12

```
        Moon 7/13/77      13°♊11'
             7/12/77    −  1°♊21'
                          11°  50'        = 3071 PLR
                                          + 0144 CL
                                       3215 =  11°27'


        Moon 7/12/77       1°♊21'
                         + 11°  27'
           corr. Moon    12°♊48'
```

Please check Formula 10 - midnight math - PM chart, and note same birthtime and date same results in TCST and planet correction.

Be sure to read all our mathematical explanations in previous lessons before you attempt to do this Quick and Easy Formula. It is very important that the logic of the steps taken in the longer methods has been understood before you take shortcuts and only do the math by rote. Also please read some of the explanations for this Quick and Easy Math as given under Formula 8, page 37.

But, What if there is No Birthtime Available?

This is one of the predicaments in Astrology. There are certain methods whereby one can rectify a horoscope, but it is a very difficult and complicated affair, and after many hours of adjusting an event to fit a particular stellar pattern, you still can never be absolutely sure that the rectified chart is correct.

There are several easy methods of erecting a chart to gain some insight, although none of these will ever reveal as much as a natal (radix) chart based on the actual known time of birth.

Flat Chart   This is the natural or flat wheel as we have taught in Volume 1. You put 0° Aries on the Ascendant, 0°Taurus on the cusp of the 2nd house, 0° Gemini on the cusp of the 3rd house, and so on around the wheel. You simply copy the position of the planets as they are listed, right out of the ephemeris for the date of birth and insert them in the proper houses. Unfortunately, the Moon moves as much as 15° per day, so you will not be able to see the true lunar relation to the other planets. Naturally, you will not be able to interpret house positions, but you can at least use the aspects from one planet to another and interpret them, as well as the sign location of each planet. This type of chart can show you some of the *natural tendencies* and *basic characteristics* for the individual, but no more than that.

Solar Equilibrium Chart   From the ephemeris for the date of birth, copy the exact position for the Sun; put that degree and sign on the Ascendant. Walt Disney, for example, was born on December 5, 1901. The ephemeris for that day puts the Sun at 12° Sagittarius 40'. Put this on the cusp of the 1st house. The 2nd house then reads 12° Capricorn 40', the 3rd house 12° Aquarius 40', and so on around all 12 houses. Again, as with the Flat Chart, copy the rest of the planets into the wheel. Aspect the planets to determine the relationships they have to each other. This chart also is no substitute for the corrected natal chart, but by putting the degree of the Sun on the Ascendant, you are able to see some of the *potentials and resources,* some of the *basic abilities* of the person in question.

By using both the FLAT and SOLAR EQUILIBRIUM CHARTS, you can get some idea of the fundamental personality you are dealing with; however, since you do not have a true Ascendant, and thus no house position for the planets, you will not be able to determine the actual areas of emphasis, nor the outer personality. You will not be able to describe the type of partner the individual wants or could be happy with, the attitude toward children, the sense of values, the need for religion or a philosophy of life, the ability to complete an education, and any of a hundred other fine points you can pinpoint through an accurate natal chart.

Refer to the examples of these chart types on page 47.

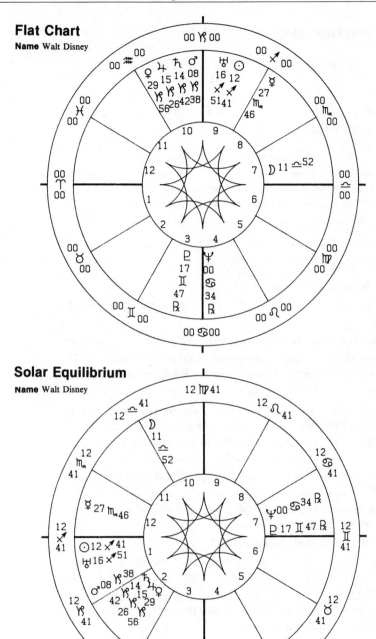

Flat Chart

Name Walt Disney

Solar Equilibrium

Name Walt Disney

Quiz for Part One - Math

1. What do the following abbreviations stand for?
    ST   PM
    LMT   CL
    GMT   TCST

2. Fill in the blanks.
    60'' = _____ = 1° or 1 hr.
           = one sign   12 signs =
           _____   _____

3. Latitude measures distances between what directions? _____
    Longitude measures distances between what directions? _____

4. How many degrees does the Sun move in 16 minutes?

5. In calculating a chart using a Noon ephemeris,
        When do you add 12 hours?
        When do you subtract 24 hours?
        When do you subtract 1 hour?

6. If a person is born at 8:30 PM, which house should the Sun be in?

7. A new degree of the zodiac crosses the MC every_____minutes.

8. Do we add or subtract corrections for WEST of Greenwich?
    Do we add or subtract corrections for EAST of Greenwich?

9. What does EGMT stand for?

10. Using a Noon ephemeris, if a person was born at 11:15 AM, on
    June 15, 1952, what date will you use for the ST?_____
    What two dates do you use to determine planetary motion?____
    _____ & _____

11. If 11°♌21' is on the 3rd house cusp, what is on the 9th house
    cusp?_____

12. If a person is born at 1:10 PM in New York City, what time is it
    in Greenwich?

13. How do you correct an Rx planet?

14. Rules for correcting planet positions - do you add or subtract?
        If GMT is AM____corrections from planet on nearest noon.

        If GMT is PM_____corrections to planet on nearest noon.

15. If a person is born at NOON or MIDNIGHT, how would you
    write this in numerals?

16. If the LMT is AM, and the GMT is also AM, what additional
    step must be taken?

17. When a person is born EAST of Greenwich, do you add or
    subtract the EGMT correction?

18. When a person is born SOUTH of the Equator, what additional step is necessary to find the TCST?

19. In using a Midnight ephemeris, when it is necessary to add 12 hours?

20. What two kinds of charts can you use if there is no birthtime available?

For the answers to this quiz, please turn to the Appendix, page 239.

Part Two

Introduction
Steps to Refine Delineation

As we stated in Volume One of "The Only Way to... Learn Astrology", we teach the mathematics of erecting a horoscope only after you have gained some fundamental understanding of interpretation. We hope that you have had a chance to practice some basic delineations as outlined and suggested in Volume One, because in this section of the book we will teach you refinements based on the fundamental principles of astrology.

Unless the nature and feeling of each planet, sign, house and aspect are familiar to you, these refinements may seem complicated or hard to understand. In order to avoid any problems, we will at this point suggest that you take any chart you have, or that of Muhammad Ali (in the back of Volume One), and delineate it according to the basic concepts we taught in Volume One.

Look first at the chart as a whole; then take it apart and interpret the Sun by sign, house ruler and aspects, and then do the same with all the other planets and houses. Refresh your memory on any keywords that may elude you at the moment. In our classes, we always have a review lesson right after we teach the math, which is a subject by itself and totally apart from astrological judgment.

After you have reviewed and familiarized yourself with basics, you should be ready to learn how to find some of the less obvious traits and characteristics that each person possesses.

Since we will be using the charts of Walt Disney, Farrah Fawcett, Hermann Hesse and Joan Sutherland for delineation purposes, it will be helpful if you copy their charts on horoscope blanks. This little exercise has a dual purpose; it is easier to follow some of our explanations with the chart in your hand, rather than flipping back and forth in the book, but even more important, as you copy a chart in your own writing, you will get a feeling of the makeup and character of the person involved. For some reason, it helps to put the cusps onto the blank wheel, to insert the planets, to aspect the chart by yourself, rather than seeing what we have already done. We are not trying to give you additional work—we are just passing on to you some of the things we have learned in our years of teaching beginning astrology.

Lesson 5
Standouts - Lack of Element, Lack of Quality, Lack of House Emphasis and Unaspected Planets

What is a standout? Actually, it can be many different things. It can be the lack of a particular quality or element, or a planet that is unaspected. It can be an obvious planetary configuration, like a stellium of planets or a T-Square. It can be anything in the horoscope that even the beginning student will zoom in on, and when the teacher asks, "What made you pick on this first?", the student will invariably answer, "Because it stands out!" In this lesson we will be discussing these standouts.

The Lack of an Element in the Horoscope

In the horoscope blanks that we used in Volume One, as well as in this volume, you will find that at the bottom of the page we have an *Aspectarian*. On the left side we do the actual aspecting of one planet to the other; on the right side there is a tabulation of certain indicators that we consider important in delineating. These include the qualities, elements, types of house (broken down into angular, succedent and cadent—relating to the qualities), types of house (broken down into life, substance, relationships and endings—relating to the elements), planetary dignities, exaltations, detriment, and fall, the chart patterns (Lesson 10), the chart ruler, final dispositor (Lesson 9), mutual receptions (Lesson 9), and the critical degrees (Lesson 18).

As you look at the horoscope and mark these areas, you will quickly notice if any of the qualities or elements, or any other important factors, are missing. If, for example, you look at the horoscope of Farrah Fawcett, you can see that she has no planets in the *Earth* element in her chart; however, if you look at the house division at the bottom of her chart you will note that she has three planets in the houses of substance (relating to the Earth element). Saturn and Pluto are in her second house, which relates to Taurus, and Venus is in her sixth house, which relates to Virgo. This tells us that the traits we associate with the Earth element are there, some of the Taurus earthiness will help her keep her feet on the ground. Venus in Sagittarius can fly off in many directions and scatter its affections, but its position in the sixth (Virgo) house adds a shade of "Let's think before we act," "Let's analyze this," and of course, "Let's buckle down to work."

Suppose that you have a horoscope in which there are no planets in Earth and none in the houses of substance either. You will find this to be an individual whose feet are not on the ground, who has trouble holding on to money because it does not mean much, someone who dreams impossible dreams but rarely puts these dreams to practical use. And most difficult of all, these people find it hard to differentiate between that which really matters ("matter" is quite earthy and practical) and that which is unimportant and passing. They make mountains out of molehills, and rarely have time to get right down to the nitty-gritty. Writer Zelda Fitzgerald, ever zany, ever flitting, always seeking and rarely finding, well represents this type of lack. Famous personalities with no earth but quite a few planets in the houses of substance include authors Mark Twain, Eugene O'Neill and Arthur Miller, reporter Ernie Pyle, the Duchess of Windsor and baseball star Joe di Maggio. These people also grope for reality, but usually manage to find facets of it. Mark Twain who was an idealist and a very impractical man, most realistically described his youth on the Mississippi in many of his books. For another example see Ernie Pyle's chart on page 57.

No Fire says it in those two words. These individuals lack that certain spark. You may feel like lighting a fire under them because they show little or no enthusiasm. They can be most dutiful, practical, ambitious, intelligent, intellectual and all else their horoscope promises, but they lack that certain flair. The motivation does not stem from a wish to expand and grow (Leo/Sagittarius) nor from that inner push to try and dare (Aries), rather it springs from a need or a wish to succeed. Scientist Louis Pasteur serves as a good example.

If the Fire element is missing but the houses of life are occupied, some of the fiery feeling is present, but it is not so obvious. Think of Jack Benny, a pioneer in his type of comedy, but do you remember that marvelous dead-pan face? Actress Merle Oberon with her beautiful yet nearly expressionless face falls in the same category. Other examples are actor Vincent Price, President Franklin Delano Roosevelt and baseball great Babe Ruth. Jack Benny's chart can be found on page 57.

No Air When there is no Air and the houses of relationships are unoccupied, the sensory and mental abilities are either lacking or hampered

No Earth

Name Ernie Pyle
Date August 3, 1900
Time 5:00 PM CST
Place Dana, IN
Long. 87W30
Lat. 39N48

Source
Biography *Story of Ernie Pyle* by Miller

B

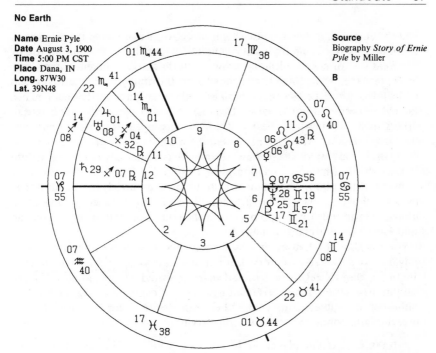

No Fire

Name Jack Benny
Date Feb. 14, 1894
Time 4:04 AM CST
Place Waukegan, ILL.
Long. 87W50
Lat. 42N22

Source
Sabian Symbols #89

C

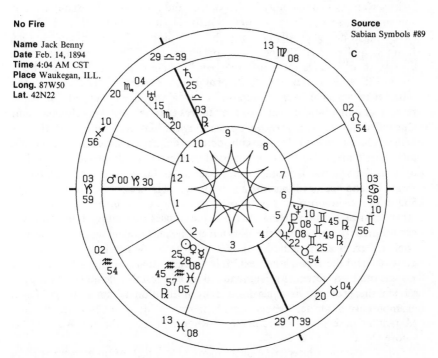

and the emphasis is directed elsewhere. Since Air is considered the element of communication (Gemini/Mercury) these persons have to find a totally different way of communicating, using whatever talent or potential they have to express themselves. Air is associated with the ability to intellectualize, to understand abstract concepts, to push aside the emotions and view matters in a factual, objective way (Aquarius/Uranus). Air also shows how we relate to others socially (Libra). If these abilities are missing, then the emotions may take over or some other manner of coping must be found. Helen Keller is a fairly drastic example. She had no Air in her chart and only one planet (Pluto in the 7th) in a house of relationships. Despite her inability to see or hear (sensory perception), she managed to become a model for handicapped persons all over the world. Artist Vincent Van Gogh is another example of an individual with no Air and no planets in the houses of relationships. You can find Helen Keller's chart on page 59.

No Air, but the houses of relationships occupied is well exemplified by Edgar Cayce. This seer (sensory) learned to relate by seeing people not as they are but as they 'were'. Another good example would be actor Marlon Brando who in his mumbling way created a new style of communicating, making his rather unintelligible diction chic. Other examples are actor Dustin Hoffman, preacher Jim Jones and writer Clifford Irving.

No Water   and no planets in the houses of endings indicates a person who lacks sensitivity or the ability to feel deeply and intuitively. It usually denotes someone whose emotions are well controlled, who is not influenced by his environment and generally does not show his moods. Every human being has feelings, and so does the person who lacks water planets, but these people express their feelings on a different level. Their motivation will not be to nurture (Cancer) or feel deeply (Scorpio) or know intuitively (Pisces), some other elements take over. Composer Ludwig van Beethoven was one such person. Anyone familiar with his life realizes that he was a very disliked man. One adjective used in nearly every biography for him was "unfeeling" (lack of feeling - lack of water). He was considered rude, hot tempered, suspicious and tactless. He had few friends and insisted he preferred to be alone. But his lack of sensitivity toward people was most certainly compensated for by his creativity and ability to feel through his music. The creativity of Fire (he had a Sagittarius stellium) took over and he will go down in history as one of the great musical geniuses. No Water but the houses of endings represented, is exemplified by actress Marlene Dietrich and boxer Muhammad Ali. Both seem cool, collected and unemotional. Yet all who know Marlene's love for her daughter and the Hausfrau streak in her, realize that a strong 4th house is at work. And by observing Muhammad Ali we can feel that behind the facade of "I am the greatest" is a caring and even emotional human being. Other examples are publisher Bennett Cerf, entertainer Maurice Chevalier, Senator Margaret Chase Smith, opera manager Rudolf Bing and dictator Adolf Hitler whose chart is on page 59.

One of the most interesting phenomena of the lack of an element is to be

No Air

Name Helen Keller
Date June 27, 1880
Time 4:02 PM LMT
Place Tuscumbia, Ala.
Long. 87W42
Lat. 34N44

Source
Dewey quotes Wemyss
"Astrological Quarterly"
December 1930

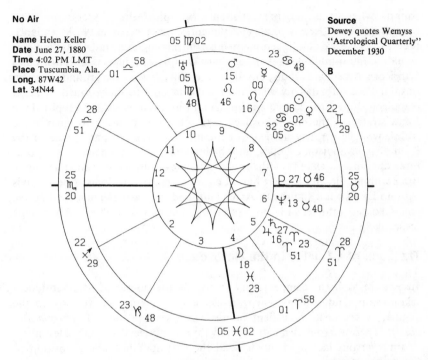

No Water

Name Adolf Hitler
Date April 20, 1889
Time 6:30 PM LMT
Place Braunau, Austria
Long. 13E03
Lat. 48N15

Source
Hitler by Alan Bullock

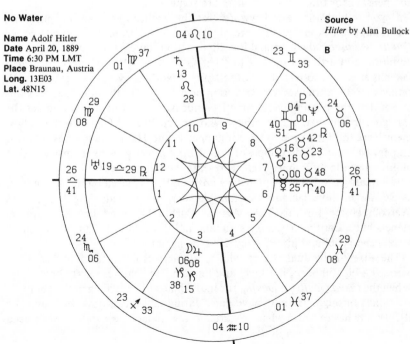

found when the lacking element occupies the Ascendant. The overcompensation seems total, and the entire outer personality (Ascendant), the way people see you, is represented by the missing element. A case in point would be multi-millionaire J. Paul Getty who had no planets in Earth but a Capricorn Ascendant. Indisputably, he kept his feet on the ground, he most certainly knew financially what mattered and how to make much of little. Napoleon Bonaparte, lacked Air but had a Libra Ascendant, and typified the Libra strategist, the man who needed to wage war in order to balance the scales, who desperately needed to communicate his ideas and beliefs in the form of the Napoleonic Codes, and the man who needed a partner, or two or three or four, to relate to. Other good examples would be comedienne Fanny Brice with no Fire in the chart but a Leo Ascendant. Nutritionist Adelle Davis with no Earth but a Capricorn Ascendant, and both artists Toulouse Lautrec and Georges Braque with no Water but Scorpio and Pisces Ascendants respectively.

The Lack of a Quality in the Horoscope

Just as we look for compensatory factors in the houses of life, substance, relationships and endings when an element is lacking, so we look to the angular, succeedent, or cadent houses when we find one of the *qualities absent.* There are four elements but only three qualities, thus you are less likely to find persons lacking a quality and the corresponding house position to compensate for this lack—but there are some.

If you rethink the basic keywords for the qualities you can imagine what might happen if some quality is totally lacking in a horoscope. If the *Cardinal Quality is absent,* the Cardinal initiative, action, quickness, pioneering spirit, ambition and ardor gives way to "Let George do it!". Whatever action *is* taken is as easily motivated out of self-pity, "Nothing ever goes right for me", rather than by a true sense of direction or priority. On the other hand, if this person has the possibility for creative endeavor or spiritual involvement, he can go further than many others who are so busy doing that they allow themsleves too little time to be. Kidnapper Bruno Hauptmann whose chart is on page 61 was a good example of the "Nothing ever goes right for me" type; philosopher Manly Palmer Hall represents the latter type.

If a quality is missing by planetary position but is placed on the Ascendant, as we saw in those lacking a certain element, the individual again seems to overcompensate for this lack. Actress Barbra Streisand has no Cardinal planets but a Cardinal (Aries) Ascendant and it would be hard to find a more active, energetic, ambitious, go-getter-type person.

The Fixed individual is one who is stable, resolute, fixed in his ways, perhaps a bit stubborn, but loyal and reliable. He achieves slowly but surely. When the *Fixed Quality is lacking* the individual will be lacking in the ability to see things through. He may have guts, daring and great ideas, but someone else usually has to finish what he starts. Yet, even lacking stability, when used

No Cardinal

Name Bruno Hauptmann
Date November 26, 1899
Time 1:00 PM MET
Place Kamenz, Germany
Long. 14E06
Lat. 51N16

Source
TP Davis quotes radio
gram "from his mother to
Paul Clancy"

A

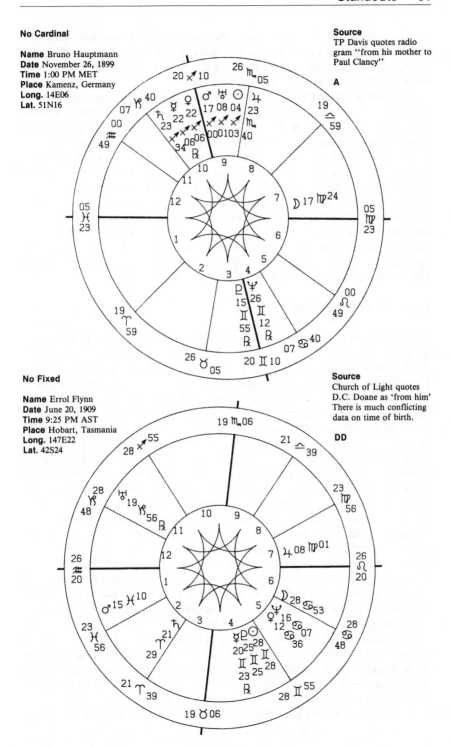

No Fixed

Name Errol Flynn
Date June 20, 1909
Time 9:25 PM AST
Place Hobart, Tasmania
Long. 147E22
Lat. 42S24

Source
Church of Light quotes
D.C. Doane as 'from him'
There is much conflicting
data on time of birth.

DD

positively he can be freer than others, less burdened by his own entrenchment, able to change and grow without the pains that so often go with changes. Actor Errol Flynn, see his chart on page 61, singer Nelson Eddy and poet Elizabeth Barrett Browning are some examples.

When the *Mutable Quality is lacking,* the individual may lack some of the versatility, adaptability and changeability so well represented in the common signs. This may indicate that he is very dependable and one-directional, often to the point of being a bore, too set in his ways and demanding that others be as perfect as he. On the other hand, the Mutable signs as a group are very involved with others, in fact nearly dependent on them; if that need is absent, it frees the individual to be his own person, to grow and evolve in his own way without worrying what others say or think. Violinist Yehudi Menuhin, child prodigy at age 9 and still diligently pursuing the same career, serves as a good example. He is one of the great violinists of the century, but he was also one of the first to embrace Eastern philosophies and music, long before it was fashionable to do so. Another pertinent example is conductor Arturo Toscanini whose chart can be found on page 63.

Lack of House Emphasis

This entails the reverse procedure from the way we handled the elements and qualities. To compensate for any lacks in the houses of life, substance, relationships and endings, look to the elements. Lacks of planets in angular, succeedent or cadent houses are helped by planets in cardinal, fixed or mutable signs. A lack of house emphasis is not as important as lacks of an element or quality, but they should be observed, since any lack indicates an imbalance.

The *houses of life* unoccupied may indicate a lack of inspiration or idealism, or even a certain difficulty in planning for the future. After all, we are talking of the first, fifth and ninth houses. Heiress Patty Hearst serves as one good example. See her chart on page 63. No planets in the *houses of substance* often denotes a person who has a hard time deciding on a vocation and tends to flounder in his sense of values. With the second, sixth and tenth houses empty, he may be catapulted into a career by circumstances rather than diligent preparation. Dictator Benito Mussolini had such a chart, so do Governor George Wallace, Nazi propaganda minister Joseph Goebbels and drug cult leader Timothy Leary whose chart is on page 64. All of them well illustrate the problem at hand. If the *houses of relationships* are not occupied, we may find someone to whom any form of relating is but a minor subject. Therefore he could be the eternal bachelor (or she the spinster), the loner or even an orphan. Teddy Roosevelt's rather eccentric daughter Alice Longworth would be one such an example. So is Sam Goldwyn whose chart is on page 64. No planets in the *houses of endings* may indicate a lack of depth or sensitivity, but most often it shows great difficulty or even fear of looking within. Actors Desi Arnaz and Orson Welles, Queen Elizabeth II and artist Vincent van Gogh all illustrate the problem. See Van Gogh's chart on page 66.

A chart of a famous person with *no planets in angular houses* is hard to

No Mutable

Name Arturo Toscanini
Date March 25, 1867
Time 2:00 AM LMT
Place Parma, Italy
Long. 10E10
Lat. 44N48

Source
Church of Light
from him personally

A

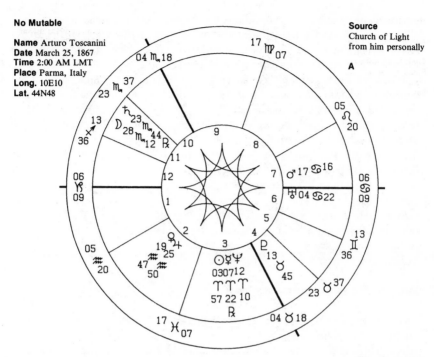

No Life

Name Patty Hearst
Date Feb. 20, 1954
Time 6:01 PM PST
Place San Francisco, CA
Long. 122W25
Lat. 37N47

Source
Contemporary Sidereal
Horoscopes

A

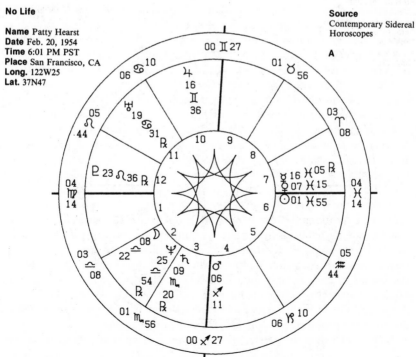

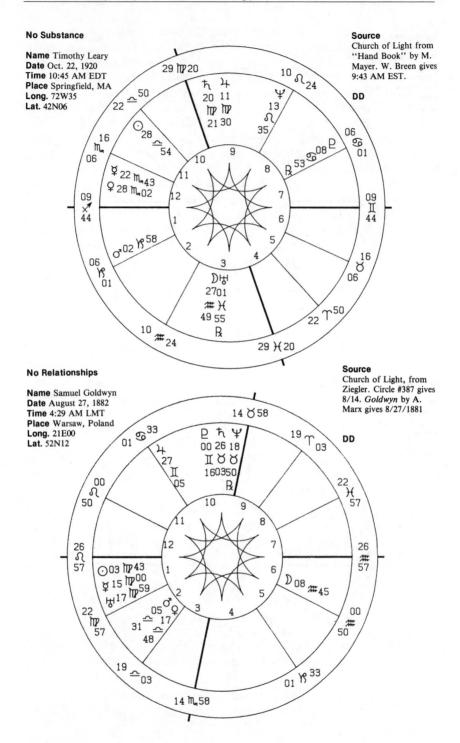

No Substance

Name Timothy Leary
Date Oct. 22, 1920
Time 10:45 AM EDT
Place Springfield, MA
Long. 72W35
Lat. 42N06

Source
Church of Light from
"Hand Book" by M.
Mayer. W. Breen gives
9:43 AM EST.

DD

No Relationships

Name Samuel Goldwyn
Date August 27, 1882
Time 4:29 AM LMT
Place Warsaw, Poland
Long. 21E00
Lat. 52N12

Source
Church of Light, from
Ziegler. Circle #387 gives
8/14. *Goldwyn* by A.
Marx gives 8/27/1881

DD

find, since the angles propel us into action and without some kind of action there is little chance of fame. Barbara Hutton is one of the few examples we came across and her fame was due to her father's wealth, not to her own initiative. You can find her chart on page 66. Lack of planets in the first, fourth, seventh and tenth houses indicates someone who rarely starts anything on his or her own, the drive seems to be missing and they need cardinal planets to help them become active.

No planets in succedent houses is less serious than no planets in the angles, and with some fixed planets in the chart the compensation is rather easy. Yet a certain balance is missing and T. E. Lawrence best known as Lawrence of Arabia exemplifies this quite well. See his chart on page 67. Though fixed in his purpose, adhering to his early principles and beliefs, he felt the need to roam, at home nowhere and everywhere.

Empty cadent houses again are far less important than empty angles and easy to balance with some mutable planets in the horoscope. The lack would show in such areas as adaptability, versatility or movability, or any other words you may chose in order to illustrate the third, sixth, ninth and twelfth houses. A good example would be television host Mike Douglas whose chart is on page 67.

The Unaspected Planet

A totally unaspected planet is nearly impossible to find; however, a planet lacking what we call major aspects to it (conjunctions, oppositions, squares, inconjuncts, trines or sextiles) does exist, and when it does, the pattern generated is most interesting. Do not conclude that such a planet is weak, because it does not integrate with the rest of the chart; to the contrary it works doubly hard, as if to compensate for the fact that it stands alone. This solo performance can sometimes be exhausting, but it is never dull! A great deal depends upon which of the planets is unaspected, the sign it is in and the house it occupies.

The Sun   representing your individuality, inner self, the heart of the chart, without aspects to other planets will manifest in several ways, all of them very important, because this is the *Inner You* we are talking about. If *You* stand by yourself, alone, and whatever you do is done without encumberance or worry about others, even the other parts of yourself—such as your thinking, feeling, ambitions, partners, family,—then you can be different. Within you can be whatever the Sun wishes you to be. You may work hard at it, but it will be relatively easy because nothing and nobody can stop you. Queen Elizabeth II who dared to be human though a queen, independent "I'll do my own thing" actress Mia Farrow, girl jockey Robyn Smith-Astaire, first to break a tabu and painter Vincent Van Gogh are good examples. See Robyn's chart on page 68.

No Endings

Name Vincent Van Gogh
Date March 30, 1853
Time 11:00 AM LMT
Place Groot-Zundert,
      Holland
Long. 4E21
Lat. 50N51

Source
Autobiography *Van Gogh,
a Self Portrait* Gauquelin
Volume 4 # 1444.

No Angular

Name Barbara Hutton
Date Nov. 14, 1912
Time 2:25 PM LMT
Place New York, NY
Long. 73W57
Lat. 40N45

Source
Blanca Holmes states from
"baby book."

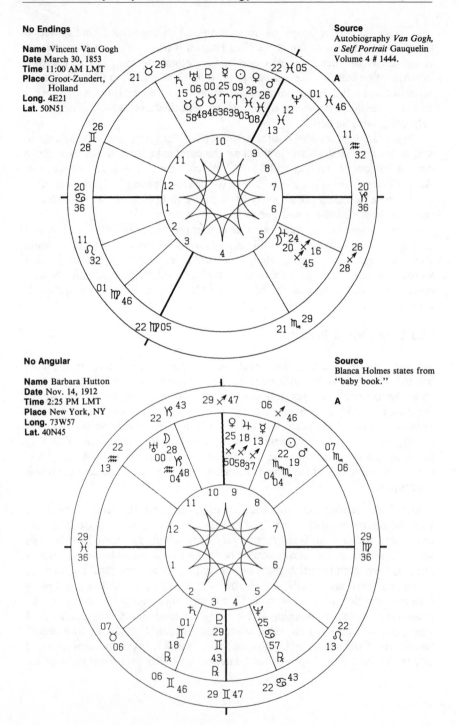

No Succedent

Name T.E. Lawrence
Date August 16, 1888
Time 5:00 AM GMT
Place Tremodoc, Wales
Long. 4W15
Lat. 52N50

Source
Biography *Secret Lives of Lawrence of Arabia* quotes early morning. Mother also stated - born small hours of AM. Tucker quotes August 15 SS # 554 says 11 PM GMT

DD

No Cadent

Name Mike Douglas
Date August 11, 1920
Time 5:30 PM CDT
Place Chicago, IL
Long. 87W39
Lat. 41N52

Source
American Astrology July, 1977 Joy Rank. Penfield gives same month and day but 1925.

C

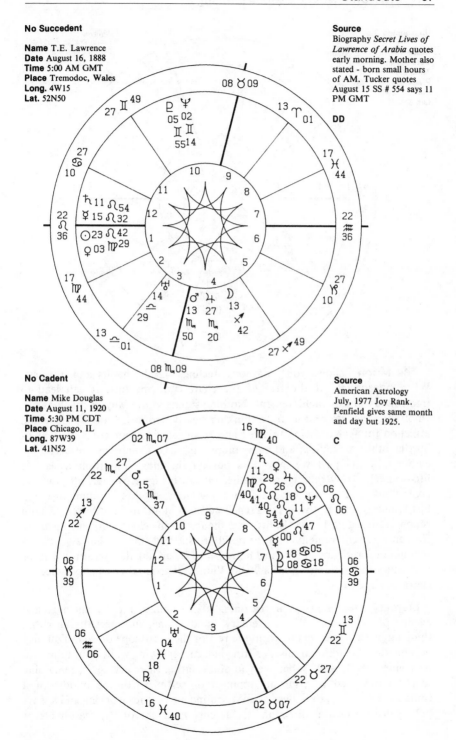

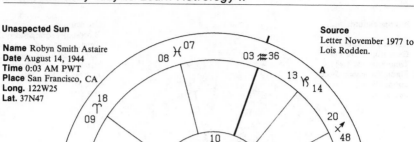

Unaspected Sun

Name Robyn Smith Astaire
Date August 14, 1944
Time 0:03 AM PWT
Place San Francisco, CA
Long. 122W25
Lat. 37N47

Source
Letter November 1977 to
Lois Rodden.

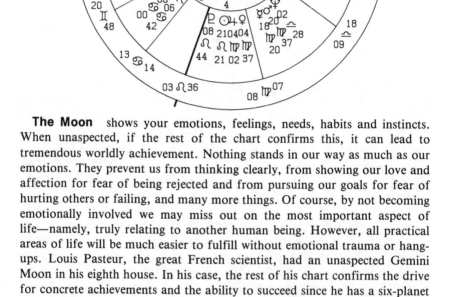

The Moon shows your emotions, feelings, needs, habits and instincts. When unaspected, if the rest of the chart confirms this, it can lead to tremendous worldly achievement. Nothing stands in our way as much as our emotions. They prevent us from thinking clearly, from showing our love and affection for fear of being rejected and from pursuing our goals for fear of hurting others or failing, and many more things. Of course, by not becoming emotionally involved we may miss out on the most important aspect of life—namely, truly relating to another human being. However, all practical areas of life will be much easier to fulfill without emotional trauma or hangups. Louis Pasteur, the great French scientist, had an unaspected Gemini Moon in his eighth house. In his case, the rest of his chart confirms the drive for concrete achievements and the ability to succeed since he has a six-planet stellium in Capricorn in his third house ruled by an angular Saturn in Taurus that trines this stellium. Baseball star Vida Blue is another example. See his chart on page 69.

Mercury represents your reasoning ability, mind, intellectual urge and avenue of expression. When Mercury stands alone, unaspected, the entire thinking process is detached from the rest of the horoscope or *you*. You may be a bundle of emotional misery sitting in a corner crying while your mind will be saying "Well, well. What are you doing sitting there crying?", remaining totally uninvolved in your unhappiness or self-pity. In the middle of a romantic adventure, or in deep sleep, the mind never stops working and always pulls you in a mental direction. If Mercury is in one of the reasonable or

Unaspected Moon

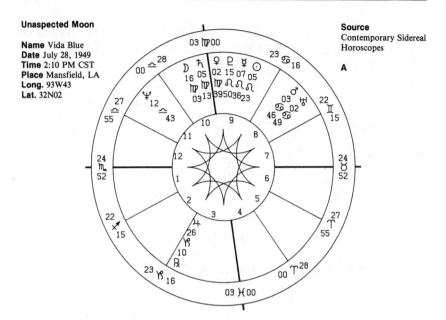

Name Vida Blue
Date July 28, 1949
Time 2:10 PM CST
Place Mansfield, LA
Long. 93W43
Lat. 32N02

Source
Contemporary Sidereal
Horoscopes

A

mental signs, the direction will be logical, cool and collected. If it is in an unstable sign, it can at times become too much for the person to handle and you either blow your stack or the nervous system suffers. These persons can benefit greatly from meditation or Yoga which gives the mind a chance to rest once in a while. Prominent persons having Mercury unaspected are Maria Montessori, the educator, with a Libran Mercury in the tenth house, and comedian Jonathan Winters with Mercury in Sagittarius in the 5th house of creativity. To illustrate a horoscope where the unaspected Mercury strengthened the mind, please see Mohandas Gandhi's chart on page 70. Gandhi, lovingly known as "Mahatma", has a 1st house unaspected Mercury in Scorpio; this helps us understand the unbelievable ability he had to put mind over matter, to stay alive through his long stints in prison, his interminable hunger strikes and still be able to lead India into independence with calmness and wisdom.

Venus the planet of affection, values and social urges, when it lacks the ability to integrate, can go one of two ways. The person may pursue his goals and objectives without a need for love and affection, detached and self-sufficient (similar to an unaspected Moon) but more obvious since the emotions are somewhat hidden, whereas affections are visible in the outer behavior pattern. Or, the person may feel a constant need to give and receive love and affection, but at the same time, regardless of how much is given or received, he still feels unloved, unwanted and alone. We find examples of both types among the famous. There is actor Mickey Rooney with Venus in Libra who kept changing partners in order to feel loved; Sammy Davis Jr. with Venus in Aquarius in his eleventh house who even changed his religion in order to be part of his friends; and there is Jean Claude-Killy, the famous French skier and athlete, with Venus in Virgo in his second house, self-sufficient and satisfied with his own value system—mostly money. See Rooney's chart on this page.

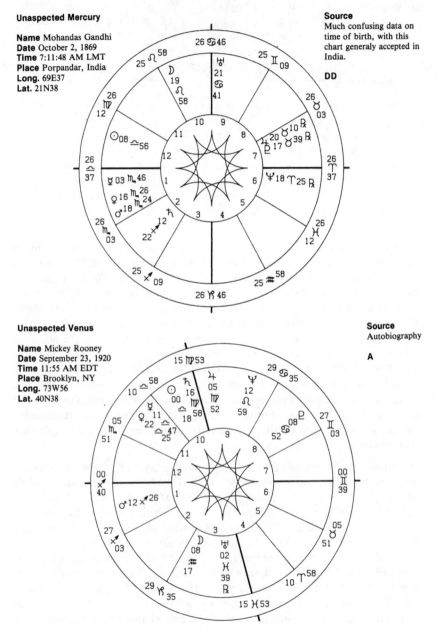

Unaspected Mercury

Name Mohandas Gandhi
Date October 2, 1869
Time 7:11:48 AM LMT
Place Porpandar, India
Long. 69E37
Lat. 21N38

Source
Much confusing data on time of birth, with this chart generaly accepted in India.

DD

Unaspected Venus

Name Mickey Rooney
Date September 23, 1920
Time 11:55 AM EDT
Place Brooklyn, NY
Long. 73W56
Lat. 40N38

Source
Autobiography

A

Mars symbolizes energy, drive, action and initiative. When these attributes work alone they often become too much of a good thing. The individual will burn the candle at both ends and thus burn himself out very quickly. When Mars is in a passive sign, it helps. These people are the explorers, pioneers, inventors, and overdoers who can scare others away with their intensity. Roald Amundson (the explorer) is one good example. So is Senate majority leader Howard Baker, who uses his unaspected Mars in Scorpio in the 7th house to influence and persuade others to his point of view. He is known as an indefatigable and diligent worker who relentlessly pursues his responsibilities in the Senate.

Jupiter We now move away from the very personal planets into a more general realm. Jupiter and Saturn stand between the personal and the transcendental planets, between self-motivating action and the abstract and impersonal sphere. However, Jupiter represents one factor of life which is important to personal growth, namely the ability to expand and use the higher mind in such directions as ideas and ideals, philosophy, and religion. When Jupiter is unaspected the person forms his own beliefs and mental images at an early age. he may seem unorthodox to his peers, even *outre,* especially since he does not seem to care what others think. If his horoscope indicates ambition, and he wishes to grow and expand, he will do it in his own way regardless of the morals and mores of the time. In a chart that is otherwise well integrated, this can signify an exciting individual who has new thoughts to offer a hungry world. However, in an already difficult horoscope, it can lead to Jupiterian excesses and Jupiter'splacement can make a difference. Witness the horoscope of murderer Richard Loeb where Jupiter in Taurus in the eleventh house was misused. By contrast, there is Oscar Wilde with Jupiter in Aries in his seventh house. Wilde may have been excessive but at least he offered humanity marvelous literature, as did humorist-poet Ogden Nash whose chart is on page 72.

Saturn though not a personal planet, is very important in any horoscope. It represents the urge for security and safety; it gives a sense of responsibility; it shapes our ambition and ego drive; it is the teacher and taskmaster needed in order for us not to overstep our boundaries. When unaspected, Saturn can become too demanding of the individual; nothing is ever good enough, we must constantly try harder and even that will not suffice. The result can be a very lonely human being, so self-disciplined that life offers no joys or pleasures, only work and duty. If the rest of the chart is light and mutable, Saturn becomes helpful by directing the person and this would be interpreted as beneficial, but in a sensitive and tension-prone horoscope, an over-bearing unaspected Saturn can be quite difficult to handle. Senator Ted Kennedy has an unaspected Saturn and both he and his family make tremendous demands on him. So, at times, he tries to escape, but never for long since Saturn always calls him back to duty. See chart on page 73.

Unaspected Mars

Name Howard Baker
Date November 15, 1925
Time 3:00 PM CST
Place Huntsville, TN
Long. 84W29
Lat. 36N25

Source
Gauquelin Book
of American
Charts

A

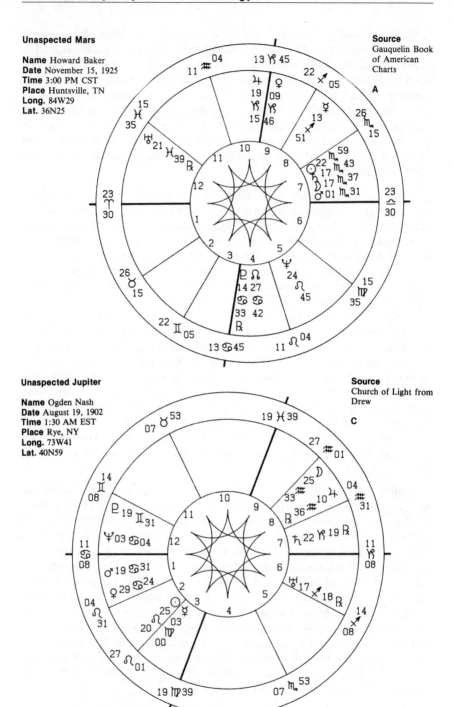

Unaspected Jupiter

Name Ogden Nash
Date August 19, 1902
Time 1:30 AM EST
Place Rye, NY
Long. 73W41
Lat. 40N59

Source
Church of Light from
Drew

C

Unaspected Saturn

Name Ted Kennedy
Date February 22, 1932
Time 3:58 AM EST
Place Dorchester, MA
Long. 71W04
Lat. 42N18

Source
Hospital Records according to AFA April 1972.

A

Unaspected Uranus

Name Sally Field
Date November 6, 1946
Time 4:23 AM PST
Place Pasadena, CA
Long. 118W09
Lat. 34N09

Source
Church of Light from birth certificate

A

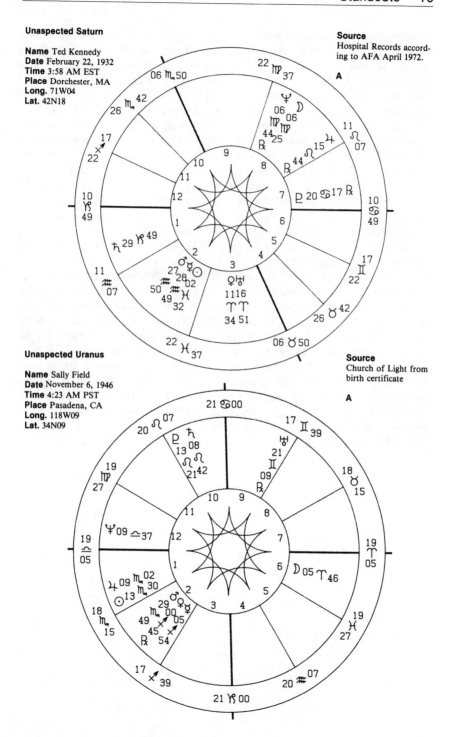

Uranus, Neptune, and Pluto   These three transcendental planets cannot be interpreted in the same vein as our previous delineations. Human beings are mostly shaped by events and happenings in their earliest years. Childhood environment, parental attitude, siblings—these are all determining factors that influence how we handle ourselves in later years. Uranus, Neptune, and Pluto are very far from Earth, very impersonal, abstract planets, and as children we do not tune in to their vibrations—not knowingly at least. Even an Aquarius child will be more influenced by Saturn, a Pisces child by Jupiter, and a Scorpio child by Mars than by their modern rulers. Whatever influence there is, it seems to be on its least evolved level. Some of the Pluto intensity rubs off on the Scorpio child, the Aquarian child may be a bit more original or rebellious than a truly Saturn-ruled person, and the Piscean child more imaginative or dreamy, but that seems to be as far as it goes. Thus, these planets standing alone and unaspected will only influence the latter part of life, after the basic personality has formed. The unintegrated Uranus enables the person to use whatever uniqueness he has already developed during his adult life, to make him stand out as being different or special at some point in life. For example general Charles de Gaulle, bishop James Pike, tenor Enrico Caruso, labor leader James Hoffa and actress Sally Field whose chart is on page 73. Neptune brings out whatever creativity, spirituality, or artistic ability has already become evident and it may throw the individual into the limelight when he starts tuning in. Singer Frank Sinatra, astronomer Johannes Kepler and actor Roddy McDowall are some examples. See Sinatra's chart on page 75. Pluto, the planet of transformation, is also the planet of the masses, mass appeal for good or bad, and as the individual becomes aware of Pluto's strength and intensity he will begin to stand out in a crowd as somebody to be reckoned with, as did Presidents John F. Kennedy and Gerald Ford. See Kennedy's chart on page 75.

Unaspected Neptune

Name Frank Sinatra
Date December 12, 1915
Time 1:19 PM EST
Place Hoboken, NJ
Long. 74W02
Lat. 40N44

Source
Karma Welch
Lynn Palmer quotes 3 AM

DD

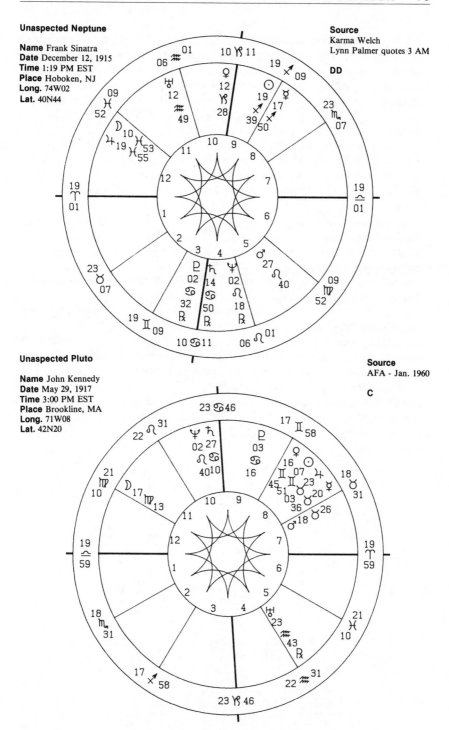

Unaspected Pluto

Name John Kennedy
Date May 29, 1917
Time 3:00 PM EST
Place Brookline, MA
Long. 71W08
Lat. 42N20

Source
AFA - Jan. 1960

C

Lesson 6
Standouts Continued, Lack of a Specific Aspect, Configurations and Final Signature

The Lack of Some Specific Aspect

A planet that has no squares, oppositions, conjunctions, inconjuncts, trines or sextiles is easy to spot in the aspectarian of your horoscope, in fact it too stands out. This lack of a specific aspect is not too important in the case of trines or sextiles, but the person with no squares or oppositions will definitely feel the lack. Anytime something is missing in the horoscope, we feel it. The question then becomes, are we able to replace this lack with something else? Can we still cope despite this lack?

Lack of Squares If we go back to the basics of any aspect and use the flat chart to guide us, we realize that the square is really Aries versus Cancer or Capricorn. Fiery, 'I' oriented Aries is squarely placed against gentle and watery Cancer. But what does water do to fire? It puts it out. How does Aries feel when someone tries to eliminate him? He gets mad, mad enough to do something about it. What about quiet, down-to-earth but ambitious Capricorn versus hot and heady Aries? What does earth do to fire? Same as water, it puts it out by trying to smother it. And again Aries, thinking of himself as the most important and best of the signs, after all, he is number 1 in the Zodiac, feels he has to fight back or be extinguished. That is why a square manifests so much tension and challenge and that is why we need squares in order to make something of ourselves, to fight for survival, even to overcome the powerful influence of our parents, astrologically represented by the 4th and 10th, the Cancer/Capricorn houses.

If there are no squares in a chart the native is not aware of the lack; in fact these people may have difficult lives, just like everyone else, but they will tell you how everything is just perfect, life is good and it's fun to be alive. The tensions or apprehensions that others innately feel seem to be absent. Since no square ever pressures them into overcoming obstacles, they choose to ignore all difficulties and happily live with the status quo. There is only one problem, when real trouble starts they do not know how to cope with it and either run away from it or internalize their feelings. They are not used to fighting or squarely facing a problem and unless their chart offers other strong points (conjunctions and/or oppositions), they may not accomplish much in this lifetime. Some famous (or infamous) people lacking squares are Lt. Calley of Mi Lai fame, who lacks both squares and oppositions, aviator Charles Lindbergh, see chart below, poet Ogden Nash, glamor queen Marlene Dietrich and opera impresario Rudolf Bing.

Lack of Oppositions   Going back to the flat chart we now see pioneering, self-oriented Aries trying to tell the world that he needs nobody, until one day he realizes that his fire cannot burn unless Libra's air fans it. He may come on too strong and make Libra mad enough to blow up a real firestorm, but eventually Aries will become aware that no man is an island - for after all Aries is represented by Mars and Libra by Venus, and what can be more fun than pairing Mars and Venus. Therefore the oppositions teach us to become aware

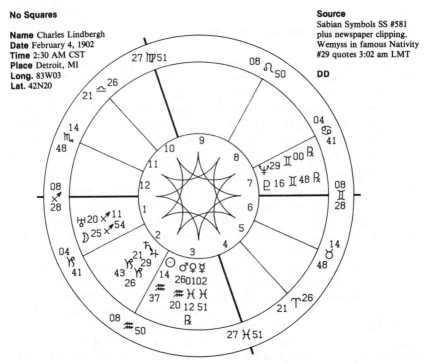

No Squares

Name Charles Lindbergh
Date February 4, 1902
Time 2:30 AM CST
Place Detroit, MI
Long. 83W03
Lat. 42N20

Source
Sabian Symbols SS #581
plus newspaper clipping.
Wemyss in famous Nativity
#29 quotes 3:02 am LMT

DD

of others and by doing that, becoming aware of our own needs too. Aries needs Libra's air, but Libra needs Aries' warmth. Aries needs Libra to add manner and style to its rather aggressive nature. Libra needs Aries to stop procrastinating and together they can benefit by each other's polarities. When there is no opposition, the need to become aware, the need to relate to others is not innately there and has to be learned on the hard road of experience. But since these people are not aware that they have a hard time relating, they really feel that they have excellent understanding of others, business or marriage partners. When suddenly faced with the fact that something is wrong, they truly do not know what the partner is talking about. As they often get burned, they may shy away from any close relationships, since "It never works out anyway." As always, look for compensating factors, such as strong squares, to spur these people on to face themselves and their shortcomings. Entertainer Fanny Brice, so ably portrayed by oppositionless Barbra Streisand (see chart below) in "Funny Girl" and "Funny Lady" serves as one good illustration. Other examples are actors Montgomery Clift and Dustin Hoffman, author and lecturer Helen Keller, atheist Madelyn Murray O'Hare, White House assistant Hamilton Jordan and dictator Benito Mussolini.

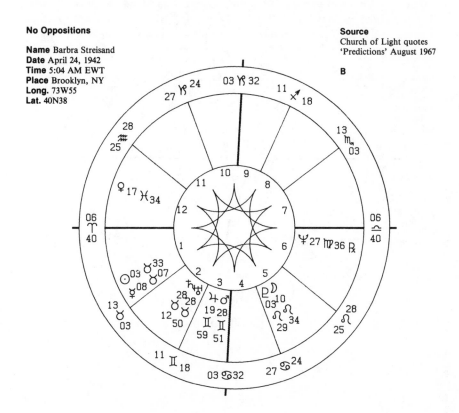

No Oppositions

Name Barbra Streisand
Date April 24, 1942
Time 5:04 AM EWT
Place Brooklyn, NY
Long. 73W55
Lat. 40N38

Source
Church of Light quotes
'Predictions' August 1967

Lack of Conjunctions   There are many charts without conjunctions. Anyone with a widely dispersed chart will not have a conjunction. This type of chart can indicate a very versatile person; as one door closes, the next one opens. The conjunction stands for the drive and action inherent in two planets placed in Aries in the first house. If that feeling is lacking, the person may scatter the energies or be too multi-faceted. Yet a good square can compensate for the lack. Actresses Nina Foch and Mia Farrow, pianist Ignace Paderewski and actor Clint Eastwood whose chart below serves as a good example.

No Conjunctions

Name Clint Eastwood
Date May 31, 1930
Time 5:35 PM PST
Place San Francisco, CA
Long. 122W25
Lat. 37N46

Source
Lockhart, birth certificate

A

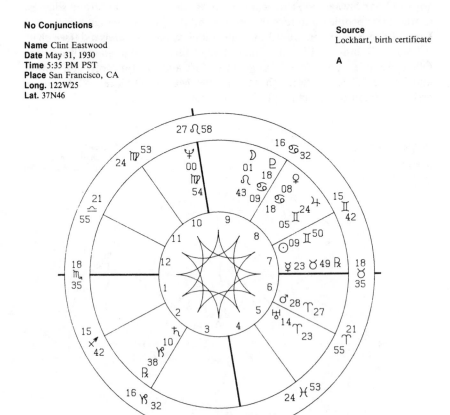

Lack of Inconjuncts   (Quincunxes) In the flat chart the inconjunct relates to the attitude of Aries versus Virgo or Aries versus Scorpio. Aries is active, cardinal and fire - Virgo is passive, mutable and earth while Scorpio is passive, fixed and water. Everything is different, there is not one thing these signs have in common, therefore they find it particularly difficult to relate to each other, understand each other's needs or wants. Again Aries is put on the defensive because earth and water threaten his fire. But the aspect is not angular, therefore the threat is more psychological (Scorpio's 8th house) or mental (Virgo's 6th house). Our favorite keywords for inconjuncts are ''adjustment'' when used positively and ''compromise'' when used negatively. People lacking inconjuncts in the chart don't even know what it feels like to adjust to someone else's needs or wishes. They may get an occasional twinge of discomfort, as if they know that something is expected of them, but they don't quite know what, because basically they think only of their own feelings. Some good examples would be French entertainer Maurice Chevalier, seer Edgar Cayce, actors Montgomery Clift and Orson Welles, author Jess Stearn and director Alfred Hitchcock. Orson Welles' chart is below.

No Inconjuncts

Source
Steinbrecher, Registrar of
Deeds/Kenosha

Name Orson Welles
Date May 6, 1915
Time 7:00 AM CST
Place Kenosha, WI
Long. 87W49
Lat. 42N35

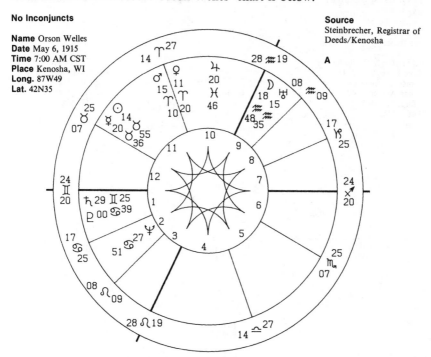

Lack of Trines or Sextiles It will be rare to find a chart which lacks both trines and sextiles. Many charts do lack one or the other and one can compensate for the other. The so-called hard aspects give us the push necessary achieve while trines bring ease and flow and sextiles bring the opportunities to make good use of the hard aspects. Sextiles and trines serve as good outlets for the tensions manifested by the harder aspects, therefore when one or the other is lacking, the individual may have to work a bit more to achieve, but unless both are missing, the compensatory factors are easy to find. If both sextiles and trines are lacking, the tension and challenge may become too much and the person gives up and does little or nothing, or tries to find another easy way which at times can mean indulging in criminal acts. Some famous personalities lacking trines are poet Emily Dickinson, author Simone de Beauvoir, actor Keenan Wynn, composer/author producer/actor Noel Coward. Examples of those lacking sextiles are authors Scott Fitzgerald, Anne Morrow Lindbergh and Gertrude Stein, boxer Muhammed Ali, Queens Elizabeth II of England and Beatrix of Holland, and former White House adviser John Dean. Emily Dickinson's chart is below and the chart of Queen Beatrix can be found on page 83.

No Trines

Name Emily Dickinson
Date December 10, 1830
Time near midnight
Place Amherst, MA
Long. 72W31
Lat. 42N22

Source
Church of Light Quotes
AFA (March 1962) as time
recorded near midnight.
Biography *The Years and Hours of Emily Dickinson* says 5:00 AM.

DD

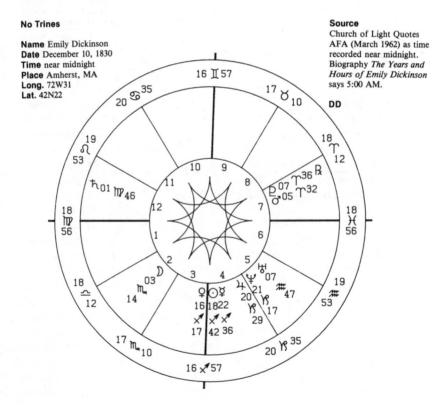

No Sextiles

Source
Church of Light, Sabian
Symbols #77.

Name Queen Beatrix, Netherlands
Date January 31, 1938
Time 9:47 AM GMT
Place Amsterdam, Holland
Long. 4E56
Lat. 52N22

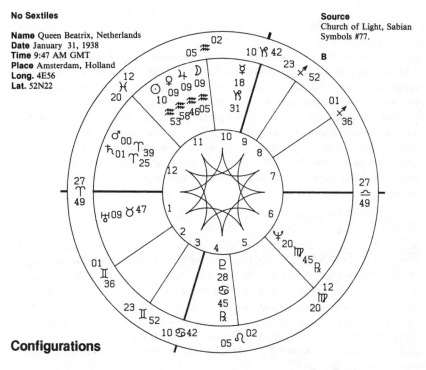

Configurations

Configurations do not stand out as obviously as some of the previous features we have discussed. Yet, configurations are one of the most important features to consider in delineating a horoscope. In Volume One we briefly described some of the major configurations. By configuration we mean - three or more planets all joined together by aspect that in so doing form a geometric pattern. For example, two planets in opposition, each squared by a third planet, form a *T-square or T-cross.* In Joan Sutherland's horoscope we find Venus at 10° Scorpio 36' in opposition to Mars at 10° Taurus 12' with both planets in square aspect to her Midheaven at 7° Aquarius. If you were to draw in lines to show these aspects you would end up with a perfect "T". Assume that she also has a planet in her fourth house in the early degrees of Leo (Neptune in her case is out of orb), then you would have another kind of configuration, called a *grand square* or *grand cross.* Again, if you connect these points you will see that it looks just like a cross—Mars opposing Venus and the Midheaven opposing some planet in Leo, Mars and Venus square the MC and planet X also square Mars and Venus. In this case we are dealing with a fixed T-square or fixed grand square, for all of the points are in fixed signs. T-squares and grand squares can occur in any of the 3 qualities. In the T-square three planets and three houses are tied together; as one acts, the other two are automatically involved. In fact we have automatic and innate integration in all configurations, all planets and houses involved are tied together, working in tandem whether or not they like it.

The Grand Cross

In the Grand Cross or grand square we are dealing with 4 planets and 4 houses; 4 planets interrelating and involving 4 areas of life and possibly ruling some other houses or areas of life and by pulling in so many facets of the chart, it becomes a most important, even overpowering factor of a horoscope.

Since the grand cross involves 4 squares and 2 oppositions, we are dealing with a person capable of tremendous effort and activity. How this effort or activity takes place depends on which quality and which houses are involved. Cardinal crosses produce quick action, fixed crosses are more deliberate in their actions and mutable crosses depend much on the action and reaction of others.

Cardinal Grand Cross   No one can be constantly active, therefore the grand cross is often compared to a windmill; capable of tremendous output and action when the wind blows, but rather idle in between. Of the 3 qualities, the Cardinal Grand Cross is probably the easiest to handle. Cardinal stands for motion, finding and solving problems; here you have the doer, both effective and purposeful. But in order to function at its best, the cardinal grand cross, or any squares and oppositions for that matter, needs an outlet, a flow to or from one of the planets involved; this can be a trine or a sextile. Without an outlet, the cardinal cross with its constant need for motion, can work itself into exhaustion. Dancer Mitzi Gaynor and Author Gore Vidal both have cardinal grand crosses.

The Fixed Grand Cross   is the most difficult of all 3 to handle. Fixed signs are purposeful, they like to plan everything and lay a good foundation on which to build. They need to be self-motivated, from the inside out, therefore if there is no flow to the fixed cross, the native can become repressed or emotionally frustrated. To overcome some of these frustrations, hobbies can be helpful. Musician John Lennon and medical missionary Albert Schweitzer (see his chart on page 85) had fixed grand crosses.

The Mutable Grand Cross   adds to the problems inherent in mutable signs: indecision, scattering of energies or working at cross purposes. Where the fixed signs depend on themselves, the mutable signs depend upon others and their lives are often not in their own hands. Flexible, they bend to the wishes of others. Undecided, they ask for everyone's advice and end up more confused than ever. Flowing aspects can lead to a very pleasant life, since getting along lies in the art of compromise. Without flow, they may end up wasting much of their potential. Two examples of famous personalities with mutable grand crosses are author James Hilton and singer Bobby Darin.

The T-Square

The T-Square involves two squares and one opposition. Whereas the grand cross is integrated at 4 corners, the T-square has the ability to balance the two

Fixed Grand Cross

Name Albert Schweitzer
Date January 14, 1875
Time 11:50 PM LMT
Place Kayserberg, Alsace
Long. 7E16
Lat. 48N09

Source
Lyndoe and Hubers quote
birth certificate.

A

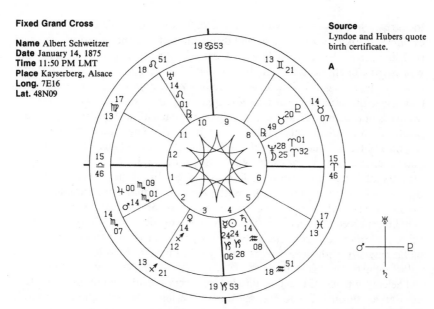

opposing planets, but the third planet is left dangling by itself. It squares two planets but has no opposition and becomes a dynamic focal point of the configuration, usually reflecting self-drive. Whereas the opposition is concerned with relationships, the square seeks action. The house and sign of the focal planet, or arm as it is sometimes called, assumes great importance.

The Cardinal T-Square is dynamic, quick and immediate. The native is little concerned with abstracts and often rushes in where angels fear to tread. He tends to stick his nose in others' business. Positively used, the native is dependable and strong in all emergencies. General George Patton, whose chart is on page 86 and psychoanalyst Sigmund Freud have cardinal T-squares.

The Fixed T-Square works in a slow and deliberate way; major problems are researched before action is taken. Unless some trine or sextile gives flow to the configuration, the native can be rigid in his approach, dogmatic and unbending. Prime Minister Winston Churchill and Queen Elizabeth II are good illustrations.

The Mutable T-Square usually makes the person idea-and-people-oriented. Since he gets along with people, he has an easier time solving his problems although indecision or wavering may be his greatest hang up. Prime Minister Indira Gandhi and comedian Groucho Marx are two examples.

Here are a few keywords describing the different focal point planets. If it is the *Moon*, the native is quite susceptible to the mood of the moment as poet Robert Browning was. With *Mercury* he is able to rationalize and handle events in a cool and collected manner like aviator Billy Mitchell. If *Venus* is the arm, he might seek some means of profiting by the situation, or, if the effort is too great, just give up. Evangelist healer Katherine Kuhlman is one good example. With the *Sun* there, he will throw himself into the situation heart and soul like actress Vanessa Redgrave. *Mars* gives plenty of energy to cope with whatever he might need to face, but he may blow up and accomplish nothing, boxer Muhammed Ali is a case in point. With *Jupiter* he will enlarge or embroider the situation, but basically treat it as an adventure, writer Norman Mailer is one example. *Saturn* makes him approach all with great caution, but patience and innate shrewdness allow him to come out a winner. The responsibilities of queens, Elizabeth of England and Juliana of Holland are good examples. With *Uranus* he will handle things in his own unique way and others had better not interfere, like 'preacher' Jim Jones who cajoled 900 people to follow him into death. With *Neptune* he may have troubles seeing the situation clearly and might come to an impasse or his great imagination can help him succeed, such as film director Vittorio de Sica. With *Pluto* he may use the situation to become a crusader not only for himself but to save mankind, or he may live with deep frustrations within himself. Astrologer Evangeline Adams illustrates this well.

The empty place of the T-square is also a very sensitive point and can often be used as an outlet. You can see this in Hermann Hesse's chart. He has a mutable T-square with Jupiter in the 1st house opposing Mercury in the 7th and both squaring Saturn and the Moon in the 3rd house. Hesse learned to use the 9th house of philosophy and religion to great advantage. Also take a few minutes to study Disney's cardinal and Joan Sutherland's fixed T-squares.

Cardinal T-Square

Name George Patton
Date November 11, 1885
Time 6:38 PM PST
Place San Marino, CA
Long. 118W06
Lat. 34N07

Source
Biography *Patton* by
Ladislas Farago. Data
from family bible.

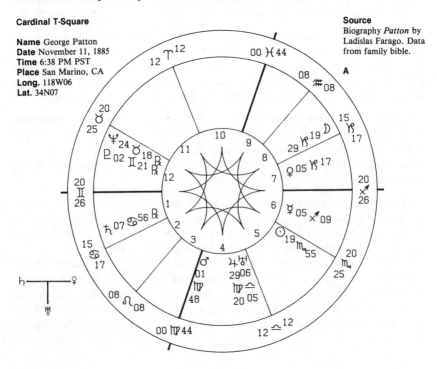

The Stellium

Another very important configuration is the Stellium. Here we find three or more planets all conjunct one another. These planets create their own emphasis and action, greatly enhancing the importance of the sign and house in which they fall. Walt Disney has Mars, Saturn and Jupiter all conjunct in Capricorn in the 4th house, (Disney's Venus is also in Capricorn, but out of orb for a conjunction). Despite Disney's creative and idealistic indications, this Capricorn stellium brought him down to earth, demanded concrete results, required recognition and solid achievements and overshadowed other tendencies in his chart.

A stellium is very strong, since it basically consists of three or more planets in the first house in Aries, regardless of what house and what sign the stellium actually falls in, this basic feeling based on the flat chart will always remain. Because the first house is considered personal, a congregation of planets will heighten the focus on the personality and self, giving us such keywords as self-centered or self-absorbed. With so many planets pulling the native in one direction, he is often quite one-sided and rarely has problems deciding which direction to take in life. He also finds any kind of compromise difficult. Because the stellium reflects that first house feeling, it also influences the appearance, no matter where the stellium occurs in the chart. Some famous people with stelliums are: Singer Della Reese and conductor Arturo Toscanini who have cardinal stelliums, actress Arlene Dahl and artist Pablo Picasso with fixed stelliums and writer-philosopher Jean Paul Sartre and playwright/actor Noel Coward with mutable stelliums. Picasso's chart is below.

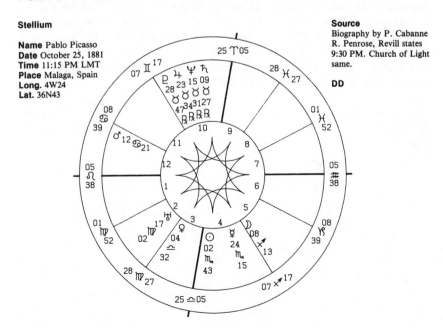

Stellium

Name Pablo Picasso
Date October 25, 1881
Time 11:15 PM LMT
Place Malaga, Spain
Long. 4W24
Lat. 36N43

Source
Biography by P. Cabanne
R. Penrose, Revill states
9:30 PM. Church of Light
same.

DD

The Yod

The Disney horoscope is also illustrative of another important configuration-the Yod. The yod consists of two planets sextile to one another, both inconjunct a third planet. In Disney's case Mercury sextiles Venus and both are inconjunct (quincunx) Neptune. As discussed in "Lack of Specific Aspects", inconjuncts always require certain adjustments or compromises; they are not the easiest aspects to handle, but in the case of the yod, the sextile of Venus and Mercury gave Disney the opportunity to learn how and when to adjust. The yod is very important in Disney's chart, since Neptune is the highest planet and is in his tenth house of career and worldly ambitions. Neptune, the planet of illusion and delusion, is brought down to earth and forced to be used through Mercury (communications) and Venus in the fifth house of creativity.

In any yod the planet receiving the two inconjuncts becomes the focal point and is often referred to as the "Finger of God". The need to act will arise through this focal planet whereas the opportunity to act lies in the two planets sextile each other. The problem of the yod is that it often produces undisciplined thinking. Yet the "finger" eventually forces the native into some sort of action. Please note that Hermann Hesse also has a strong yod with Pluto sextiling Venus and both planets inconjunct Jupiter. Since we are dealing with a 1st/6th or 1st/8th house involvement, we must take personal action (1st house) by examining our mental and physical habit pattern (6th house) and our emotional desire pattern (8th house). If changes, adjustments or reorganization are not brought about, the person can have mental, emotional or health problems. Through knowledge (Virgo/6th house) and psychological understanding (Scorpio/8th house) this can best be solved.

Yods are fairly common and here are a few famous people who have them: entertainer Frank Sinatra, Governor Jerry Brown and his father, former Governor Pat Brown, San Francisco Mayor Diane Feinstein, Indian leader Jawaharlal Nehru, Senator Robert Kennedy, actress Ellen Burstyn and actor Charles Chaplin. See Nehru's chart below.

Yod

Name Jawaharlal Nehru
Date Nov. 14, 1889
Time 10:05 PM LMT
Place Allahabad, India
Long. 81E58
Lat. 25N30

Source
From Premier Joshi in 1948 to Church of Light. No source for time.

C

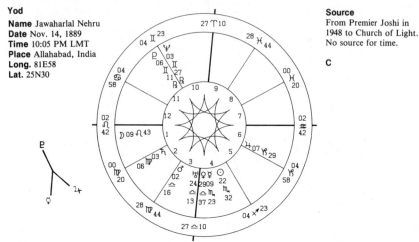

The Grand Trine

The Grand Trine is the last of the major configurations. As the word implies, a minimum of three planets is involved, each trining the other. Usually all of the planets are in the same element and we classify the trine, as for example in Farrah Fawcett's case, a grand air trine. Her Sun at 13° Aquarius 11' trines Uranus at 17° Gemini 58' and both are trine Neptune at 10° Libra 41'. All three planets are in air signs, giving Farrah inspiration and creative ability. In a way we have the reverse situation of the grand cross or T-square. The 3 planets harmoniously interconnected need the challenge and tension of a square or opposition to be spurred into action. Otherwise the person may happily bask in the sunshine of doing nothing, wasting all their natal potentials. In Farrah's case the Sun has an exact opposition to Pluto and Neptune squares the Moon, just what is needed to push her into action and let her utilize the talents indicated in her horoscope.

The Grand Fire Trine gives much self-confidence, physical activity, enthusiasm, a certain dramatic flair and a very outgoing nature. Fire people are quite perceptive and can inspire others; they usually aim high. Labor leader Caesar Chavez and actor Marlon Brando both have grand trines in fire. Brando's chart is as follows.

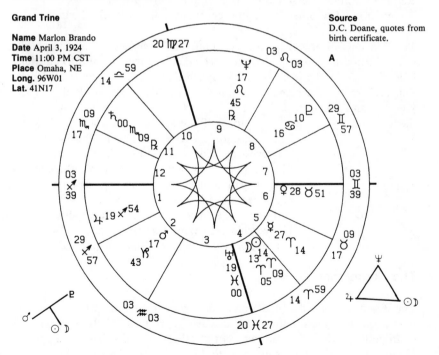

Grand Trine

Name Marlon Brando
Date April 3, 1924
Time 11:00 PM CST
Place Omaha, NE
Long. 96W01
Lat. 41N17

Source
D.C. Doane, quotes from birth certificate.

The Grand Earth Trine natives like material comfort, are dependable, hard workers and can be quite psychic; possibly because the earth element is related to practical matters they are able to see reality in a larger dimension than others. Actress Vanessa Redgrave and Russian leader Joseph Stalin are two examples.

The Grand Air Trine produces highly idealistic and individualistic people, but they are apt to drift and be subject to frustrations. With a strong chart, they have excellent mental faculties, great ease and ability of communication and they like to influence others through ideas and ideals. They dislike routine and menial work. Two examples are former White House advisor John Dean and composer George Gershwin.

The Grand Water Trine bears the most creative potential. These people have the subtle and intuitive understanding of mass consciousness. They are instinctive and sympathetic and need a productive outlet, else they suffer from the hidden uncertainties and anxieties inherent in the water element. Cautious, they only act when confident of the results. Water natives are very sensual. Since water embraces all and knows no barriers, these people rarely know when to stop, regardless of what they are doing. Secretary of State Henry Kissinger and etertainer Johnny Carson both have Grand Water trines.

Here are a few other interesting configurations to think about:

The Kite consists of a grand trine with one of the planets having an opposition to it. If you draw a line linking the three planets in trine it will form a triangle. Now draw a line between the two opposing planets and connect the planets that each sextile the planet in opposition and the result will look just like a kite. Farrah Fawcett has a kite. Her Uranus trines her Neptune and both trine the Sun, but the Sun opposes Pluto and Pluto sextiles both Uranus and Neptune.

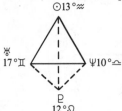

The opposition between the Sun and Pluto gives her the awareness needed to utilize the trines and sextiles. The biggest problem of the kite is that is has three different aspects within itself and therefore can be too self-contained and the rest of the chart may not be used to full advantage. Actress Rosemarie Guy also has a kite in her chart, so does Russian dictator Joseph Stalin whose horoscope you will find on page 92.

The Boomerang

The Boomerang is a configuration coined by Joan McEvers who kept watching its action for years before she decided that it definitely worked like a configuration. It is a yod where the 'finger' planet has an opposition. Hermann Hesse's chart can serve to illustrate. We discussed his yod with Pluto sextiling Venus and both inconjuncting Jupiter. Please note that Jupiter is opposed by Mercury. This configuration does exactly what its name implies. The action for the focal planet, Jupiter boomerangs to Mercury and the

tendency is to work all problems out between the two
oppositions, and take advantage to do so through the
sextiles, but ignore the inconjuncts. This can be
dangerous in the long run, because adjustments that are
not handled can become deep frustrations.

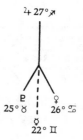

Author Henry David Thoreau also had a boomerang,
so does much-married actress Zsa Zsa Gabor whose
chart is on page 92.

The Grand Sextile

The Grand Sextile is one of the rarest configurations, and if you keep the orb
we recommend for sextiles (5° and 6° for the luminaries) we have not come
across any one who has this configuration. It would imply six sextiles, linking
the entire horoscope and when drawn visually, the result looks like the Star of
David. The configuration gives the native tremendous opportunities, excellent
ability to communicate and a breezy and people-oriented attitude. The danger
in this configuration is the scattering of energies since too much versatility and
opportunity is available. Some squares and/or oppositions and/or
conjunctions can be very helpful.

The Mystic Rectangle

Another interesting yet rare configuration is called the Mystic Rectangle.
Why 'mystic' is a mystery, since it works on a very practical level. It consists of
four planets interconnecting by two trines, two sextiles and two oppositions.
When you link them the resulting figure really looks like a rectangle. For
example if you have Mars at 14° Aries opposing Saturn at 20° Libra, trining
Neptune at 16° Leo and sextiling the Sun at 19° Aquarius, you would also
have Neptune opposing the Sun and sextiling Saturn. At the same time Saturn

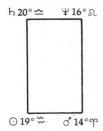

trines the Sun. So the result is two trines, two sextiles
and two oppositions and it tends to work similarly to the
kite. Again we have the oppositions (this time two, the
kite only has one) to give us awareness and help us
utilize the flow of the trines and the opportunity of the
sextiles in a useful way. And again, just like the kite, the
danger of this configuration is that it is too self-
contained and may overpower the rest of the chart.

The Final Signature (or Type)

This last category doesn't stand out at all; in fact, you have to do some
figuring in order to find it. What then is this final type? Using the horoscope
of Hermann Hesse as an example, we see that he had five mutable planets and
five planets in water. In other words, more mutability and water than any

Kite

Name Josef Stalin
Date January 2, 1880 NS
Time 8:15 AM Zone 2
Place Gori, Russia
Long. 44E05
Lat. 42N00

Source
Date recorded but time is
unknown and speculative.

DD

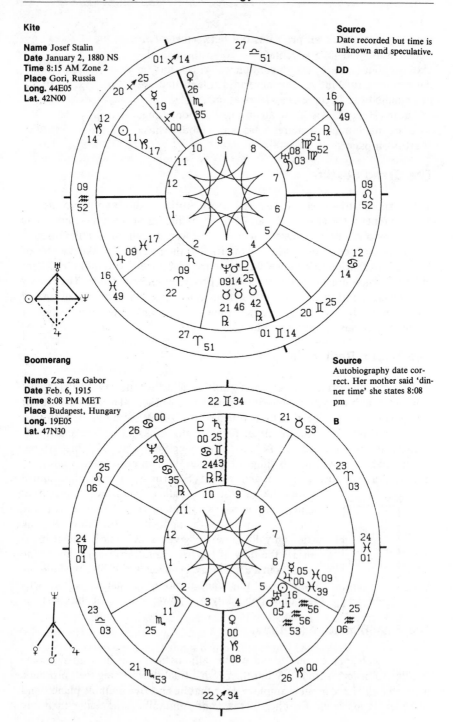

Boomerang

Name Zsa Zsa Gabor
Date Feb. 6, 1915
Time 8:08 PM MET
Place Budapest, Hungary
Long. 19E05
Lat. 47N30

Source
Autobiography date cor-
rect. Her mother said 'din-
ner time' she states 8:08
pm

B

other quality or element. There is only one mutable water sign in the zodiac: Pisces; therefore, Hesse's signature was Pisces.

This is not always evident in looking at the chart. Yet, by arriving at this signature, we realize that Hesse was very sensitive, intuitive, emotional, introspective, and any other words you wish to use to describe the Pisces feeling.

Walt Disney had six cardinal and four earth planets as his predominant factors, which leads us to a Capricorn signature for him. This confirms what we've already observed regarding his Capricorn stellium. Joan Sutherland has six fixed and five water planets, giving her a Scorpio signature, which is not too surprising since her Sun and two other planets are in Scorpio. Farrah Fawcett has an Aquarian signature, also not unexpected with her Sun and two other planets in Aquarius.

Sometimes, you will end up with a very different signature than you might expect, as in the case of Helen Keller (whose horoscope is included in Lesson 5). This will give you an additional blend and insight into the personality you are dealing with. At times, the final signature is difficult to ascertain because the division is fairly even. In such cases, we suggest that you use the Ascendant to break the tie. If there is no signature, do not be concerned. It is just one extra way to gain insight.

Following are descriptions of how the various signatures behave. Remember, the whole chart must be taken into account, but generally this is an added insight into the person's personality and behavior pattern. If there is no signature, do not be concerned, it just means the chart is very well balanced and does not fit into any definite category. But when there is a signature, be sure to consider it. If the signature is the same sign as the Sun, Moon or Ascendant, the person will find it easier to express that particular sign.

Cardinal Fire (Aries) This is the warmest, most active combination and you usually have a kind and winning personality. Quick and agile mentally, you are an independent thinker. Your temperament is fiery and if the water element is prominent, you must work at forgiving others. Your mind is penetrative and you have high ideals and aspirations.

Cardinal Earth (Capricorn) Ambitious and social, it is important that you develop a sense of material achievement. You are a "take charge" person, not always verbally, but tacitly. Capable and dependable, you are the salt of the earth.

Cardinal Air (Libra) Your intuition is strong and your mind rules your action. Cleverness is pronounced and this produces skill and favors a professional career. You are verbal and to the point and may be a good speaker. Your disposition is honest and refined and you are a stickler for perfection. Always courteous in speech, you exhibit much manual and mental dexterity.

Cardinal Water (Cancer) Romantic and sensitive, you feel according to the weather, personal contacts and the current situation. Expressive, you show anger and hurt; your feelings cannot be hidden. You often absorb the moods of others and can become very attached, affectionate and sentimental. Your experiences have a deep and lasting effect.

Fixed Fire (Leo) You are the strongest-willed individual in the Zodiac. Your temperament is tinged with ambition and there is a persistence of force and energy that enables you to accomplish your ends, whatever they are. Somewhat reserved, your pride is evident in all your undertakings. You generally do not scatter your love nor your career efforts.

Fixed Earth (Taurus) Overly rigid, you find it hard to flow with the tides. If any other element is strong, especially air, this quality may be modified. Often you display an overconfident temperament with too much self-esteem. Less emphasis should be placed on your own accomplishments or you will lose the insight needed for success. Sometimes quiet, reserved and even sad, your true personality comes through only in close contacts.

Fixed Air (Aquarius) Noble, refined and peace-loving, you are the artistocrat who brings elegance to your surroundings. Often a fine artist, you have patience for work that involves nature, sculpture, painting or related fields. Your temperament is subtle with a basic conservativeness and your disposition is firm and deliberate. If you have some earth planets, you may turn success into fame.

Fixed Water (Scorpio) A receptive soul, you have an uncanny sense of knowing where the world is headed. Negatively, you can be jealous, suspicious and even treacherous; but on the other hand, you can be a saint or a master of all things. Your temperament is moody and depressive, running to high and low extremes. Your disposition is dramatic and mysterious, making you hard to understand. Often this combination makes a procrastinator.

Mutable Fire (Sagittarius) Expressive, you exhibit great enthusiasm and promote others into action but rarely push yourself to great achievement. With enough earth planets to balance the fiery zest, you can be a prodigious doer. You have a keen, independent temperament and an even disposition, but you always need encouragement from others and someone to lean on.

Mutable Earth (Virgo) Conservative, with a rather nervous temperament, you like to lead a formal type of life that can become monotonous, leading to stagnation. If earth is stronger than mutability, you can express a good business mind, your disposition settles into a harmonious state of being and you will be stable and consistent. If not, worry and hesitation are predominant forces.

Mutable Air (Gemini) You are a dreamer, the student who goes to school for life because you never tire of learning. Your temperament is complacent, your disposition eager. A scientific or literary career is what you seek, but to become prominent or rise to any great height, you must have some fire or earth planets. You should always be alert to and aware of your environment, because you are easily swayed by others.

Mutable Water (Pisces) You have an uncanny sense of seeking out the undesirables, so many problems could come your way. Your temperament fluctuates according to your early home life and strong discipline in your young years would have been helpful. Your disposition can be self-pitying on one side and very loving when things go your way. Here, more than with any other combination, the other elements and qualities as well as the planetary aspects must be taken into consideration.

Sub-Signature

You may get an additional insight by using the house positions to get a "sub-signature". Check if there is a preponderance of angular or succedent or cadent planets. Then see if the houses of life or substance or relationships or endings are the most occupied and the sub-signature will reveal which area of life (house) is really important to the native. Hermann Hesse has predominantly angular planets with a majority in houses of relationships. Therefore all 7th house matters would be very important to him. Joan Sutherland has a sub-signature of six angular/five houses of substance resulting in a 10th house emphasis. Walt Disney with five angular planets but the houses of life, substance and ending holding three planets each, has no final sub-signature. Farrah Fawcett has six succedent and six houses of endings planets giving her an 8th house sub-signature. She represents a sex symbol to the public, one of the interpretations of the 8th house.

We are not giving you any actual homework with this lesson, but we do urge you to look at all of the other horoscopes in this book and try to determine some of the stand-outs in them for yourself.

Lesson 7
Retrograde Planets

We have mentioned the term retrograde quite a few times, and in calculating the horoscope you have seen the Rx and D symbols in the ephemeris—but, what does this really mean? Is there some special way that one must delineate a retrograde planet?

The word retrograde means going backward (retro = back and gradi = go). But, how can a planet go backwards? For, after all, we know that in our solar system everything continues to move in an ecliptic forward motion. The retrograde planet does not suddenly reverse its motion and go backwards; it only appears to do so. It is apparent because as these planets decrease in longitudinal motion (as viewed from the Earth), they appear first to slow down and finally to move backward. This phenomenon can best be explained by thinking of two trains passing or paralleling each other. If you are sitting in the faster train, you will at first feel that the slower train is standing still, and then you will suddenly think that the slower train is moving backwards.

In Volume 1, lesson 3, we give you the speed of all the planets. Venus for example takes 224½ days to complete one orbit of the Sun. The Earth, as you know, takes 365¼ days. So at some point Venus will be the faster train passing the Earth. But from Earth it will look like Venus is first standing still and then going backwards. Since Mars takes 22 months, or almost two years to complete the orbit, now Earth will be the faster train while Mars will seem to slow down and finally appear to have regressed in its path.

This same visual illusion happens at certain times when a planet changes its angular position in relationship to the Earth. Since we judge our horoscopes from the viewpoint of the Earth, we have to take this illusion into account and record this fact.

This retrograde motion is noted in three stages. As the planet apparently slows down, it eventually becomes stationary. In the ephemeris you will note that certain planets are at the same degree for one, two or three days, some even for a week or more. The second stage is the retrograde stage. As it is ready to turn again, we observe a second stationary period, and then the planet appears to go direct again.

Be sure that you mark your horoscope with Rx or D and SRx when the planet is standing still and ready to turn retrograde, with SD when standing still and ready to move forward again. All of these different motions can be found in the ephemeris by checking a few days back and a few days forward.

In the early teachings of astrology, a retrograde planet was attributed characteristics like debilitated, weak, unfortunate and other dire meanings. In observing retrograde motion in horoscopes, modern astrologers have found that these terms hardly apply. By using your own logic (which we always urge you to do), you can analyze it for yourself. If the planet is retrograde, it is not moving in its usual overt fashion. Therefore, its action will be less obvious, less open, and much more inwardly oriented. In certain cases this can be a blessing; in other cases, it may slow down the outward process of maturation. If many of the personal planets (Mercury, Venus, Mars) are retrograde in the natal chart, the true nature of the person will be less obvious on the outside, because much of the action takes place on the inside. If a Rx planet rules the Sun, Moon or Ascendant, the person may seem shy or evidence a certain hesitancy in facing new situations. The average horoscope has two retrograde planets.

Students ask what happens when there are no retrograde planets in a chart. All other things being equal, the person seems to be quite direct, outgoing and uncomplicated. What you see is what you get, so to speak. See chart of Linda Rondstadt on page 99. She has no retrograde planets at all. Very unusual is Graham Nash's chart with six retrograde planets, see page 99. That many retrogrades would add a subtle nuance of mystery, the person being less open. We will give you a few keywords to explain where the planet in retrograde motion differs from direct planets, but as always, we urge you to use your own common sense when delineating and think of the nature of the planet(s) involved.

By the way - we did say "planets" in the very real sense of this term. The Sun and Moon are luminaries, not planets, and they never appear to be in retrograde motion.

Mercury retrograde   This is the planet of reasoning ability, the mind and communication. When it is retrograde, the thinking process seems deeper and more sensitive. There is some innate ability to relate to other people's feelings and thoughts making you less likely to jump to conclusions. Many writers have Mercury retrograde, because for many of these people it is easier to express

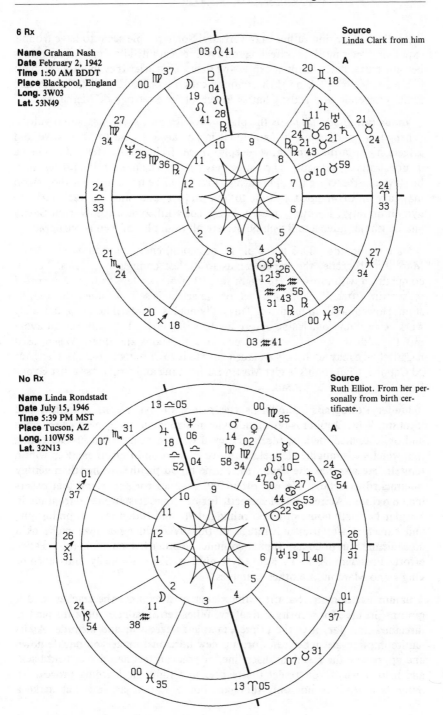

6 Rx

Name Graham Nash
Date February 2, 1942
Time 1:50 AM BDDT
Place Blackpool, England
Long. 3W03
Lat. 53N49

Source
Linda Clark from him

A

No Rx

Name Linda Rondstadt
Date July 15, 1946
Time 5:39 PM MST
Place Tucson, AZ
Long. 110W58
Lat. 32N13

Source
Ruth Elliot. From her personally from birth certificate.

A

themselves in writing rather than verbally. Some people seem to have trouble explaining their motives or feelings and will retreat into silence, whereas others become particularly adept at expressing their needs after they mature and have had a chance to work on their communication gap. Authors Pearl Buck and Zelda Fitzgerald and actor Charles Boyer all have retrograde Mercuries.

Venus retrograde   This is the planet of affection, social urges and values. When it is retrograde, the individual is not always able to show love and affection, regardless of how deeply these feelings are felt. Just being demonstrative is difficult. The native may be shy. The maturation process may be slow and therefore the approach to love could be immature. Or the person may take an off-handed attitude to love and romance and this can mark the nymph or satyr. Former 1st Lady Mary Todd Lincoln, actor Warren Beatty and consumer advocate Ralph Nader are all examples of Venus retrograde.

Mars retrograde   This is the planet of action, energy and initiative. When Mars is retrograde, the person tends to be less competitive, unless he's in competition with himself. He might say, "I swam ten laps today; tomorrow I must swim fifteen". Since so much of the action is self- or inner-oriented, he seems slowed down in his drive. This individual is more deliberate and usually works everything out inside before he does it overtly. This way he can avoid pitfalls and so quickly catches up with the constant doer. When used negatively, he may act hastily and then have to redo or retrace his steps. Gangster Al Capone, Civil Rights leader Martin Luther King and strip tease artist Gypsy Rose Lee all have retrograde Mars.

Jupiter Retrograde   Jupiter is the planet of expansion, optimism and idealism. When Jupiter is retrograde, the individual develops his own religious and philosophical beliefs, ideals and even morals, rather than just accepting that which he is taught. He seeks intuitive answers and finds them deep within himself. He also has the ability to see the broad picture, rather than getting sidetracked in details. He will often find avenues for expansion that others may overlook. Actress Carol Burnett, for example, has Jupiter retrograde in Virgo in her sixth house of work, ruling her 9th and 10th houses of philosophy and career. Carol took advantage of this by finding her own niche as a comedienne, but of course Jupiter conjunct Neptune helped her in this creative effort. President John F. Kennedy's mother, Rose Kennedy and inventor Guglielmo Marconi are other examples.

Saturn Retrograde   Saturn is the planet of discipline, the teacher, and it governs the urge for security and safety. When retrograde, of all of the planets discussed thus far, it is the prime example of free will and attitude. As its nature implies, a teacher can open up new horizons, make you buckle down and appreciate the resultant discipline, or you can feel hampered, held back, and held down if you resent the teacher and fight the learning process. In Saturn's case, it is not only the sign, house and its aspects that make a difference, but your own response to it. Therefore, when it is retrograde, it can have the opposite effect. Negatively used, you may feel insecure or even inferior, because as you look within you don't like what you see. You fear rejection and therefore expose yourself as little as possible to situations that may result in a rebuff or make you feel this way. You seem to need constant encouragement and you lack the ambition usually innate in Saturn. However, used positively, you will look within and at an early age already be fairly clear as to who you are, where you are going, and what you will do about getting there. You are more deliberate in attaining your goals in a quiet and unobtrusive way—but you do attain them! Some may consider you to be too serious; however, you do have a sense of humor, only it is self directed. Poet Emily Dickinson, scientist Albert Einstein and author Thomas Mann have Saturn retrograde.

Uranus Retrograde   Here we are dealing with the planet of freedom, the awakener. When Uranus is retrograde its inward direction reinforces the urge to be different, to break the chains of tradition at an early age. The need to be special or unique is reinforced. The need to achieve personal freedom, strangely enough, creates the urge to dominate others. Many politicians, heads of state, dictators, and social leaders have Uranus retrograde. How much domination they are able to achieve, of course, depends on the placement of Uranus in the chart; it certainly helps to have retrograde Uranus in an angular house. Examples of political leaders with Uranus retrograde are legion: Adolf Hitler, Winston Churchill, Franklin D. Roosevelt, Lyndon B. Johnson, Nelson Rockefeller, Robert Kennedy, and Hubert Humphrey.

Neptune Retrograde   Neptune is the planet of intuition, illusion or delusion, and of spiritual awakening. Neptune's aspects take on utmost importance when it is retrograde. If Neptune, by aspect, is foggy or clouded, going inward will not help to clear matters up; on the contrary, the person can live in a deep dream world of unreality or delude himself completely. The martyrdom nature of Neptune may become stronger, or the person may only feel worthy when he is sacrificing himself for the good of others. With positive aspects to support the retrograde Neptune, the inward action can produce tremendous personal insight; any talent present at birth can be utilized easily and at a relatively early age. Many artists, composers, poets and religious personalities have this position: artists Pablo Picasso and Toulouse Lautrec, writers Eugene O'Neill, Elizabeth Barrett Browning and Robert Browning, psychologist Carl Jung, scientist Mme. Curie, composer Johannes Brahms.

Pluto Retrograde   Pluto is the planet of transformation and obsession. Since Pluto is retrograde as much as six months out of the year, nearly half of all people born have it retrograde. Therefore, it is impossible to ascribe definite tendencies to the motion. You might try to assess for yourself if you see definite traits these people have in common. From our own observations, we can only state that, since Pluto is very far away and very erratic in its orbit, its effects are usually felt at a later point in life. Children do not seem to react to Pluto's deep and transforming nature, but only to the intensity or obsessiveness inherent to the planet, which is an outer manifestation. Therefore, a retrograde action, which demands going inward or inside will not manifest itself until the person is well past childhood. By then so many other factors come into play that it is difficult to pinpoint the retrograde action as the culprit or benefactor.

To briefly illustrate the retrogrades in the charts of those we are using in this book as our examples, let us look at the horoscope of Hermann Hesse. Hesse's Jupiter is retrograde in his 1st house. Jupiter also rules his Ascendant and as his chart ruler assumes great importance. If you read our description of a retrograde Jupiter, you will see that it fits Hesse totally. Because it is his chart ruler, it establishes the basis for his personality; always searching, always doubting those pat answers, looking for that illusive something from the days of his early youth. His Saturn is stationary, ready to go retrograde the next day. Saturn's station is relatively short - three days only. It has a difficult position in Hesse's chart; flanked by Mars on one side, egging it on to act, and the Moon on the other, urging it to be emotional. Saturn is stronger than either of these; it tends to hamper Mars (one foot on the gas - the other on the brake), and it dampens the emotional Moon, leading either to self-pity or a feeling of not being loved and denied tenderness by his parents. Saturn is also a part of his mutable T-square to the Ascendant (outer personality) and Mercury (reasoning ability). With all of these difficulties we can understand that Hesse used the more negative attributes of Saturn as a young man. However, as Jupiter helped him to find himself and some of the answers he was seeking, he became more certain of who he was and where he had to go; he deliberately went after his goals and most certainly was able to reach many of them.

Walt Disney's retrograde Neptune works similarly to the way we've described it here, with one exception. His way of living in a dream world of fantasy was used in a most positive way—by allowing others to share this grand illusion with him. The challenge to make something of himself, generated by the many squares to his natal Moon in the first house, prevented him from retreating into his private dream world. Instead, he utilized his dreams to create for children and the eternal child within him.

Time Spent By Each Planet In One Sign Of The Zodiac

Moon   Moves 12-15° per day; thus is in one sign for 2¼ to 2½ days.

Mercury   Can traverse a sign in as little as 14 days, but since it is never more than 28° away from the Sun, it retrogrades approximately 3 times per year, as if to get in line again.

Venus   Requires approximately 26-30 days. Venus is never more than 46° away from the Sun and retrogrades once or twice per year. At these times it may take 2 months to go through a sign.

Sun   Moves at the rate of 28-31 days per sign (our Earth month).

Mars   As fast as 40 days, or as slow as 6 months in a sign. The average movement is approximately 2 months depending upon whether it goes retrograde or not. Mars does not go retrograde every year.

Jupiter   As quickly as 6 months, or as slowly as 18 months, depending if it goes retrograde, which it does not do every year. The average motion is about one sign per year.

Saturn   spends approximately 2½ years in each sign retrograding 2 or 3 times within that period.

Uranus   requires approximately 7 years to go through each sign, during which period it retrogrades as many as 7 times, or about once per year.

Neptune   Requires 14-15 years to go through each sign, and it retrogrades about once each year, often for as long as 5 months.

Pluto   Pluto's orbit is so eccentric that it takes anywhere from 12-25 years per sign. It required 25 years to go through Cancer, but it will require only about 12 years to go through Scorpio. Pluto retrogrades about once each year and for about 6 months.

The planets can go retrograde only when at a certain critical distance from the Sun. Here are these distances:

Mars	-	133°
Jupiter	-	116°
Saturn	-	104°
Uranus	-	104°
Neptune	-	101°
Pluto	-	101°

There is no critical distance between the Sun and Mercury or the Sun and Venus. These two planets basically move faster than the Sun, so at certain times they seem to slow up or even move backward as their distance from the Earth increases. As a result, they never exceed their distance of 28° or 46° respectively from the Sun, despite their inherently faster motion.

From this data you should note the following facts:

1. Any planet that is in opposition to the Sun MUST be in retrograde motion.

2. Jupiter, Saturn, Uranus, Neptune, and Pluto, when trine or inconjunct to the Sun MUST be in retrograde motion. Mars when inconjunct the Sun must also be in retrograde motion. Occasionally, Jupiter when in trine to the Sun may be in direct motion, but this is infrequent.

3. Because of the variance of the planets' retrograde periods there will be certain years during which it is impossible for a person to be born without retrograde planets in their horoscope; example: 1975.

4. When a planet is in direct motion, its distance from the Earth is increasing; when retrograde, its distance from the Earth is decreasing.

Review Question: Delineate Joan Sutherland's retrograde Mars and Uranus briefly. Please refer to the Appendix for our delineation on page 239.

Lesson 8
Intercepted Signs and Houses

Because of the tilt of the Earth on its axis, and its distortion from being a perfect sphere, there is often a distortion of house sizes as we move North or South from the equator. When this happens some signs are found to be completely contained within a house; i.e., the sign does not appear on any cusp, and we refer to this phenomena as INTERCEPTION. In latitudes of more than 50° North or South, two or more signs may be intercepted in one house or there may be two sets of houses with intercepted signs.

If one house has an intercepted sign, the opposite house will also contain an interception sign. An interception widens the house in which it occurs and therefore complicates the affairs of that house because of the added signs involved. For example, in the horoscope of Farrah Fawcett, the 4th-10th house axis contains intercepted signs—Libra and Aries. Mercury (ruler of Virgo) rules the cusp of the 4th house; Libra is intercepted and thus Venus co-rules this house; Neptune actually occupies this house. In delineating the 4th house all of these factors must be considered. Thus, you can see that the delineation of a house that contains an intercepted sign can become quite complex.

Often, the house axis containing intercepted signs is the most activated axis in the horoscope. And, nearly always, it is the largest house; it contains the greatest number of degrees from cusp to cusp. Again referring to the chart of Farrah Fawcett, notice that the 4th house contains 8° of Virgo + 30° of Libra + a little over 2° of Scorpio = 40+ °. Compare this to her 2nd house, which contains only a little over 26°, all in the sign of Leo.

Although the meaning of planets in intercepted signs becomes more subtle, the force of such planets often becomes more powerful. An intercepted planet, once it gains momentum, will brook no interference. A planet contained within an intercepted sign is like being fenced in or held in restraint, until the individual learns to use the force or power generated by this planet; then he can forge ahead at full steam. If the Sun, Moon, ruler of the Ascendant, or the ruler of the intercepted sign is also intercepted, there may be some delay in getting that area of the life started in the right direction. If, for example, in Farrah Fawcett's chart we were to discover Mars in Aries (which is intercepted) in her 10th house, it would be much more difficult to release Mars' energies. Tensions and frustrations must be worked out, and often the best avenue is through the house that the planet rules.

If there are no planets in the horoscope in intercepted signs, the house itself needs attention.

In Farrah Fawcett's chart, Neptune is the only intercepted planet. It rules her 10th house of status and career. Thus, one avenue for coming out of the interception is through the 10th house. Of course, the aspects to Neptune should also be considered.

The Sun intercepted   indicates one who is under restraint, especially in the early years of life. The need for this person is to find a special field or place in life to be comfortable and stand alone. Often there is a feeling of some lack within the self, and it is harder for this individual to relate to others. Usually he is personally involved in matters pertaining to the Sun's sign and house and with dedication and direction he can go directly to his goals. Assassin Lee Harvey Oswald is an example of an intercepted Sun. So are artist Vincent van Gogh, baseball player Vida Blue and Prime Minister Jawaharlal Nehru whose charts are on pages 66, 69 and 88.

The Moon intercepted   indicates emotional intensification. Feeling is accentuated but there may be a problem in communicating and at times even a speech impediment (though other factors in the horoscope would be needed to confirm this). There is some withdrawal at the emotional level and feelings of rejection are intensified. When this person does communicate emotionally, he can be very effective and others will listen. Religious leader Mary Baker Eddy and author Fanny Hurst have intercepted Moons. So do comedian Lenny Bruce and singer Linda Ronstadt whose charts are on pages 123 and 99.

Mercury intercepted   indicates that the thinking processes are not the same as those of others. Often this person feels misunderstood or out-of-step with his peers. When he has learned to accept his own concepts, others come to admire his gift for intellectual specialization. He is very good at appraising values. Scientists Louis Pasteur and Albert Einstein and horticulturist Luther Burbank are some examples. So is conductor Arturo Toscanini whose chart can be found on page 63.

Venus intercepted   the individual seeks love in an entirely personal way and the love life is often kept secret, sacred and hidden, or is held apart from all other phases of the life. This person may feel that he has never experienced real love, for his idea of love is too intense and limited. A creative outlet is of great benefit. Former Beatle John Lennon and architect Frank Lloyd Wright have this interception. So do Senator Ted Kennedy and psychoanalyst Sigmund Freud whose charts are on pages 73 and 124.

Mars intercepted   shows intense power and energy. This individual needs a definitely specialized goal toward which to channel his aggressive energies. He has the ability to make whatever he does become a personal triumph. Some examples are psychic Peter Hurkos, Emperor Hirohito and mystery writer Agatha Christie. Also lecturer Helen Keller whose chart is on page 59.

Jupiter intercepted   may indicate difficulties in early life and a bottling up of natural enthusiasm. This person has a sense of value that is uniquely his. When opportunity knocks he is capable of taking advantage of it in a different way than his contemporaries would. General Erwin Rommel, consumer advocate Ralph Nader and child specialist Benjamin Spock serve as good illustrations. So does artist Pablo Picasso whose chart is on page 87.

Saturn intercepted   gives great sensitivity to other's problems and an uncanny knack for solving them. However, things that upset others rarely bother this individual. He tends to face his own difficulties with fatalism. Wherever you find Saturn there is a tendency to hold back or a tendency toward congestion. This person must develop his outer expression to enable him to take risks to achieve his goals. Two examples are magician Harry Houdini and actor Dustin Hoffman. Also writer Hermann Hesse and singer Linda Ronstadt whose charts are on pages 31 and 99.

Uranus intercepted   indicates a certain timidity of expression, particularly where originality is concerned. There is a fear of ridicule. Although the individual is creative and idealistic, there is a need to overcome the sensitivity that will not let him express his humanitarian zeal. Murderer Charles Manson, educator Maria Montessori and White House advisor John Dean have this placement. So does Queen Beatrix of the Netherlands whose chart is on page 83.

Neptune intercepted   indicates a desire to avoid leadership. This is the person who would rather take a back seat and must be urged to step out and assert himself. Or, he can become a hermit or a dreamer completely introspective. If Neptune is angular, there is a strong need to reach out to others and this should be encouraged. This is a very good placement for writers, musicians or anyone who works alone. Authors Arthur Conan Doyle and Joseph Wambaugh and composer Igor Stravinsky have Neptune intercepted. So does actress Barbra Streisand whose chart is on page 79.

Pluto intercepted shows that the life motivation is different from that which spurs others. This person's need for action often comes from a group feeling and his giant need for approval. Regeneration is very important, and he has a deep sense of obligation to investigate life thoroughly and completely, which he should be urged to use. Some examples are socialist Karl Marx, band leader Guy Lombardo and baseball player Stan Musial. So is movie producer Sam Goldwyn whose chart is on page 64.

Depending on which Table of Houses you use, the interceptions may change or in some cases even be eliminated. All the charts in this book are based on the Koch Birthplace Table of Houses.

Whenever there are intercepted signs in a horoscope, you will find that two sets of houses are linked together because they have the same sign on adjacent house cusps. In Farrah Fawcett's chart the 2nd and 3rd houses are linked together as are her 8th and 9th houses. Leo and Aquarius are the signs involved. In Hermann Hesse's chart the 6th and 7th and 12th and 1st houses are linked with Gemini and Sagittarius respectively on the cusps.

The activities of the two houses that share the same sign on their cusps are tied together in many ways. The affairs ruled by these two houses tend to blend and intermingle:

First with Second   The person earns his own way in life, determines his own value structure, or sets much store on material comforts. Skating champion Sonja Henie, movie producer Alfred Hitchcock have this, as well as actor Marlon Brando whose chart is on page 89.

Second with Third   This person earns through the transportation or communication fields; his values may be influenced by, or may influence, a sibling, or he could go into business with a brother or sister. Singer Cher Bono and author Leo Tolstoy have this, so do actress Farrah Fawcett and humorist Ogden Nash whose charts are on pages 238 and 72.

Third with Fourth   A sibling may have taken a parent's place; there may have been an unsettled early childhood with attendance at different schools, or a brother or sister may share this person's home. Expression and communication may seem easier when in the home. Some examples are Attorney General Robert Kennedy, artist Vincent Van Gogh and actor Orson Welles whose charts can be found on pages 66 and 81.

Fourth with Fifth   This person's children always come home to roost; he is very creative in the home environment, or may even be an artisan who works out of his home. Author Henry Miller and composer Georg Friedrich Handel serve as examples, so do conductor Arturo Toscanini and singer Barbra Streisand whose charts are on pages 63 and 79.

Fifth with Sixth   This person works in a creative field and through his work gives service to young people (for example - as a teacher), or he may work in sports or coach a team. His work becomes his first love. Author Joseph Wambaugh and sculptor Auguste Rodin have this placement; so do ballplayer Vida Blue and blind author Helen Keller whose charts are found on pages 69 and 59.

Sixth with Seventh   This person works with his spouse or in partnership, or with the public in general (often in a service capacity). His work may involve the law. Former Beatle Ringo Starr and statesman Benjamin Disraeli have this; so do skier Jean-Claude Killy and footballer Joe Namath whose charts are on pages 123 and 121.

Seventh with Eighth   This person could go far in politics with the support (8th) of the public (7th); he may go into business partnership or he may inherit money through a partner. Labor leader Walter Reuther and satanist Aleister Crowley serve as examples; also producer Samuel Goldwyn whose chart is on page 64.

Eighth with Ninth   Publishing or writing could be tied to mystery or sex novels. He could be a financial tycoon or expert, and he may have a great affinity for or teach the psychic, mystic or occult. Child evangelist Marjoe Gortner and scientists Enrico Fermi and Albert Einstein are some examples; so is statesman Jawaharlal Nehru whose chart is on page 88.

Ninth with Tenth   This individual may travel extensively on career matters, education or law may play a significant role in his work, or a foreign born parent or person may be helpful to him in his career. Murderer Nathan Leopold and Prime Minister Harold Wilson have this placement, so do politician Robert Kennedy and artist Vincent van Gogh whose chart is on page 66.

Tenth with Eleventh   Friends and social relationships may help this person in his job or career; he may work for the government in some capacity (often in the military or in politics); he is usually very active in group efforts in a leadership capacity. Former Vice President Spiro Agnew and flying ace Eddie Rickenbacker serve as examples, so do Senator Ted Kennedy and entertainer Barbra Streisand whose charts are on pages 73 and 79.

Eleventh with Twelfth   He is often drawn to charitable work, or to the job of social or welfare worker. He needs to have time for himself or forces outside of his control may cause confinement. He is comfortable working behind the scenes. Authors Robert Louis Stevenson and James Joyce and movie director Vittorio de Sica have this placement; so does dictator Josef Stalin whose chart is on page 92.

Twelfth with First   This individual has much inner strength that he can call upon; his personality may require sharpening or defining; shyness or introversion may have to be dealth with. Misused, he can become his own worst enemy. Some examples are murderer Richard Loeb and Field Marshall Hermann Goering as well as singer Linda Ronstadt and conductor Henry Mancini whose charts can be found on pages 99 and 121

Review Question: On this page is the horoscope of singer Bob Dylan. Interpret his horoscope for the interceptions, the two sets of houses sharing the same sign on their cusps, and do not forget to include your interpretation of his intercepted Mars and Neptune. When you have completed this assignment, compare it with our answers in the appendix on page 240.

Name Bob Dylan
Date May 24, 1941
Time 9:05 PM CST
Place Duluth, MN
Long. 92W06
Lat. 46N47

Source
Contemporary Sidereal Horoscopes

A

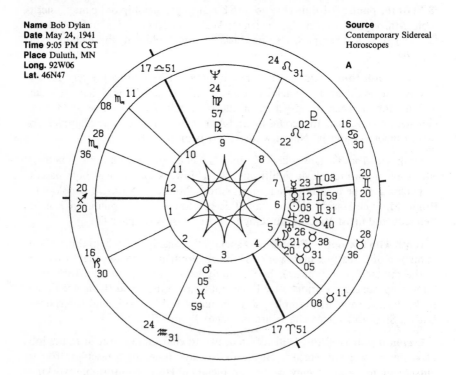

Lesson 9
Mutual Reception, Final Dispositor, Chart Ruler, Planet in High Focus

Mutual Reception

Mutual reception is a term used when two planets are placed in each other's sign of dignity or rulership. For example, if Venus is in Aries and Mars is in Taurus — Venus rules Taurus and Mars rules Aries — the two planets are in mutual reception, or mutually involved in each other's rulers. This is considered a very beneficial and harmonious relationship between two planets. It is as if the forces emanating from each planet are geared into one line of action. In interpreting this placement, some astrologers will read Mars in Aries and Venus in Taurus, reasoning that the two planets are so interlocked or integrated through mutual reception, that they function as if located in their own dignities. We do not quite agree with this.

To give you a few examples: Jean Claude Killy has Venus in Virgo and Mercury in Libra, therefore the planets are in each others' sign of dignity and in Mutual Reception. Both are in his second house (refer to Killy's horoscope page 123 in Lesson 10, "Chart Patterns"). Venus in the second house is accidentally dignified, therefore already quite well placed; however, Venus in Virgo is not in her happiest sign position, but in her fall. Venus is also retrograde, working in an inward direction, which is not the way Venus is supposed to work. By interchanging the two planets and delineating Venus as if it were in Libra, you would be disregarding the Virgo nature, yet much of Killy's self-criticism and self-imposed discipline, so necessary for a competition skier, comes from that Venus in Virgo, demanding perfection, and since it is also retrograde, demanding perfection from himself.

Our interpretation of a mutual reception is that the harmony of the two planets gives an overlay or additional help in bringing out the best that each planet has to give in whatever sign and house it may be and whatever aspects it has. In other words, it makes it easier for the individual to use the most positive qualities possible within the limitations of the horoscope. In Killy's case you may say that, because of the mutual reception, he was demanding of himself instead of pushing his demands and criticisms on others, which is of course a much more positive approach. His Mercury in Libra is so well aspected that it would be easy for him to communicate well and think clearly—but—he does have a bundle pattern, which makes it hard to function in relationship to others, since the energies are so concentrated in one area. But with Mercury in Libra, the wish and ability to relate and cooperate, the Libra need to function in society, are made easier by being in mutual reception to Venus in Virgo.

In Walt Disney's horoscope on page 236 there is a mutual reception between Pluto in Gemini and Mercury in Scorpio. Pluto has very few outlets through which to channel the energies generated in the square to his Ascendant, the opposition to Uranus and the Sun, the conjunction to his Midheaven. Nor do the two inconjuncts to Jupiter and Saturn give much outlet. At best, he can function through the wide trine from Pluto to the Moon. This is where the mutual reception really helps. It enabled Disney to use all the Pluto intensity and depth in the most positive way. By the same token, it brought out the best in Mercury. His mind functioned in a probing, searching way; he communicated and expressed himself without stinging or being excessively sarcastic, qualities very inherent in Mercury in Scorpio when used negatively.

Some astrologers also use planetary exaltations in mutual reception. For example, the Moon in Libra and Saturn in Taurus—Moon exalted in Taurus and Saturn exalted in Libra. We have not found this to work as strongly as the exchange or mutual reception of dignities. But, like everything else in Astrology, don't just take our word for this. See if it works for you.

Review Questions: Briefly describe how the mutual reception works in the Farrah Fawcett's horoscope. Compare it with our analysis in the Appendix on page 241.

Final Dispositor and High-Focus Planet

In observing a chart sometimes one planet stands out, perhaps it is *elevated* (in the 9th or 10th house) or because it receives and makes more aspects than any other planet, or because it is the **Final Dispositor** of the horoscope.

Very few charts have a **Final Dispositor**. To find it, see if there is a dignified planet. There must be *only one dignified planet,* and *no mutual reception* to have a final dispositor. To illustrate final dispositorship we will use Bob Dylan's horoscope on page 110.

Bob Dylan has the required dignified planet—Mercury in Gemini. The Sun and Venus are also in Gemini, so they are said to be disposed of by Mercury. Jupiter, Uranus, Saturn, and the Moon are all in Taurus, which is ruled by Venus in Gemini which leads back to Mercury. Mars is in Pisces, ruled by Neptune in Virgo ruled by Mercury in Gemini. Pluto is in Leo, ruled by the Sun in Gemini again leading back to Mercury. As you can see, each planet is finally disposed of by Mercury in Gemini, and so Mercury becomes the final dispositor of Bob Dylan's horoscope.

In Howard Cosell's chart on this page, you see that Mars is the handle of the bucket pattern. Mars is also involved in eight aspects, so Mars is a *very important* planet in Cosell's chart. This is considered to be a **Planet In High Focus.**

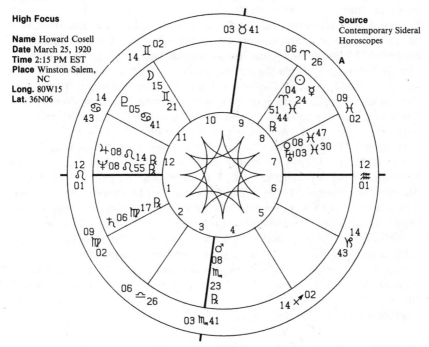

High Focus

Name Howard Cosell
Date March 25, 1920
Time 2:15 PM EST
Place Winston Salem, NC
Long. 80W15
Lat. 36N06

Source
Contemporary Sideral
Horoscopes

Any time that you have this situation—a final dispositor or a high-focus planet—that planet becomes very significant in the horoscope and needs special attention in your delineation. Mercury, Dylan's final dispositor, is in the seventh house and has only two aspects; it opposes the Ascendant and squares Neptune. But it definitely shows his musical ability and his need and opportunity to use this ability to appear before the public.

In Howard Cosell's horoscope, the high-focus Mars with its many aspects accounts, in part, for his interest in sports and his somewhat abrasive personality, since it is his Sun ruler and it squares Jupiter and Neptune. These aspects are also responsible for his spellbinding way with words.

Review Question: Try the final dispositor method with Walt Disney's, Joan Sutherland's, and Farrah Fawcett's horoscopes and see why they *do not* have a final dispositor. Our answers will be found in the Appendix on page 241.

The Chart Ruler

The ruler of the chart, sometimes referred to as the personal ruler, is the planet that rules the Ascendant. If this planet is actually located in the rising sign, the person is typical of the sign. If, however, this planet is in another sign (which is more often the case), you have to blend the two to gain an understanding of the personality. This is why no two people are alike, even though they may share the same rising sign.

For example, Hermann Hesse, (see chart, page 31) Lenny Bruce, and Henry Mancini all have Sagittarius rising. (For Bruce and Mancini, see the horoscopes on pages 123 and 121). Hesse has Jupiter in Sagittarius in the 1st house; Mancini's Jupiter is also in Sagittarius, but in his 12th house; Bruce's Jupiter is in his 1st house, but in Capricorn. Quite a difference when it comes to delineating the character, appearance, and personality of these three people. The house that the ruler of the Ascendant is in shows where the person is particularly active and where he really wants to be.

Composer Frederic Chopin's chart ruler is Mercury in Aquarius in the 6th house. He started his musical career at the ripe age of six and true to a sixth house chart ruler, worked and worked. He composed more than 27 etudes, 24 preludes, 20 nocturnes, 59 mazurkas, 16 polonaises, 14 waltzes to mention but a few. All of this he accomplished in a life span of less than forty years. This hyperactive and highly nervous genius (Mercury square Uranus) had a burning love affair with Madame Dudevant, better known as George Sand and he succumbed to tuberculosis in October 1849. (See chart, page 115).

Here are a few keywords to show you how the chart ruler expresses in the different houses, but *be sure to look at aspects too* as you delineate (Hesse's Jupiter for example is part of a mutable T-cross which has to be taken into consideration).

Chart Ruler in the 1st House   This is the self made, do-it-yourselfer, who expresses his or her own view actively.

Chart Ruler in the 2nd House   Assets, money and possessions are important as well as establishing one's own value system. Security and self worth will be prime motivations.

Chart Ruler in the 3rd House   There is a need to communicate in every which way, to be mentally or intellectually active; dealings with relatives may become important.

Chart Ruler in the 4th House   This person really needs a home base and is often very involved with family, foundations or real estate.

Chart Ruler in the 5th House   Self-expression through love, creativity or children is one of this person's needs as well as fun, games and romance in many forms.

Chart Ruler in the 6th House   This can be the workaholic of the zodiac or a hypochondriac if not working. Routine and method are also important.

Chart Ruler in the 7th House   Other people — the public and partners — are important. There is a need to share activity and to engage in competition, friendly or otherwise. The individual expresses with or through another person.

Chart Ruler in the 8th House   This person works well with the resources of others (monetary affairs, banking, etc.) or attracts support from others (politicians). Sex or research may become predominant factors.

Chart Ruler in the 9th House   Higher education, travel, law, religion, philosophy, ideas and ideals are important to this person.

Chart Ruler in the 10th House   Ego expression and career fulfillment are foremost needs. Government, prestige, politics or one of the parents may play a vital role.

Chart Ruler in the 11th House   Work with groups, humanitarian causes, goals, friends, outer circumstances and social activities all may affect the life.

Chart Ruler in the 12th House   This person may thrive on behind-the-scenes activity or be somewhat withdrawn, preferring to keep personal affairs private. The individual has much inner strength to draw on when needed.

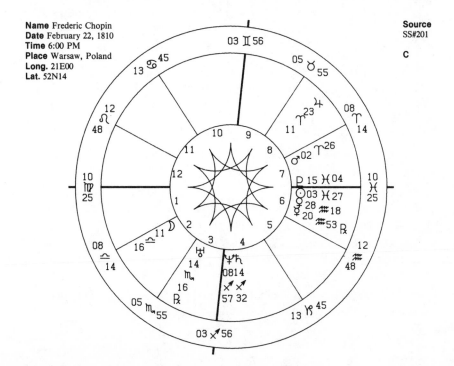

Name Frederic Chopin
Date February 22, 1810
Time 6:00 PM
Place Warsaw, Poland
Long. 21E00
Lat. 52N14

Source
SS#201

C

Lesson 10
Chart Patterns

A horoscope is like the individual it represents; it should first be seen as a whole before we take it apart. The fact that the Sun is in Virgo and the Moon and the other planets likewise placed at various points in the zodiac, is of no real value until they are seen in relation to the pattern of the entire chart and therefore applied to the whole context of a person's life. Ultimately the delineating of any chart is broken down into the details of signs, houses, aspects, and other factors. This can be done much more intelligently if the interpreter has a total concept of the horoscope, or, as we choose to call it, an overview.

Astrologer Marc Edmund Jones was the first one to make use of patterns which he called focal determinators. Jones' books, "The Guide to Horoscope Interpretation" and "Essentials of Astrological Analysis" give much insight into the subject which we outline in this lesson. Jones classified these focal determinators, which are basically geometric forms, into *seven basic types* which can be recognized at a glance. Astrologer Robert Carl Jansky did much in-depth research on Jones' original material, and added *an eighth type*. His book "Planetary Patterns" is must reading for anyone wishing more complete information on this subject.

In our own research, we have found the eight basic types of patterns to be important, because they seem to pull the entire chart or the entire individual into a definite direction. The keywords we give for each pattern will show you the direction. We have found that certain horoscopes do not fall into any of these eight patterns, and that is exactly what makes the pattern reading valuable—not every chart has an overall motivation, and only those that truly do should be interpreted as having a set pattern.

In establishing the pattern, we *use only the 10 planets.* In drawing your charts, it is wise to put the planets in one color and any additional factors (nodes, parts, etc.) in another. Jones uses a totally visual approach; Jansky uses a visual and mathematical approach. For example, the SPLAY pattern (which Jansky calls TRIPOD) divides the chart into three distinct areas where planets are bunched together, the rest of the chart being empty. Jones feels that if it looks like three areas, that's good enough. Jansky feels that in order to be a perfect TRIPOD, the three areas should be linked by trines from at least one of the planets in each bunch. Obviously Jansky's method is even more potent, since not only do we have a visual, but also an astrological direction. However, we find that both approaches work.

The Splash Pattern (See conductor Henry Mancini's horoscope.) All ten planets are well divided around the wheel. Ideally, there is no conjunction anywhere. It makes no difference which planet is where; it's the pattern that counts. This shows a universal type person who can do many things well; as one door closes, he can open the next one. He can create order out of confusion. At its most negative, the splash chart indicates a scattering of energies or a person who is off in all directions.

The Bowl Pattern (See athlete Joe Namath's horoscope.) The planets all lie to one side of the zodiac and occupy only one-half of the chart. This pattern is even more pronounced when the angles are involved (division by Equator or Meridian). Ideally the two planets forming the rim of the bowl should form an opposition to each other. The bowl person is very self-contained, quite subjective, and often self-satisfied. He may need to further some cause or fulfill a mission. The unoccupied portion of the chart becomes his challenge—the unknown quality the individual wishes to and needs to understand in order to function properly.

The Bucket Pattern (See conductor Zubin Mehta's horoscope.) This pattern looks like a bowl with a handle on it. The handle becomes all important; it represents the outlet for the energies stored in the bowl. It is the singleton that can indicate the special capacity or talent through which the individual will express himself. The position of this singleton is important too. If it stands straight up, in relationship to the bowl, the person knows what to do and how to go after it. If it leans to the left, he knows and feels what he wants, but loses steam half way in going after it and so has to try harder. If it leans to the right, he overdoes and puts forth more effort than is really necessary. Operating positively the bucket person can inspire or teach others; at its worst, the bucket person becomes an agitator. The bucket pattern is the second most common pattern.

The See-Saw Pattern   (See actor Richard Chamberlain's horoscope.) Called the hourglass pattern by Jansky. Here we find two groups of planets opposed to each other, as for example two houses with planets opposing three houses with planets. According to Jansky, this pattern requires a square of open space on one side and more than a sextile of open space on the other side. This is the most common of all of the patterns. Here the person needs to learn how to weigh and balance his life, because his natural pattern is that of the teeter-totter, always being pulled first in one direction and then the other. He is prone to act under a consideration of the opposing view and therefore tends to live in a world of conflict. Yet, when this energy is positively used, he is capable of unique achievements, because he can learn true awareness by understanding and using the opposite polarity. Used negatively, he will waste time and energy.

The Locomotive Pattern   (See comedian Lenny Bruce's horoscope.) All ten planets are placed within 2/3rds of the chart leaving an empty trine (120° segment). According to Jansky this formation is not valid if within the pattern there is an open space that exceeds 65°. The Locomotive gives a certain balance, since the empty trine symbolically gives a free span of experience set against the limited span embraced by the 2/3rds. Yet this can give a strong sense of lack forcing the individual to solve problems or perform tasks. This shows a self-driving person who brings much power to bear in order to achieve. He is often found moved by external factors rather than his own tendencies. Yet he has much practical capacity and can go far when he uses this ability positively. This pattern is the third most common one.

It is important to determine the 'engine' of this pattern, the planet that will motivate the locomotive into action. In Lenny Bruce's chart Pluto is the engine. Through the years, the planets move on (Uranus progresses through Pisces and Jupiter through Capricorn and so on); yet as the whole chart moves forward in a clockwise direction, Capricorn will come to the Ascendant, then Aquarius; therefore Pluto will pull the planets just as any engine pulls any train.

The Bundle Pattern   (See skier Jean Claude Killy's horoscope.) Called the wedge pattern by Jansky, this horoscope pattern is nearly the opposite of the splash. All ten planets are concentrated within the narrow confines of a trine; therefore, the focus is very one-sided, the energies tremendously concentrated and confined. Yet this individual is capable of making much of very little and often gets unanticipated results. Used positively, he can start with small beginnings, and as he works himself out of the bounds of the pattern, build on solid ground. Negatively, he may be rather inhibited or try to force his limited views on others.

The Splay Pattern   (See former first lady Rosalynn Carter's horoscope.) Called the tripod pattern by Jansky, this pattern has three distinct points in the chart, and if perfect, some of the planets within the three points form a grand trine. This pattern has tremendous momentum and can produce geniuses. But even the average person will be able to make his own anchorage in existence, and with a rather intensive and fiery nature, can rarely be limited to one point of application. The harmonious flow created by the three points, where one reaches out for the other will always be helpful.

The Fan Pattern   (See psychiatrist Sigmund Freud's horoscope.) This pattern coined by Jansky is similiar to the bucket pattern, only instead of a bowl, we have a tight bundle and one singleton planet as an outlet for all the energies. But there is one more difference in the two patterns. In the bucket the singleton really seems to work as an outlet or channel for the nine planets contained in the bowl. In the fan pattern, it seems to rather act as input to the bundle, as if it were in the driver's seat directing the bundle into action. Jansky feels the handle of the bundle is the effect whereas the handle of the bowl is the cause. The resulting interpretation is therefore nearly the opposite and the momentum generated is even greater.

Review Question: Please interpret the bundle pattern for Jean Claude Killy. Our interpretation is given in the Appendix on page 242. For additional learning, try to delineate the other charts in this chapter for yourself as well.

Splash

Name Henry Mancini
Date April 16, 1924
Time 0:10 AM EST
Date Cleveland, OH
Long. 81W43
Lat. 41N30

Source
Jansky/from him

A

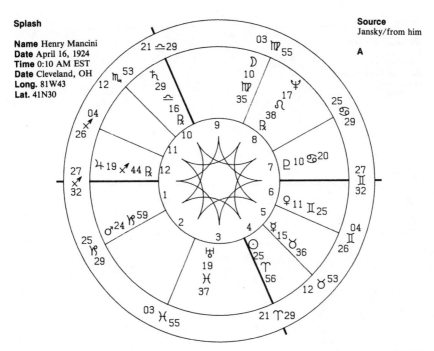

Bowl

Name Joe Namath
Date May 31, 1943
Time 6:20 AM EST
Place Beaver Falls, PA
Long. 80W19
Lat. 40N45

Source
Jansky, birth certificate.
Penfield says 'from
mother' personally 0:30 AM
EST

DD

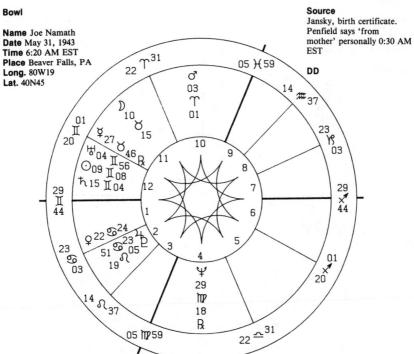

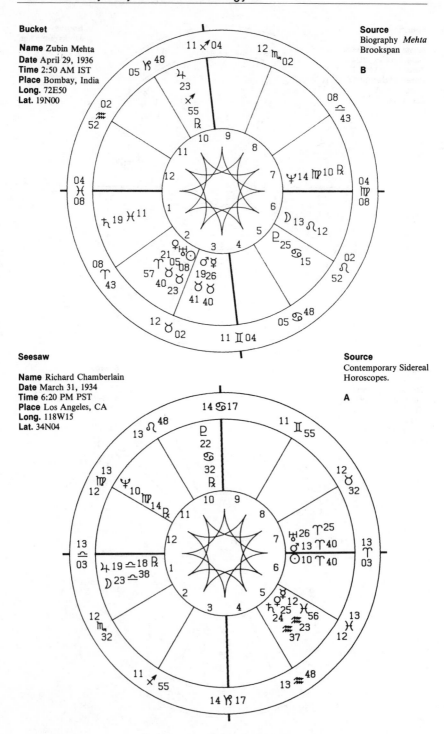

Bucket

Name Zubin Mehta
Date April 29, 1936
Time 2:50 AM IST
Place Bombay, India
Long. 72E50
Lat. 19N00

Source
Biography *Mehta*
Brookspan

B

Seesaw

Name Richard Chamberlain
Date March 31, 1934
Time 6:20 PM PST
Place Los Angeles, CA
Long. 118W15
Lat. 34N04

Source
Contemporary Sidereal
Horoscopes.

A

Locomotive

Name Lenny Bruce
Date October 13, 1925
Time 11:25 AM EST
Place Mineola, NY
Long. 73W38
Lat. 40N45

Source
Contemporary Sidereal
Horoscopes

A

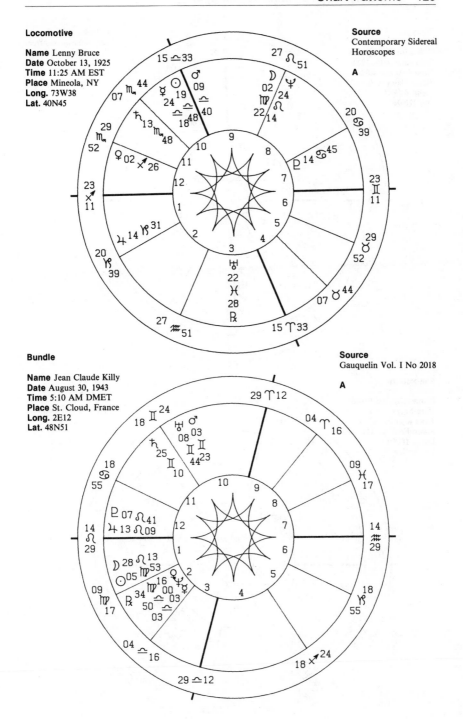

Bundle

Name Jean Claude Killy
Date August 30, 1943
Time 5:10 AM DMET
Place St. Cloud, France
Long. 2E12
Lat. 48N51

Source
Gauquelin Vol. I No 2018

A

Splay

Name Rosalynn Carter
Date August 18, 1927
Time 6:00 AM CST
Place Plains, GA
Long. 84W24
Lat. 32N02

Source
Horoscope quotes from
her mother.

A

Fan Pattern

Name Sigmund Freud
Date May 6, 1856
Time 6:30 PM LMT
Place Freiberg, Germany
Long. 18E09
Lat. 49N38

Source
Photograph of fathers
diary. Data written in
Hebrew and German.

A

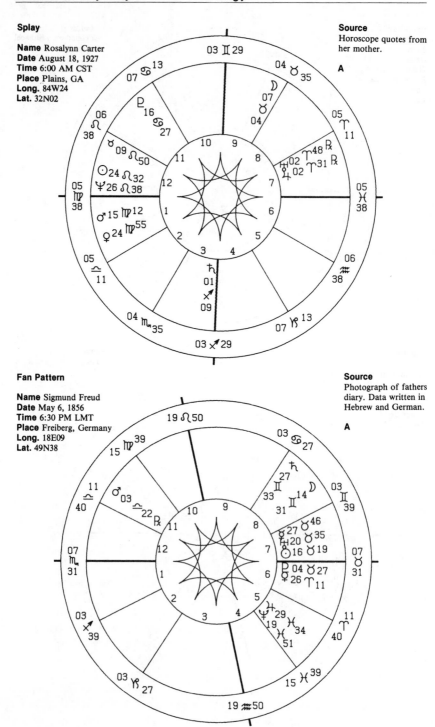

Lesson 11
The Overview of the Chart

We have talked time and time again of looking at the chart as a whole and examining the basic overview of the horoscope. In Volume One, before we asked you to delineate Judy Garland's horoscope with us, we gave a brief overview based on the knowledge you had at that point. Then, and now, we stress again that each person is unique; therefore, we must first look at the overall picture before dissecting it. This overall picture, which we call the overview, has to be kept in mind *at all times* as you delineate planet by planet and aspect by aspect. It is this overview that enables you to discriminate and judge in selecting your keywords and key phrases.

To really see the person as a whole, we start with the most obvious — a pictorial look at the horoscope. How many planets are there above and how many below the horizon; how many planets are East and how many West of the Meridian? Does the horoscope have a planetary pattern? (See Lesson 10.) How are the qualities and elements distributed, are there compensations by house position, and does this person equate to a certain signature? (See Lesson 6.) Is there a final dispositor, a mutual reception? Which planet rules the chart, or is there a planet in high focus? (See Lesson 9.) Are there any interceptions? Are there many or no retrograde planets? (See Lessons 7 and 8.) How many planets are dignified or exalted, or in detriment or fall? Are these planets of great importance in the chart? Are there any configurations in the chart and how many houses do they involve? (See Lesson 6.) If there are no configurations, which are the most exact aspects? They will create the greatest energy and have much to do with the basic character of the individual.

After you have determined all of these facts, you should already have a pretty good idea of the kind of person you are dealing with. NEVER FORGET THIS! If the overview shows a rather mutable person, versatile, and with a splash-type chart, even the most fixed Sun will have to be delineated accordingly. That fixed Sun may help to hold down the scattering tendency, but it will not be as set in its way as a fixed Sun in a very fixed chart.

Learning is easiest by example. Let's take the overview of Hermann Hesse's horoscope, see page 31. There are four planets above and six planets below the horizon, a fairly even division, showing integration between objectivity and subjectivity, the ability to look within and yet be able to act without. There are four planets East and six planets West of the Meridian. Again, a rather unimportant division, indicating that though at times dependent on or needing others, he can also be his own man with free will to choose his destiny.

Hesse's horoscope has a definite planetary pattern—a bucket, with Jupiter as the handle. Jupiter is already important in this chart since it is angular (in the 1st house) and is the chart ruler, dignified in Sagittarius. Now we see that Jupiter gains additional emphasis by serving as the outlet for the stored energies of the rest of the chart. This handle or singleton is leaning to the left of center; though Hesse seemed to know what he wanted, he may have had trouble following through at times, a point substantiated by the great mutability in this chart.

Since the singleton can indicate the special talent or capacity through which Hesse could express himself, we also observe that Jupiter is retrograde (see our delineation in Lesson 7 - Retrogrades) and also involved in two configurations—a T-square and a yod. The tremendous energies generated with the T-square can be used positively through the trine to Uranus (the awakener) in the dramatic sign of Leo in the often occult and always deep 8th house. Uranus makes a sextile to Mercury, which is part of the T-square, substantiating the ability to utilize Uranus. The yod, involving an inconjunct from Jupiter to Pluto and to Venus (Pluto and Venus are sextile), makes Jupiter the finger or focal planet toward which both Pluto and Venus have to adjust.

This indicates personal expansion (Jupiter in the 1st house) through 8th house matters, but in a feeling (Cancerian) way, and through creativity (5th house) and regeneration (Pluto), but in a tangible (Taurus) fashion. So his special talent had to develop from within (Jupiter is retrograde), with all of the idealism and philosophical inclination inherent in Sagittarius expanding the personality as Hesse grew and matured, challenged by Saturn in the 3rd house of communication in the sensitive sign Pisces, but also giving him the discipline needed to stick to his guns.

The square to the Moon is less productive, sometimes even self-indulging, but giving a certain generosity of spirit and much nervous energy. Since both of these planets are in an intercepted sign, the emotions and sensitivities are intensified and directed inward. The uncertainties and imbalances between Jupiter's optimism and wishful thinking and Mercury's rational thinking (in

Gemini) and wish to learn and communicate its learning, can be applied the moment this opposition is used to become aware of his own and other's needs.

Hesse had no final dispositor, no mutual reception, and we have already discussed Jupiter as a planet in high focus, chart ruler, and a part of two configurations. His five mutable planets and five planets in water signs equate to a Pisces signature, re-emphasizing the sensitivity of his nature, already evident in a Cancer Sun. With four planets in angular houses, we see that Hesse had enough get-up-and-go to accomplish, and with five planets in the houses of relationships he could communicate, reason, and think well. He had no planets in the houses of substance, but two planets in the earth element; therefore, there was no lack of earthiness but still some of the practicality was missing. As we mentioned in Lesson 5, it was harder for Hesse to find his true vocation in life.

We have discussed Jupiter's dignity, but Mercury is also dignified in Gemini. It is also angular and it rules the 7th house of partners and the public in which it is placed. Mercury is a part of the T-square; it makes an exact sextile to Uranus. Thus, Mercury becomes another very important planet in Hesse's horoscope. Mercury in Gemini demands detached and cool logic; the Pisces type he equates to and the Pisces planets that square Mercury want feelings, emotions, and poetic expression. Therefore, regardless of aspects, we have to keep this inner dichotomy in mind when we proceed to delineate Hesse's horoscope.

We also note that Uranus and Pluto are in the signs of their detriment. Uranus is in the 8th house (Scorpio) where it functions quite well, and it makes two trines and two sextiles which are very helpful. Pluto is not too happy in Taurus and it is not at home in the 5th house (Leo). Yet, the inner tensions and struggles of Hesse's life were all finally expressed in an intense (Pluto) creativity (5th house). In other words, just because something is difficult does not mean it cannot or will not work; quite the contrary, if the chart is as active and integrated as Hermann Hesse's chart, this can be the challenge necessary to force him to produce.

Hesse also had two nearly exact trines, Sun trine Mars and Uranus trine Ascendant; these served as good outlets for the tensions created by the T-square and yod. The trine from the public 7th house Sun to Mars in the 3rd house obviously helped Hesse to communicate and express himself; wherever we find Mars in the horoscope is where we want to act and do. Hesse most certainly did express himself, and in a very Piscean way as all of his books prove.

After familiarizing yourself through the overview, you should have a pretty good idea of who this man Hesse was what made him tick and why. Now is a good time to take the chart apart, to delineate it step-by-step, and as you do, always keep the overview in mind. After you have finished the basic delineation, as we taught you in Volume 1 continue with the additional learning we give you in this book.

Review Question: Interpret the overview in Joan Sutherland's horoscope. You'll find our interpretation in the Appendix on Page 243.

Lesson 12
Decanates and Dwads

Decanates

To further refine the reading of a horoscope, there is a method called decanates. Decanates (derived from the word "deca", meaning 10) divides each sign (each of which contain exactly 30°) into thirds of 10° each. The ruler of the first 10° of the sign is the ruler of that sign. For example, Aries from 0° to 9°59' is pure Aries, ruled by Mars. The second, or Leo, decanate, from 10° to 19°59' Aries, is ruled by the Sun, and the third, or Sagittarius, decanate, from 20° to 29°59', is ruled by Jupiter. As you can see, each decanate is ruled by the planets associated with the other two signs of the triplicity - in this case, by the fire sign triplicity of Aries/Leo/Sagittarius.

Thus, a person whose Sun is at 15° Aries will act differently from a person whose Sun is located at 22° Aries. In the first instance, you must add some of the Leo/Sun attributes; in the second case, you look to Jupiter (ruler of Sagittarius) to see what qualities should be added. The following is a table to make decanates easy to determine:

	0° - 9° 59'	10° - 19° 59'	20° - 29° 59'
Aries	Mars (Aries)	Sun (Leo)	Jupiter (Sagittarius)
Taurus	Venus (Taurus)	Mercury (Virgo)	Saturn (Capricorn)
Gemini	Mercury (Gemini)	Venus (Libra)	Uranus (Aquarius)
Cancer	Moon (Cancer)	Pluto (Scorpio)	Neptune (Pisces)
Leo	Sun (Leo)	Jupiter (Sagittarius)	Mars (Aries)
Virgo	Mercury (Virgo)	Saturn (Capricorn)	Venus (Taurus)
Libra	Venus (Libra)	Uranus (Aquarius)	Mercury (Gemini)
Scorpio	Pluto (Scorpio)	Neptune (Pisces)	Moon (Cancer)
Sagittarius	Jupiter (Sagittarius)	Mars (Aries)	Sun (Leo)
Capricorn	Saturn (Capricorn)	Venus (Taurus)	Mercury (Virgo)
Aquarius	Uranus (Aquarius)	Mercury (Gemini)	Venus (Libra)
Pisces	Neptune (Pisces)	Moon (Cancer)	Pluto (Scorpio)

As you can see from the table on page 129, the first 10° of each sign have the pure feeling of that sign and its ruler, whereas the next 10° adds a shading of the next sign within that triplicity of element you are dealing with. The air triplicity is from Gemini/Mercury to Libra/Venus to Aquarius/Uranus. Or, if we start in Libra, the next decanate is Aquarius/Uranus followed by Gemini/Mercury. If you know your elements, you should not have any trouble understanding the principle involved.

In Walt Disney's horoscope, the Sun is at 12° 26' of Sagittarius; therefore, it is in the second, or Mars-ruled, decanate of Sagittarius. He had more drive and daring than would at first be noticed by looking at the Sun's sign. With Mars in Capricorn, his daring and drive had a very practical orientation. Both the Moon and Ascendant are in Venus-ruled decanates (Moon in the Libra/Venus decanate and the Ascendant in the Taurus/Venus decanate). Venus is in his 5th house of creativity, so it is easy to see why Disney directed his activities to the creative fields. Since Venus is in Capricorn, he was able to do this in a business like way.

To give one more illustration: Joan Sutherland's Sun is at 14° 08' Scorpio, in the second, or Pisces, decanate of Scorpio ruled by Neptune in Leo. To the rather intense and deeply feeling Sun, we must add the sensitivity of Pisces. Since Pisces is a mutable sign, we must also blend in the ability to unflex the rather rigid and fixed Scorpio tendency. Her Neptune is in Leo, it is ruled by the Sun, reinforcing the already existing solar tendencies.

You can, of course, use this decanate method with all ten planets. In our teaching we suggest using it as a minimum with the Sun, Moon and Ascendant—these three representing the most important facets of a person.

Review Question: Delineate Hermann Hesse's Sun by decanate. Our interpretation will be found in the Appendix on page 244.

Dwads   There is another method of sign division, called dwads, an abbreviation for the word Dwadasamas which, loosely translated from the Sanskrit, means duo-decimal or divided into 12ths. This very old system, dating to Chaldean times, focuses on an even narrower area of each planet and permits a yet finer interpretation.

We do not advocate that you use this method for general delineation purposes, but there are instances where dwads can be very valuable—for example, in the case of twins, where there is little difference in planetary position. The decanate is helpful, but the dwad can pinpoint the very fine differences.

For your convenience, we have included a complete table of dwads on page 131. The principle is easy to understand: each 2½° of the sign takes on an overlay of another sign, this time not by element but in the order of the signs of the zodiac. The first 2½° dwad of Aries is pure Aries, the next 2½° dwad adds a nuance of Taurus, the next dwad, Gemini and so forth through the entire 12 signs.

DWAD TABLE

Signs	Aries	Taurus	Gemini	Cancer	Leo	Virgo	Libra	Scorpio	Sag	Cap	Aquarius	Pisces
0° - 2½°	♈	♉	♊	♋	♌	♍	♎	♏	♐	♑	♒	♓
2½° - 5°	♉	♊	♋	♌	♍	♎	♏	♐	♑	♒	♓	♈
5° - 7½°	♊	♋	♌	♍	♎	♏	♐	♑	♒	♓	♈	♉
7½° - 10°	♋	♌	♍	♎	♏	♐	♑	♒	♓	♈	♉	♊
10° - 12½°	♌	♍	♎	♏	♐	♑	♒	♓	♈	♉	♊	♋
12½° - 15°	♍	♎	♏	♐	♑	♒	♓	♈	♉	♊	♋	♌
15° - 17½°	♎	♏	♐	♑	♒	♓	♈	♉	♊	♋	♌	♍
17½° - 20°	♏	♐	♑	♒	♓	♈	♉	♊	♋	♌	♍	♎
20° - 22½°	♐	♑	♒	♓	♈	♉	♊	♋	♌	♍	♎	♏
22½° - 25°	♑	♒	♓	♈	♉	♊	♋	♌	♍	♎	♏	♐
25° - 27½°	♒	♓	♈	♉	♊	♋	♌	♍	♎	♏	♐	♑
27½° - 30°	♓	♈	♉	♊	♋	♌	♍	♎	♏	♐	♑	♒

Again, using Disney's horoscope, his Virgo Ascendant was in the Gemini dwad, giving dexterity and an ability to communicate, which reinforced his 3rd house Sun. Assume that Walt Disney had a twin brother born 4 minutes later. The Ascendant in this case would be approximately 1° later, or at 25° Virgo 53'. This would still be in the third decanate of Virgo and not give you much help; however, it is in the Cancer dwad, and functions on a different level than Disney's Gemini dwad.

Review Question: Delineate the dwads for Farrah Fawcett's Moon and Ascendant. Compare your answer with ours in the Appendix on page 245.

Lesson 13
The Lunar Nodes

In Volume One, Lesson 3—Planets, we gave you a brief description of the Nodes of the Moon. We explained that they are not planets but instead planes in celestial longitude where the Moon crosses over the path of the Sun (the ecliptic). We told you that the North Node (also called the Dragon's Head) is considered to be a point of gain, increase and added confidence—the point where you take in or are given to, the point in your horoscope you should strive toward to find fulfillment. The South Node (or Dragon's Tail) is a point of release or letting go; it is where you must give or are taken from, and where it is found in the horoscope is where you may take the easy way out.

Since we use the Moon's Nodes in our beginning teaching and basic delineation, we would like to give you a few more key phrases to help you understand the nature of these sensitive points in a chart.

If you visualize a dragon, you can understand that at the head he starts to take in or ingest. As he eats, the food is ingested through the mouth which is located in the head. This is how the North Node works; it is the point where you take in new knowledge, new ideas and ideals, everything that is new to you—therefore, it is the point of gain or increase. As you gain in knowledge, you automatically gain confidence; as you gain confidence, you gain inner security and eventually reach the highest point of inner peace or fulfillment that your horoscope promises.

If the North Node, or Dragon's Head, is the point of taking in then obviously the South Node, or Dragon's Tail, is the point of giving out or egesting. But we are not egesting the knowledge gained through the North Node; instead, we are giving out that which is already within, the knowledge, ideas, attitudes, morals that are already a part of us, based upon our past, our memories, our childhood, or if you wish to use the esoteric approach—on our past throughout the ages. Being taken from or having to give may not sound like points we flee to or take the easy way out of, but think about this. Don't most of us prefer to stay with what we know or are familiar with, rather than reaching out toward the new and therefore unknown? Don't we hang on to that old comfortable pair of shoes as long as possible before we buy a new pair which may pinch or squeeze our feet? That's one part of the problem. The other one is based on the fact that most people find it easier to give graciously than to receive gracefully. To accept without feeling a sense of obligation seems harder than to give, which makes us feel good and important. If you keep these points in mind, you will understand why we tend to flee into the South Node, rather than using the North Node to grow or evolve.

In the ephemeris you may encounter two kinds of Nodes. All American ephemerides carry what is commonly referred to as the True Nodes. These Nodes move forward and backward alternately. They can move backwards as little as 2 minutes in one month or as much as 2½ degrees. But over the years their motion is always backwards. Most other ephemerides carry the Mean Nodes. These Nodes always move backwards and always at a mean motion of approximately 3 1/3 minutes per day or 10 minutes every three days.

Neither Node is "truer" than the other. As the Moon orbits around the Earth, it does not do so in a smooth motion, but with wobbles called perturbations. The Mean Nodes are figured as though there were no perturbations, evening out the orbit by taking a "mean" average. The True Nodes are refigured every time there is a wobble in the orbit by calculating a new orbit for each perturbation. Neil Michelsen who produced the *American Ephemerides*, prefers the "True Node", because he wouldn't think of using the "Mean" Moon position, though it is much easier to calculate.

The difference can be a few degrees from one ephemeris to the other. Walt Disney's Mean North Node is 11° Scorpio 55', his True North Node is 13° Scorpio 20'. Farrah Fawcett's Mean North Node is 8° Gemini 27', her True Node is 9° Gemini 46'.

Since in our delineation of the Nodes we stress house position more than aspects, we feel that either system is fine.

As you become more proficient in Astrology, you might wish to read some very interesting books written on the Nodes of the Moon based on a more esoteric or karmic interpretation. Isabel Hickey touches on this subject in her book "Astrology, a Cosmic Science". Martin Schulman's book "Karmic Astrology—The Nodes and Reincarnation" goes into great detail. So does Bernice Prill Grebner's "Lunar Nodes - New Concepts". These books include the position of the Nodes in the different signs of the zodiac, the house positions and the aspects they make to natal planets.

We don't feel that any of this is necessary in basic beginning delineation. In fact, it might put too much weight on something that should only be interpreted as a sensitive point or area in the chart until you are ready to go into a much deeper delineation.

We do feel that you should look at the positions occupied by the Nodes and put your main emphasis on the houses they are in, then look at the sign to interpret in which manner they will express.

To illustrate: Hermann Hesse's South Node is at 4° Virgo in his 9th house, his North Node at 4° Pisces in his 3rd house. His early and rather automatic response therefore would be to express through the 9th house (the higher mind, his philosophies and beliefs) but he would do it in a Virgo way, being rather critical of himself and others, always analyzing and taking everything apart. Eventually though, to reach his highest potential, he has to use the North Node and communicate (verbally, in writing or painting) his feelings, emotions, and spirituality. In his case it should have been made easier, because Saturn and the Moon in Pisces are the arm or focal points of his T-square (Lesson 6).

Farrah Fawcett has the North Node in the 12th house at 8° Gemini 26'(or 9°♊46'). She is expressing herself through her work in the 6th house where she has the South Node in Sagittarius. Her eventual fulfillment though will be found by reaching for or tuning in on her 12th house North Node. The 12th house when interpreting any sensitive point has to be seen as the subconscious, often the inner, hidden self. When she really looks within in a Gemini (intellectual, detached, mental) way, she will find peace of mind and true inner security.

The nodal axis as it falls across each pair of houses seems to give some indication of family interaction. To give you a few examples:

Nodal Axis in the 1st and 7th houses: The person has visible character, personality or appearance traits in common with one of the parents or grandparents.

Nodal Axis in the 2nd and 8th houses: The person's value system is similar to that of one or both of the parents. They often earn their income in the same field as a parent.

Nodal Axis in the 3rd and 9th houses: Here the person shares a religious or philosophical outlook with a parent and the lines of communication with this parent are open and operative.

Nodal Axis in the 4th and 10th houses: This individual often follows in one of the parent's footsteps in a career. Also the parental ties are very strong.

Nodal Axis in the 5th and 11th houses: Here we find a person who socializes with the family, particularly their own children, often to the exclusion of others.

Nodal Axis in the 6th and 12th houses: This placement may indicate a hereditary tendency to illness, both the individual and a parent showing the same symptoms.

In some astrological books you will find the Nodes interpreted as social relationships or involvement; how the individual relates to society as a whole or his social mores, morals, and attitudes. We have not observed this to be as relevant as the interpretation we use, except in progressed aspects, which we will cover in another book.

Review Question: Delineate the Moon's Nodes in the horoscope of Walt Disney. For our delineation, refer to the Appendix, page 245.

Lesson 14
Delineating The House Cusps

The Cusps

Up to now, in Volume One and in this book, we have talked about houses, signs on the cusp of these houses, meanings of the houses and the planets in them, but we have not really explained the importance of the sign on each cusp. We explain it in this lesson.

The procedure is simple and logical, like everything else in Astrology. Take the meaning of the house, blend it with the sign on the cusp, and then add some shading for the ruler of that sign.

For example: Walt Disney has Libra on the 2nd house cusp. The keywords for the 2nd houses are—values, possessions, financial affairs, earning power, inner talents and resources. With Libra on the cusp, ruled by Venus in Capricorn, how would he feel about all 2nd house matters? Libra likes harmony and balance, does things in relation to others rather than by himself, but despite this need for others, Libra likes to balance the scale his way. Libra also needs beauty around him, dislikes crass behavior, and has a mental orientation (Air Sign). Add some of the Capricorn feeling to this and you know that this Libra on the 2nd house cusp will be ambitious, serious and disciplined in his financial affairs. Or, he will be able to put some of the Venusian principles on an earthy and practical plane.

Take a look at the aspects that Venus makes. Does it have flow? Energy? Now, apply some of the keywords for the Libra/Capricorn combination to the 2nd house areas and you might say: "Values and possessions are quite important to Disney. He likes to be surrounded by beautiful things, but he has enough good sense not to squander his money in order to indulge (Libra could indulge but with the ruler in Capricorn, it won't). His earning power is good;

Venus sextiles Mercury, which rules the Midheaven and Ascendant, giving him the opportunity to earn—the will and ambition are there with Venus in Capricorn. Venus square the Ascendant gives him the get-up-and-go needed. The inconjunct to Neptune, highest planet in the chart in the 10th house of career, will force him to adjust at some point to use Neptune through his career to earn money in some Neptunian way (like motion pictures). This could be artistic or possibly connected with show business, or if the rest of the chart indicates—spiritual. The earning power is linked to the inner resources and talents, since the ruler of the 2nd house (Venus) is in the 5th house of creativity.

Does this sound complicated? It really isn't if you always remember the basic meaning of each sign, house and aspect, and then blend them together as we've just done.

In this lesson we give you key sentences for each sign on each house cusp. However, we urge you not to use them verbatim because that is not the way they function. As we've just shown you with Walt Disney's 2nd house, it does not function only on the Libra level. It works instead on a Libra/Capricorn level plus the house position of Venus and its aspects. If there are any planets in the house, they give added emphasis. The only time you would have a pure Libra reading is when Venus is in the sign of Libra and in the 7th house. Since this happens very rarely, you have to blend in order to understand the fine points that make each individual unique.

Aries ♈ on the House Cusps

Since the 1st house is your identity, outer personality, physical body, the face that you present to the world, it is the most important house and should be carefully analyzed. We will not give you keywords here for appearance in this volume since many factors have to be considered; the subject is too complex at this level.

Always blend the interpretation with the ruler - Mars ♂

Aries ♈ on the Cusp of the First House   Basically restless, you approach the world in a direct rather than a diplomatic fashion. Quite extroverted and headstrong, you have little or no physical fear; in fact, you tend to irritate others with your aggressiveness. Courageous and dynamic, you will fight for your beliefs when it is necessary, but you prefer to use your wits. Usually, you are a self-starter, but you have trouble finishing what you start since it bores you quickly and you're off to the next thing. Stick-to-it-iveness is an art you need to cultivate. If Mars is in a passive sign, Pisces for example, you will appear softer and you may be mildly assertive, less impulsive, more understanding and feeling. Be sure to blend in the position of Mars. *Actress Barbra Streisand, Senator Howard Baker, tennis pro Don Budge.*

Aries ♈ on the Cusp of the Second House (Values, possessions, financial affairs, earning power, talents and resources). If you have Pisces rising, inner talents and resources will be important to you, but with Aries on the 2nd house cusp you may not be patient enough to take good care of your assets and may end up with financial headaches. You may have many good and new ideas of how to make money. If Mars is in a stable sign, you will learn to budget properly and hold on to some of it. Impulsive, you must learn financial conservatism since material possessions are important to you and provide inner security until you are able to use your other resources, as indicated by the horoscope. *Secretary of State Edmund Muskie, ex-mayor Joseph Alioto, actress Carol Burnett.*

Aries ♈ on the Cusp of the Third House (Communications, siblings, local and early environment, education, short trips). Your mind is energetic, active and constructive. If you have Aquarius rising, the combination of being different, with open and direct Aries on the cusp of the house of communications, leads to a very outspoken and interesting person.

You are a good conversationalist who can hold his own in any argument, but are better at dishing it out than taking it. Unless Mars is well aspected, you find it hard to take criticism. A stable Saturn will help you use your facile mind for greater concentration. You may do much moving around during your early years, and if you have any siblings, the atmosphere was likely quite lively in your youth. *Ventriloquist Edgar Bergen, TV actress Cindy Williams, commentator Edward R. Murrow.*

Aries ♈ on the Cusp of the Fourth House (Home, one of the parents; your roots, foundation, and real property). If you have Capricorn on the Ascendant, your adolescent years may have seemed difficult; you may have been so restless that you considered running away from home despite a strong link with one of your parents. You may have many changes of residence during your lifetime and they might not all be welcome. Unless Mars is very favorably aspected, you tend to feel a lack of love and tenderness. However, this would not be so likely with Sagittarius or Aquarius rising. In any case, you will feel a great need to expand and will not always have the ability to do so. In your later years, you'll tend to rule the roost and the placement of Mars will show whether you will do so constructively or not. Unless you cultivate outside interests, you may use all of your energy at home and become too demanding of your loved ones. Rarely will you spend a dull or lonely old age. *General Erwin Rommel, comedian Jack Benny, writer Joseph Wambaugh.*

Aries ♈ on the Cusp of the Fifth House (Children, love affairs and romance, creativity, amusements, speculative matters). Enthusiastic, with a great zest for life, you give your all in fun, pleasure, sports, creative outlets and physical activity. You'd make a great coach or manager as you can inspire others with your enthusiasm. Though you like children, you get along best with them when they have reached the age of reason, else your impatience shows. Since you love life and love, you may use your energy in excessive sexual activity and jump from one love affair to another. If Sagittarius is rising, and Mars is well placed, you will want to channel some of your idealism into a creative outlet—or you may be quite daring and try to shoot for the stars, be it in a hobby, gambling, or a life pursuit. *Aviator Charles Lindbergh, astronaut John Glenn, composer George Gershwin.*

Aries ♈ on the Cusp of the Sixth House   (Work, health and nutrition, habits, service given, employees). You are a great and tireless worker; in fact, work is a natural for you and you'll enjoy utilizing your energies in this area. However, with your nearly superhuman drive, you may push others as mercilessly as you push yourself, and this is not always well received. You do better when you are self-employed or in an executive position since you resent authority and dislike interference, especially if you have Scorpio rising or if Mars is very active in your chart. Despite appearing strong, you need reassurance and function best when you feel appreciated. If you do not use the energies of Mars in work or some other constructive fashion, you may bring on quick illnesses or headaches, but since your basic nature is hardy, you recover quickly, though you are prone to very high temperatures when ill. *Author-composer Noel Coward, Cuban leader Fidel Castro, actor Charlie Chaplin.*

Aries ♈ on the Cusp of the Seventh House   (Partners, both business and marital; dealings with the public, legal affairs). In order to have Aries here, you *must* have Libra rising - so partners and dealing with others is most important. This need often leads to a hasty or early marriage, before you are mature enough to know what you really want and need. You seek a strong partner, but when you have found one you resent that person's strength because your Libra Ascendant likes peace and harmony (as long as it is your way). If you do find a partner who suits you, or if you have grown to accept what your partner can offer you, life will seem richer and more meaningful because cooperation and sharing is very important to your well being. Be sure to blend in not only Mars but also Venus, which rules the Ascendant, to get a good picture of the attitude toward marriage and partnership. *Ex-president Jimmy Carter, dictator Adolf Hitler, humanitarian Albert Schweitzer.*

Aries ♈ on the Cusp of the Eighth House   (Support from others, sex, legacies and inheritance, taxes, occult matters, endings, regeneration). If you have Leo or Libra rising, excessive sexual energy may need to be channeled into some other constructive outlet. With Virgo rising, you may suffer some feelings of insecurity or even inferiority, with alternating periods of brashness. To achieve inner peace and security becomes a deep psychological need that you may find only by learning to serve others, instead of taking for yourself. If you have a sensitive partner, he may help you in your search for identity. If any creative talent is evident in the chart, Aries on the 8th house cusp can express in a dramatic and deep, even occult, way. You may be preoccupied with death but are rarely afraid, merely ready to investigate it. *Authors Ernest Hemingway, Ralph Waldo Emerson, Thomas Mann.*

Aries ♈ on the Cusp of the Ninth House (Higher mind, philosophy, ideals, higher education, long trips, religion). If Leo is on your Ascendant, Aries here will express in a very individualistic and enthusiastic, even pioneering, way. You could blaze new trails in your approaches to life. Leo and Aries trine, therefore you can express your own personality easily in all 9th house matters, unless Mars is very weak or has many difficult aspects. Travel, or any avenue that broadens your horizons will be welcomed. If you tend toward the legal professions, you would do better as a trial lawyer, rather than handling taxes or corporate matters. Your philosophy will not be a dogmatic or traditional one, as you prefer anything that offers a new approach. You could even be an agnostic or atheist rather than accept the accepted. *Governor Jerry Brown, explorer Robert Peary, boxer Muhammad Ali.*

Aries ♈ on the Cusp of the Tenth House (Profession, status, reputation, ego, authority, one parent). Aries on the cusp of the house of profession and career makes you a dynamo going full force after your desired goals, or you may start ten careers, ten new inventions, ten things that have never been tried before—and finish none of them. Much will depend not only on Mars' position but also on the Moon if you have Cancer rising. A Cancer Ascendant makes you tenacious or you may give in to the ups and downs of your emotions. Sometimes this gives a domineering parent who wants you to follow in his footsteps. Since Aries and Cancer square each other by quality, you should have enough challenge and push to succeed, but be sure to blend the other factors in the chart carefully before deciding that this is so. If Leo or Gemini is on the Ascendant, the career outlook takes on a different coloration. Leo trines Aries, so success should not be difficult. With Gemini, the only real obstacle is the versatility of Gemini combined with Aries lack of perseverance. However, used constructively, this combination is excellent, especially for sales work. Since the 10th is a very public house, the Aries tendency to be bossy and argumentative needs to be curbed or you will have to fight hostility and combat rivalry on your road to success as you find that other people just don't like to be bossed around. *Football coach Knute Rockne, industrialist Henry Kaiser, actor Robert Stack.*

Aries ♈ on the Cusp of the Eleventh House (Friends, hopes and wishes, humanitarian interests, goals, circumstances, organizations). Many people with Aries here are involved with large groups or organizations, especially with Gemini rising. If Mars is strong in the chart, you seem to exert authority over others and can become a leader without really trying. You seem to manage this leadership well, and since you base your appeal on a mental approach your friends or groups follow gladly. With Taurus or Cancer rising, you tend to lack diplomacy and get involved in quarrels and gossip, which can cause emotional problems you would rather avoid. Either of these Ascendants gives more ambition and you aim high. Often, this placement is good for politics as it gives the ability to sway the masses. *Senator George McGovern, Secretary of State Henry Kissinger, general George Patton.*

Aries ♈ on the Cusp of the Twelfth House   (The subconscious, hidden strength, failings, behind-the-scenes activities). This can be the house of self-undoing, and with Aries here, you may be too restless to look within, always wanting to act without—yet, if you don't get to know yourself, you may always lack inner security which can cause great frustration. With Taurus on the Ascendant, a stable outlook and an outer affectionate nature offsets this somewhat, depending of course on the placements of Venus and Mars. With Gemini or Aries rising, the nervous system is taxed and looking within becomes imperative. When young, you need to watch your health and protect yourself from accidents. It is very important that you find the proper kind of work as a release from nervous tension. *President Gerald Ford, actress Mia Farrow, author William Saroyan.*

Taurus ♉ On The House Cusps

Always blend the interpretation with the ruler - Venus ♀

Taurus ♉ on the Cusp of the First House   (Outer personality, identity, physical body). You have a calm and peaceful nature, unless Mars or Uranus are in the 1st house. Regardless of your Sun's sign or the placement of Venus, you need time to learn and time to absorb impressions; however, once learned, they are seldom forgotten. Careful in your appraisals, disinclined to spend money, you don't like to jump to conclusions. If Venus is in a self-indulgent sign (Leo, Libra, Taurus or Sagittarius) you may over indulge in physical or material pleasures, or give in to laziness and inertia. Taurus seeks values, and eventually you will find a true purpose in life and pursue it in a tenacious and steadfast manner. Both men and women are often attracted by and like to adorn themselves with fine jewelry. *Bon vivant Diamond Jim Brady, singer Elvis Presley, cult leader Charles Manson.*

Taurus ♉ on the Cusp of the Second House   (Values, possessions, financial affairs, earnings power, talent and resources). This is the natural position for Taurus and unless Venus is very challenged all 2nd house matters flow quite well. With Aries rising, Taurus on the 2nd house cusp is just what you need to make you buckle down and stick to things, especially in the area of money and earning. With Aries' drive, you should be able to make a good living. Taurus loves luxury, and possessions are important to your general well-being. You always know a bargain because you are a very good business person with a practical approach to resources. With a stable Venus, you will be able to hold on to what is yours since your attitude toward 2nd house matters is down to earth and very practical. If you have Pisces rising, your aims may be more idealistic, but unless Venus is very weak in your chart the wish for stability in financial matters will win out. This may also indicate that you have a very fine singing voice. *Entertainer Liza Minelli, actress-singer Deanna Durbin, writer Rabindranath Tagore.*

Taurus ♉ on the Cusp of the Third House   (Communications, siblings, local and early environment, early education, short trips). This placement gives personal magnetism. Though you may seem easy and pliable, you can be as stubborn as a mule unless you have a Pisces Ascendant and Mercury in a mutable sign. You are very artistic, musical and creative, especially if Aquarius or Pisces is rising. You should use these talents in such areas as writing or in music. You seem to have an intuitive understanding of others, especially if Venus is well placed. Your early years were pleasant and your youth was quite stable without too many moves or changes unless Venus is very poorly aspected. If you have brothers and sisters, you enjoy their company and remain good friends with them. You thrive in a relaxed and pleasant atmosphere and you always try to show your appreciation for the values of other people. *Psychoanalyst Karl Jung, actress Mary Martin, labor leader James Hoffa.*

Taurus ♉ on the Cusp of the Fourth House   (Your home, one of the parents, your roots, your foundations and property). Your home is stable and on the conservative side. Heredity and parental influences are strong and lasting. You enjoy your home as a place of quiet, yet you also like to show it off with beautiful possessions, good food and such, especially if Capricorn is rising. You accumulate possessions which you rarely relinquish, in fact, you are a collector extraordinaire. With Aquarius rising, your home will serve as a refuge for you from the ups and downs you bring upon yourself. With a well aspected Venus, your old age should be fairly secure and happy, particularly if you have learned to value that which really counts in life, and not rely only upon material comforts and belongings. *Actor Alan Alda, writer F. Scott Fitzgerald, religious leader Vivekananda.*

Taurus ♉ on the Cusp of the Fifth House   (Children, love affairs and romance, creativity, avocation, self-expression, speculation). Amorous, earthy and fruitful, you are fond of children and sensual pleasures. Your tactile senses are strong; you need to touch things for full enjoyment. With Capricorn rising, the placement of Venus makes a big difference in your approach to love affairs and romance; if it is in Virgo or Capricorn, you can be reluctant to show your true feelings, which are rather lusty, for fear of rejection. Yet, if your emotional outlet is thwarted, much frustration can result. With a well-placed Venus, there is the promise of much happiness through love and children. If Venus aspects Neptune, or if Neptune is otherwise important in the chart, you can be very creative, especially musically. Though you enjoy the nice things of life, you can be happy with relatively simple pleasures. You are not a gambler at heart. *Nutritionist Adelle Davis, comedian Jack Benny, violinist Yehudi Menuhin.*

Taurus ♉ on the Cusp of the Sixth House (Work, health and nutrition, habits, wardrobe, pets, employees). Taurus on the cusp of the 6th house gives you great physical stamina, but you may tend to indulge yourself unless Venus has some challenging aspects. Self-discipline is important or you may develop a weight problem. This discipline will also aid you in achieving your goals; without it, you may drift idly. In the earlier years of life, throat problems are not uncommon, but are rarely too serious. At work you are reliable and good at detail, though also a bit dogmatic and not prone to change your ways. You are easy to get along with as long as others respect your habits. If you have breezy Sagittarius rising, people expecting something different from you will be surprised at your diligent work habits. With Venus dignified or in one of the water signs, you may wish to work at some creative endeavor. *Authors Philip Roth and Claire Booth Luce, financier Bernard Baruch.*

Taurus ♉ on the Cusp of the Seventh House (Partners, business or marital, dealing with the public, legal affairs). In order to have Taurus on this house cusp, you *must* have Scorpio rising. This makes your personality quite intense, demanding and deep. You want a partner who brings you affection, sensuality, charm, and enjoys beautiful surroundings, yet one who is also practical and down-to-earth. With your basic stubbornness and fixity of purpose, partnership may lead to difficulties unless you are allowed to have your own way or you learn to bend a bit. However, that same fixity makes you very loyal; once you give your affections, you do not change unless forced to. The 7th house has airy Libra on it in the flat chart (you should never forget this when delineating). Libra is a fairly sentimental yet detached sign; with Taurus here, the earthy matter-of-factness conflicts and romance can be snuffed out by realism. *Tennis star Chris Evert Lloyd, philanthropist Andrew Carnegie, former first Lady Jacqueline Kennedy Onassis.*

Taurus ♉ on the Cusp of the Eighth House (Support from others, sex, legacy, and inheritance, taxes, occult matters, endings, regenerations). If Libra rises, Taurus on your 8th house cusp is also ruled by Venus; Venus will make a great difference by position and aspects. With Venus well placed, you should benefit through your partner's resources as well as being helpful to your partner. Trying circumstances have a way of working out well and you usually feel confident in your ability to handle them. Sexual matters should present no problems. If Venus is challenged in the chart, you tend to be selfish. Beware of being too money-oriented. With Scorpio rising, you may use some of your faculties for a deeper probing into occult matters or have the ability to regenerate yourself, but with Virgo or Libra rising, you will prefer to tend to more definite and concrete matters. You need to know that those upon whom you rely are behind you in a practical and helpful way. *Entertainer Johnny Carson, labor leader Caesar Chavez, actor Richard Chamberlain.*

Taurus ♉ on the Cusp of the Ninth House (The higher mind, philosophy, law, ideals, long trips, higher education, religion). With Virgo rising, practical thinking is important to you. Your philosophies must make sense. You tend to be critical of that which cannot be proven. Yet, with a sensitive Venus, you may still be quite poetic; if Mercury in the chart confirms, you could be a writer. You have high standards and principles and you adhere faithfully to them, to the point of ignoring any conflicts of conscience they may bring. With Leo rising, Taurus (by sign) would square the Ascendant and the resulting energy should be channeled through work, some hobby or physical outlet. Your ideas and sentiments are stable, but the mystic sense and appreciation of intangibles are often lacking in your makeup. *Baseball great Babe Ruth, writer Anne Morrow Lindbergh, pianist Ignace Paderewski.*

Taurus ♉ on the Cusp of the Tenth House (Profession, status, reputation, ego, authority, one of the parents). With Leo rising, all 10th house matters are of importance to you—you like and need status and your ego needs expressing. If the rest of your chart indicates a commercial orientation, you may benefit from lucky coups in the financial field. You would make a good executive since you are better at giving than taking orders, but you have to learn to delegate instead of trying to do everything yourself. Prestige is very important to you. You will never let anyone know it if you don't succeed since you keep up a good front and have a generous, even lavish, attitude. With Cancer or Virgo rising, your ego needs are less obvious but your ambition remains just as strong, only less overt. *Baseball star Jackie Robinson, genius Albert Einstein, author Eugene O'Neill.*

Taurus ♉ on the Cusp of the Eleventh House (Friends, hopes and wishes, circumstances out of your control, large groups and organizations). You are very good at combining business and social relationships; however, if you have Cancer rising, you may tend to mother your friends and be too possessive of them. Your basic insecurity causes you to hold on too much and you eventually drive them away. With Leo rising, you have a deep-seated need to come first. Your ambitions are high. You want to shine among groups and friends. However, with Gemini rising, your expectations and dreams are more reasonable. If Venus is mutable, you are a good organizer and capable of a great amount of effort expended in work involving group activity; such as PTA, The Elks and others. *Governor Jerry Brown, comedian Jonathan Winters, actor Beau Bridges.*

Taurus ♉ on the Cusp of the Twelfth House (The subconscious, hidden strengths, self-undoing, behind-the-scenes activities). If you have Cancer rising, you will need money to feel protected since you have many hidden fears about lack of finances. You are very emotional and find it hard to face yourself honestly. You need to be approached gently and lovingly. With Gemini on the Ascendant, you can analyze and reason things out but not always with objectivity or complete honesty. The way to your subconscious in this case is through common sense and logic - not emotions. Yet, there is a stubborn streak within you that resists change; you'll suffer through with the status quo, rather than try something new. A bit gullible, you must watch out for schemes or you may be victimized in the area you fear most - your pocketbook. *Baseball star Henry Aaron, writer Mary Shelley, actress Shirley Temple.*

Gemini Ⅱ on the House Cusps

Always blend the interpretation with the ruler—Mercury ☿

Gemini Ⅱ on the Cusp of the First House   (Outer personality, identity, the physical body). You are pliable as a violin string, changeable as the weather, here today - gone tomorrow! However, if Mercury is in a fixed sign, this tendency is held down considerably. Your sense of the practical is very well developed, and your changeability is due to second, and often wiser, thoughts. You can get the best out of others through quick deduction. Seldom crude or coarse, you are versatile but need to learn concentration and not act in spurts. With a well-aspected Mercury, you are dexterous and have a gift of imitation. You can be a non-stop talker, and by applying your more than considerable abilities practically, you can indeed be a gifted writer or raconteur. *Actor Edward G. Robinson, basketball star Wilt Chamberlain, entertainer Phyllis Diller.*

Gemini Ⅱ on the Cusp of the Second House   (Income, possessions, talents and resources, financial abilities, values, self-worth). Financial fluctuations haunt you, though because of your resourceful earning ability, you may hold two jobs at once, and are seldom broke. If Aries or Gemini is rising, you are a good salesman, especially of yourself, and you could do well in the political arena. If Mercury is poorly placed, you tend to spread yourself too thin in an attempt to operate in too many fields at once—especially the artistic, literary, transportation, or communication field. If Taurus rises, your financial situation is more secure but you have difficulty finding true values, since you feel that money won't solve all your problems. When you learn to limit and focus your many talents in one or two directions, you will discover that financial success comes much more easily. *President Ulysses S. Grant, singer Peggy Lee, writer Taylor Caldwell.*

Gemini Ⅱ on the Cusp of the Third House   (Siblings, short trips, the conscious mind, early education and environment, communication). Gemini feels at home in this 3rd house position, and all areas of life attributable to the 3rd house assume greater importance in your life. You are interested in nearly everything. You can comprehend the most difficult of jobs and problems with very little difficulty. Quick of mind, glib with words, facile with pen, and clever at twisting most situations to personal advantage, you are seemingly never at a loss in any situation that confronts you, especially if Mercury is well aspected. If Taurus rises, you may have an unusually fine singing voice, but school learning will be a slow process. With Aries on the Ascendant, it is usually necessary to cultivate your staying power; your span-of-attention is short. There is often much involvement with siblings; you may bear responsibility for them, or they may make their home with you. *Singers Johnny Cash and Pearl Bailey, astrologer Carroll Righter.*

Gemini Ⅱ on the Cusp of the Fourth House   (One of the parents, your home, real property, foundations, roots, ultimate security). Family traditions, parental relations, and cultural background are strong factors in your life. Often when Pisces rises there is great interest in the ancestral heritage. You may have two homes, or you may have had a relative living with you when you were young. If Mercury has challenging aspects, or if Aquarius rises, there will be many changes of residence and extensive activity in your old age. Many times, with Gemini here, you may use a pen name in your activities as an author who works from his home. Your parents found it necessary to provide you with books and intellectual stimulation. If Aries rises, you enjoy the variety an active home life can offer you. *Philosopher Karl Marx, rock star Mick Jagger, actor Robert Redford.*

Gemini Ⅱ on the Cusp of the Fifth House   (Love, romance, children, creativity, avocations, fun and games, and speculation). As a parent you are more intellectually than emotionally involved with your children, particularly if you have Aquarius rising. Twin children are not uncommon. You have a purposeful nature, are ambitious, and have a sympathetic personality. With Capricorn rising, you may be musically gifted. Since you learn rapidly from experience and demonstrate a good attitude toward what you undertake, you'll usually do well in any metier, but you are especially adept at arts and handicrafts. If Pisces rises, you may be attracted to endeavors in the higher realms of thought, such as teaching, ministering, or the philosophies. *Composer George F. Handel, singer Diahann Carroll, author James Joyce.*

Gemini Ⅱ on the Cusp of the Sixth House   (work, health and nutrition, habits, service given, wardrobe, pets, employees). You are well suited to scientific research due to your quick and easy understanding of intellectual matters and complex problems, especially when Capricorn rises. When Sagittarius or Aquarius rises, non-routine occupations appeal to you; there may be many work changes. If Mercury has challenging aspects, or if it is in a mutable sign, you may well have to deal with irritability and nervousness, and job worries. Your health depends greatly upon your mental outlook. Drudgery is intolerable to you, so you'll function best in a field that allows motion and flexibility. *Entertainer Steve Allen, explorer Richard Byrd, scientist Jonas Salk.*

Gemini Ⅱ on the Cusp of the Seventh House   (Partnerships, marital and business, dealing with the public, open enemies, legal matters). With Gemini here, you *must* have Sagittarius rising. You are thus a freedom-loving soul, and you need intellectual and sympathetic companionship. Passion rarely carries you away. Age, social and financial conditions don't matter at all in your one-to-one relationships; your need is more for moral support and appreciation. Any strong irritability you have with others is rarely long-lasting; you have a "live-and-let-live" philosophy. If Mercury has good aspects you may do well in the legal field, counseling, acting, or anything to do with public relations. Jupiter's position in the chart is as important as Mercury's position in determining the ideal partner for you. *Religious leader Mary Baker Eddy, actor Robert Reed, Emperor Hirohito.*

Gemini Ⅱ on the Cusp of the Eighth House   (Support from others, sex, legacy and inheritance, taxes, occult matters, endings, regeneration). If Scorpio rises, you are curious about the mysteries of life and death, and you're restless until you gain a higher understanding. Any morbid tendencies must be wisely handled. You may have a deep and abiding interest in the occult. If Sagittarius rises, you are more interested in the mental rather than the sexual, but you still like to talk about the latter and are often the teller of double entendre stories. You show little mercy in your judgement of others, but it is hard for you to face up to your own mistakes, especially if you have Libra rising. If Mercury is well aspected, you may find that writing is your metier, particularly in the fields of sex, science or research. *Author Charles Dickens, cult leader Werner Erhardt, preacher Billy Sunday.*

Gemini Ⅱ on the Cusp of the Ninth House   (Law, religion, the higher mind, education, long trips, in-laws). In dealing with your inner conflict between faith and reason, you will rarely go in for a mystical or religious approach to life, unless Scorpio rises. You remain curious about life's mysteries, and you want to experience every facet of life. You are very adept at influencing others through your facility with words, which may attract you to the political arena. When Virgo rises, Mercury becomes doubly important, and if it is involved with challenging aspects, you can be the victim of gossip and strife with your in-laws. You love to travel; if you are unable to explore and see the world, then you will be an avid reader who at least indulges in travel of the arm-chair variety. *President Harry S. Truman, predictor Criswell, rock star Alice Cooper.*

Gemini Ⅱ on the Cusp of the Tenth House   (Career, status, prestige, ego, one of the parents, reputation). You like to work with others and you have a gift for diplomacy. You need a variety of interests to be truly satisfied, especially if Virgo rises. There are often many career changes. You are the doer who must be doing. You are likely an excellent speaker, and you should develop this ability; people enjoy listening to you. You might make a successful teacher. However, you also have a tendency to overwork yourself, which could lead to a nervous breakdown. With a Leo or Libra Ascendant, your field could be art, acting or design. Often, Gemini on this house cusp leads to two interchangeable careers, such as the writer who is also a commentator, or the singer who writes his own songs. *Publisher Bennett Cerf, writer Guy de Maupassant, actress Brooke Shields.*

Gemini Ⅱ on the Cusp of the Eleventh House   (Friends, large groups and organizations, hopes and wishes, goals, unexpected circumstances). Good public and private relations help to lead you up the ladder to success. Charming and friendly, you have a good sense of humor and the ability to laugh at yourself. With Cancer or Leo rising, you click with younger people as you are ever the child yourself. Since you rarely hold grudges, you are usually surrounded with many pleasant friends and associates. If Mercury has difficult aspects, you may be victimized by your so-called friends, and often you'll feel alone in a crowd. *Actress Liv Ullman, child evangelist Marjoe Gortner, musician Herb Albert.*

Gemini on the Cusp of the Twelfth House (Behind-the-scenes activities, inner resources, the subconscious mind, secret enemies). This placement favors self-expression. You are often inclined to morbidity and moodiness, especially when Gemini or Cancer rises. You tend to function more through the instinctive unconscious than from reason, and with Cancer rising you can be quite psychic and should work to develop this ability. Your intuitive ability is also good for such areas as psychology and psychiatry. It is difficult for you to learn by rote, but you do soak up knowledge just by listening. When Mercury is afflicted, you may have problems with the law or in developing inner security. You can be shallow and easily led. *Actress Hedy Lamarr, murderers Richard Loeb and William Heirens.*

Cancer ♋ on the House Cusps

Always blend the interpretation with the ruler - The Moon ☽

Cancer ♋ on the Cusp of the First House (Outer personality, identity, the physical body). You have a strong attachment to your home and your mother, especially if the Moon is in an angular house. Patriotism and tradition are very important to you; you love to collect and rummage in the past. You have a good imagination, and how you develop it will depend upon the placement of the Moon and its aspects. Being basically timid, you need love and encouragement in order to blossom out. You will retreat from anything unpleasant due to your innate insecurity. Your demeanor is gracious and charming, but you tend to withdraw into your shell when offended by unpleasantness. You are influenced by your surroundings because of your sensitivity. *Song writer Carrie Jacobs Bond, humorist Will Rogers, artist Salvador Dali.*

Cancer ♋ on the Cusp of the Second House (Income, finances, possessions, talents and resources, values, self-worth). You hold on to what you have, characteristically always saving for a rainy day, especially when Taurus or Cancer rises. You have a natural flair for real estate and dealing in commodities, sales and with the public. However, with challenging aspects to the Moon, you may experience financial fluctuations. Frugal but not stingy, you give freely of all your resources, mental and material, if you are emotionally involved. In spite of a natural ability to earn money, you always fear financial reverses. *Commentator Tom Snyder, British Prime Minister Harold Wilson, opera star Cesare Siepi.*

Cancer ♋ on the Cusp of the Third House   (Communication, short trips, siblings, the conscious mind, early and immediate environment). If Taurus is rising, you lack academic ability due to laziness and inattention as a youngster, but you do have a good memory and can learn through absorption and reading. Your marked likes and dislikes make you quite difficult to deal with. You are so sensitive that feeling, rather than thinking, is your keyword. With Aries or Gemini rising, you are fond of local travel. It is often hard to find you at home because you are so involved in community activities. Sometimes, this placement will indicate a good cook and an interest in gardening. *Chef Julia Child, labor leader Walter Reuther, Nazi criminal Adolf Eichmann.*

Cancer ♋ on the Cusp of the Fourth House   (The home, one of the parents, real estate, foundations, endings). This is the natural house of Cancer and therefore harmonious unless the Moon has challenging aspects. Sentimental, emotional, and traditional are words that describe you well. You need roots, yet you may have left your family home at an early age, especially if Aries rises. The moral influence of your parents upon you is powerful. It is possible that you may suffer from some hereditary afflictions. Males often fall into a kind of servitude to the distaff side of the family, taking care of mother, sister or an old-maid aunt. If Pisces or Taurus is on the Ascendant, family heirlooms are treasured and you are often the retainer of the old family home. You may live near the water in your later years. With Cancer on this house cusp, it is possible that you may choose celibacy as a way of life. *Trumpeter Louis Armstrong, entertainer Ann-Margaret, TV actress Mary Crosby.*

Cancer ♋ on the Cusp of the Fifth House   (Love and romance, children, speculation, amusement, avocation). Unless the Moon is in a fixed sign, you are inclined to be sentimentally fickle and inconstant. However, once your affections are focused, you can be strongly maternal and loving. Musical, imaginative, and dramatic, your creative efforts often appeal to the public, especially when Aquarius or Pisces rises. You have a strong cultural sense. You often do your best work late at night. If the Moon is afflicted, you must curb your intense love of gambling before it causes financial difficulties. *Singer Nelson Eddy, former Beatle Paul McCartney, kidnapper Bruno Hauptmann.*

Cancer ♋ on the Cusp of the Sixth House   (Work, health and nutrition, habits, wardrobe, service given, employees, pets). You are usually very involved in work and career, but are unhappy unless you really enjoy what you're doing, particularly if Capricorn or Aquarius rises. You tend to work well in subordinate positions, but you have great material ambition which is not always apparent to others. If Pisces rises and the Moon is in a Mutable sign, you would do well in the medical field or in some area dealing with dietetics and nutrition. Proper digestion is important—an afflicted Moon may indicate ulcers, allergies or compulsive eating. Often with Cancer here there is an interest in labor causes. This is the position of one who may be concerned with helping the underdog. *Actress Leslie Caron, pediatrician Dr. Benjamin Spock, philosopher Karl Marx.*

Cancer ♋ on the Cusp of the Seventh House   (Partnership, marital and business, dealings with the public, legal matters). Deep emotional needs urge you to seek a homeloving mate who is also a good provider. With Cancer here, Capricorn *must* be your rising sign. If you are a man, you want a partner who will mother you; if you are a woman, you need a strong mate (unless you have a very prominent Moon) and yet will often pick one who is passive or very gentle. Although you appear somewhat diffident and retiring, you desire popularity or some public exposure, so you may do well in a public career because you have a natural flair for knowing what appeals to the masses. If you do not have a career of your own, you may be a perfect helper for your mate both at home and at work. *President Zachary Taylor, comedian Jack Benny, Queen Elizabeth II.*

Cancer ♋ on the Cusp of the Eighth House   (Support from others, sex, legacy and inheritance, endings, taxes, occult matters, regeneration). If Scorpio or Capricorn is rising, unexpected events may complicate your life. This placement gives a remarkable ability for premonition, but the shadow of coming events can cause you to have fits of depression and morbidity. If the Moon is in a stable sign, this tendency is somewhat held down. You need to keep constant control over your emotions and feelings, as self-indulgence is an everpresent danger with Cancer here. When Sagittarius rises, improved well-being is always possible for you through inheritance or gifts from others. Sex may not always be easy since you need constant reassurance of being loved and loved and loved. *Drug cult leader Timothy Leary, Vice President Spiro Agnew, singer Linda Ronstadt.*

Cancer ♋ on the Cusp of the Ninth House   (The higher mind, higher education, long trips, foreign lands, in-laws, philosophy and religion). Unless Scorpio is rising, you were easily led by your elders as a youngster, but as you mature you are capable of having much influence yourself over others because of your intuition and persuasiveness. A fine teacher, you understand the needs of the public and will do well in any field where self-esteem and social acceptance are important. You are fond of travel and it is quite likely that you will do a great deal of it. You may even spend time in a foreign country, particularly if the Moon is in a mutable sign. If Libra or Sagittarius is rising, you may be led into the field of law, and from there into politics. *Secretary of State John Foster Dulles, Justice Oliver Wendell Holmes, labor leader John L. Lewis.*

Cancer ♋ on the Cusp of the Tenth House   (Profession, one of the parents, authority, ego, prestige and reputation). To have Cancer on the 10th house cusp, Capricorn must be on the 4th—your parental home. You have a traditional upbringing and your parents expect quite a bit from you. Because of this, you may be somewhat unsure of yourself and slow in settling on a career, so there can be many changes in this area, especially if Pluto is in the 10th. If the Moon is angular or otherwise strong in the chart, feminine influences are important and helpful in your ultimate success. You have a strong sense of duty and responsibility, and thus you function well in positions of authority. Early trials and obstacles enhance a tendency to philanthropy when you are earning well. *Singer Bing Crosby, President John Kennedy, actress Norma Shearer.*

Cancer ♋ on the Cusp of the Eleventh House   (Friends, hopes and wishes, aims and objectives, large groups and organizations, unexpected occurrences). With Leo or Libra rising, you are socially active, good friends with your own family, and have a binding attachment to your children. With Virgo rising, you are strongly conscious of money and material things. You have good hunches, influential friends, and you prefer intimate and friendly gatherings to large social functions. You are quite maternal and willing to help others. Often, friends come to live with you. You are always a willing and a gracious host. *Author Oscar Wilde, baseball great Hank Aaron, nurse Florence Nightingale.*

Cancer ♋ on the Cusp of the Twelfth House   (The subconscious, hidden strengths, behind-the-scenes activity). You are strongly sensitive, but pride and a fear of being hurt may keep you from showing it, especially if either Cancer or Virgo is on the Ascendant. If the Moon is poorly aspected, or in a mutable sign, there may have been a denial of love from your mother in your youth, leaving you now with great insecurities. You are very kind to those who are in trouble, and would thus do well in the medical and nursing fields. If Leo rises, you'll go to great lengths not to allow others to see your areas of vulnerability. The placement of the Moon in the chart is very important here because your subconscious emotions and feelings shape your future life. *Murderer Dean Corll, playwright Eugene O'Neill, President Lyndon B. Johnson.*

Leo ♌ on the House Cusps

Always blend the interpretation with the ruler - the Sun

Leo ♌ on the Cusp of the First House   (Personality, appearance, identity, the physical body). You have a strong personality and can easily dominate others, especially if your Sun is angular or strongly placed by sign. You are honest and direct, romantic and idealistic, yet if you have not learned the lesson of generosity you can be egotistic, willful, and undisciplined.

Naturally showy, ego-centered and proud, you have a flair for presenting yourself well, and since you enjoy applause you are often attracted to the acting profession. If your Sun is in a shy sign, you may vacillate between showiness and reticence, and those around you never know for sure whom they are dealing with. *Entertainer Fanny Brice, adventurer T. E. Lawrence, explorer Robert Peary.*

Leo ♌ on the Cusp of the Second House (Finances, self-worth, talents and resources, values, possessions). You are hopeful concerning money, but can be extravagant and are liable to suffer financial reverses. You'd prefer to work for yourself, rather than in partnership, or for someone else, especially if you have Leo rising. Wherever Leo is placed in the chart, there the drive to shine is accentuated; however the drive for money alone seldom brings Leo any happiness. Often, you succeed more through your charm than through your integrity, yet you should learn by honestly assessing your natural talent and ability. With Cancer rising, you'll do well in any field involving money management. If Gemini rises, you don't take money that seriously; you're more concerned with intellectual matters, values and personal freedom unless Mercury is in a very practical and earthy sign, like Capricorn. *Author Truman Capote, Secretary of HEW Oveta Culp Hobby, actress Lucille Ball.*

Leo ♌ on the Cusp of the Third House (Siblings, short trips, early education and environment, communication). Ambitious and enterprising, and with a good, clear-thinking mind, you are eager in your pursuit of knowledge; you like to be well read and informed. If Gemini is rising, you are a good conversationalist and have a keen wit and the power of self-expression. Usually, your childhood is happy and active; you were the center of attention in your family. This is often the placement for the successful author who lets his Sun shine through in communication. With Taurus rising, you tend to become too set in your ways and people may think you are too showy or stubborn. When Cancer rises, you may use the 3rd house as an escape from your own true ways and play a role to the hilt. *Writers A.J. Cronin and Jack London, actor Edward G. Robinson.*

Leo ♌ on the Cusp of the Fourth House (The home, one of the parents, real estate, the latter years, foundations). You like to entertain in a regal manner, even when you cannot afford it. You want and need the best of everything—food, wine, clothes, particularly if you have Taurus rising or if the Sun is in a fixed sign. You will usually have a strong inner faith acquired through the lessons of experience. Your parental home was lively, and your father probably seemed quite strong and dramatic to you. Children play an important role in your declining years, often helping to provide you with the good life. Your mother may be the sunshine of your life and she may live in your home during her later years. *Entertainer Phyllis Diller, heiress Christina Onassis, golfer Lee Trevino.*

Leo ♌ on the Cusp of the Fifth House   (Love and romance, children, sports and gambling, avocation, self-expression). This is the natural house of Leo and it operates well here unless the Sun is challenged in the chart. The natural outreach of the Sun is best expressed in 5th house matters. Even though you may seem indulgent and playful, you have great courage in the face of adversity. Being eager for attention, you are naive in your acceptance of flattery, and this may cause you some romantic problems. Your sunny nature and pleasing personality make you a natural actor and a good teacher. You are fond of children, but even though the Sun is the natural ruler of the 5th house, you rarely have many offspring of your own; especially if Aries rises because you may be too busy doing your own thing! *Singers Helen Reddy and Joan Baez, actress Joan Blondell.*

Leo ♌ on the Cusp of the Sixth House   (Work, health and nutrition, service given, employees, habits, wardrobe, pets). You go to work with a smile, and you can certainly become a leader in your field; however, if Aquarius or Aries rises, you are not happy in a subordinate position. You are rarely completely satisfied with your work, and this dissatisfaction can make you testy and hard to deal with. With Pisces rising, you feel that work is one area where you can prove yourself and you are willing to work hard. Guard your health well; you are prone to heart problems and back problems, especially if the Sun is afflicted by Saturn. The Sun, as ruler of the 6th house, is not strong here, and often indicates a lowered vitality. It is important that you learn balance in your activities. *Actors James Arness, Robert Redford and Keir Dullea.*

Leo ♌ on the Cusp of the Seventh House   (Partners - marital and business, dealings with the public, public enemies, legal affairs). To have Leo here, you *must* have Aquarius rising. With the Sun ruling your house of partnership, you expect complete devotion from your mate, and you have trouble compromising here. You'll usually attract a strong partner, and with Aquarius on your Ascendant, you are much more fixed in nature than is at first noticeable; and this can create problems as neither of you wants to give in to the other. Look for a partner who acts more with his or her heart than with his or her head, because you need love and applause, and plenty of both. Romance and candlelight are right up your alley. Usually, a woman fares better under this placement than a man. *Rock star Janis Joplin, actor Charles Boyer, President James Monroe.*

Leo ♌ on the Cusp of the Eighth House   (Support from others, partners' assets, taxes, sex, death, regeneration). If Aquarius is rising, you are adventurous, love to take risks, and may have contempt for death. You may suffer from the abuse of pleasure, which will lower your vitality. Since sex to you is an expression of your whole personality, you may like a great variety of it. It must be a sharing, not a taking experience if it is to have meaning for you. With Capricorn on the Ascendant, you want full control over your partner's assets, yet you are also generous and giving with your own belongings. You must guard against over-exertion and heart strain, especially when the Sun has challenging aspects. With Leo here, you are often drawn to serve the public in financial fields, and with a well aspected Sun, you are likely to get great public support. *Millionaire J. Paul Getty, FBI Chief J. Edgar Hoover, senator Ted Kennedy.*

Leo ♌ on the Cusp of the Ninth House   (Religion, philosophy, law, foreign travel, commerce). Your great love of truth provides an idealistic philosophy, but it is built on the concept of the benevolent despot. Optimistically faithful, particularly with Sagittarius rising, you make a good teacher and you love to travel. An afflicted Sun can make you arrogant and conceited. All higher-mind areas are very important to you and you will work hard to grow mentally. If Scorpio or Capricorn is on the Ascendant, you have great faith in yourself. You rarely will accept defeat, no matter how bad the events of the moment may appear. *Dancer Fred Astaire, actor Hal Holbrook, President James Madison.*

Leo ♌ on the Cusp of the Tenth House   (Profession, ego, one of the parents, authority, rank, status and reputation). You are well liked in your profession and others readily accept your leadership. You both need and desire power, but you'll have to work for it as it won't always come easily. If Scorpio is rising, you must learn to understand the other fellow, and you are at your best when you rule through love and not discipline. Popularity may be forced upon you and you have to learn the lesson of humility. You may have a very successful or strong parent who tries to dominate your life, especially if Sagittarius rises. You achieve status and prestige fairly easily. With Libra rising, you can charm your way to the top, but once there, you may have trouble exerting your authority since you want so much to be liked and loved. *Princess Anne, boxer Max Baer, actor Charlie Chaplin.*

Leo ♌ on the Cusp of the Eleventh House   (Aims and objectives, hopes and wishes, friends, large organizations, unexpected events). You are capable of success and personal popularity, but you are not good at mass leadership-no matter what sign is rising. You are friendly and outgoing, you want to please people and be liked by them, but difficult aspects to the Sun can give too much pride and egotism, denying achievement, and frustrating Leo's need to shine through friendships. This placement can give the ability to work for humanitarian goals and the drive to succeed in group activity. Friendship with males will likely predominate. *Actor William Holden, swimmer Marilyn Bell, composer Wolfgang Amadeus Mozart.*

Leo ♌ on the Cusp of the Twelfth House   (Behind-the scenes activity, hidden strengths, fears, the subconscious mind). This is often the placement for actors, since they shine through the roles they play without ever revealing their true selves. Depression or powerful enemies can be major pitfalls with Leo here. Your greatest success comes through things that are hidden—research, history, the movies, archeology, and similar subjects. With Virgo rising, you are often the power behind the throne, but sorrow can come through love, children, and gambling or speculation. As long as you are willing to let your light shine through others, happiness can be achieved. With Leo or Libra rising, you may be tempted to fritter away your talents, unless your Sun is well placed. *Film director Federico Fellini, former First Lady Rosalynn Carter, actor Montgomery Clift.*

Virgo ♍ on the House Cusps

Always blend the interpretation with the ruler - Mercury ☿

Virgo ♍ on the Cusp of the First House   (Personality, identity, the physical body). You have common sense and initiative; you are orderly and organized, but you tend to waste your time on non-essentials. The gift of eternal youth is yours, and so is the ability to see another's weaknesses and capitalize on them. Usually you'll do this with diplomacy and tact; the other person is often unaware that you possess this talent. With challenging aspects to Mercury, you can be too picky and fault-finding. You'll do well as an analyst, comedian or writer; with your incisive mind you can detect what shapes another's personality and makes him or her tick, especially if Mercury is well aspected. *Nurse Florence Nightingale, author Ernest Hemingway, actor Robert Taylor.*

Virgo ♍ on the Cusp of the Second House   (Your possessions, talents and resources, values, self-worth, financial abilities). You manage finances naturally, so you make a good agent in this area, being a natural banker, accountant, or tax assessor. Once you've discovered that honesty is the best policy, you can go far in this field. You can be financially manipulative, especially if Mercury has challenging aspects from Neptune or Jupiter. You're ambitious, but also cautious; rarely will you risk your own capital. If Cancer is rising, money and the security it brings are very important to you; you will often succeed in fields that require financial acumen. With Leo rising, people are surprised that showy and generous you can be so exact and particular when it comes to your pocketbook. *Emcee Hugh Downs, congressman Phillip Crane, senator Henry M. Jackson.*

Virgo ♍ on the Cusp of the Third House   (Communication, early and immediate environment, schooling, short trips, siblings, the conscious mind). Analytical, critical and scientific—you are the question-asker who has trouble making up your mind until you've gathered all of the facts. You function well in critical situations. You are able to learn rapidly and you communicate well, especially after you've overcome a sense of inferiority. If Gemini or Cancer rises, there is great concern for siblings; you often maintain an extensive correspondence with them after you leave the family home. Gemini rising with a prominent Mercury often signifies success at writing. With Leo rising, your innate dramatic ability can be put to practical use. *Writer Alexandre Dumas, actresses Lily Tomlin and Liv Ullman.*

Virgo ♍ on the Cusp of the Fourth House   (Home and family, one of the parents, real property, foundations, the end of life). Virgo unoccupied here gives little stability, much uncertainty, sometimes an impoverished childhood. You may have felt neglected and unloved by your parents. With Gemini rising, you can be of two minds on many issues. With Taurus or Cancer rising, there is a tendency to be dominated by family cares. You are always willing to serve your family and often work long after retirement age as you feel that keeping active keeps you young. You may do much of your work from your home. *Assassin Lee Harvey Oswald, boxer Joe Louis.*

Virgo ♍ on the Cusp of the Fifth House   (Love and romance, creativity, children, speculation, avocation). Discriminating in love, you tend to be prudish and over-analyze your emotions, particularly when Taurus rises. When Aries rises, your natural ebullience is held back in showing your love and affection. Too much patience and forebearance are particularly obvious in the charts of parents who let their children run wild. You hate change and anything else that upsets your routine, unless Mercury is in a mutable sign. This is a good placement for poets, but not for teachers as it is difficult for them to command obedience in the classroom. Especially with women, this placement may give a dread of solitude. It can also be the placement for prostitution, because Virgo can detach itself and treat love as a business. *Writer William Saroyan, President Herbert Hoover, actor George Peppard.*

Virgo ♍ on the Cusp of the Sixth House   (Health and nutrition, work, habits, service given, pets, employees). This is the natural house position of Virgo in the flat chart, and thus you too feel naturally at home in all sixth house matters. Hygienic, accurate and painstaking in your work, you are good at details and have an interest in diet, mechanics or research. You're a born historian and a stickler for neatness, even though you may be impatient and irritable at times if Mercury has challenging aspects. Still, you give willing service. If Aries or Gemini is on the Ascendant, it will be important for you to work at some job, else your energies will turn into frustrations and affect your health. Pay proper attention to your diet and your eating habits in order to avoid the digestive and liver problems that this placement often brings. *Writer Marcel Proust, President Andrew Jackson, opera star Beverly Sills.*

Virgo ♍ on the Cusp of the Seventh House   (Partnerships - marital and business, public relations, legal affairs). With Virgo on the 7th house cusp, Pisces *must* be rising. You have a compassionate and somewhat retiring personality, but you tend to marry a critical partner or you are critical of the partner you choose. You look for security in your partner, and you may marry too early; often there are two marriages, with the second one much happier than the first, since you grow more realistic as you mature. You must learn service in your partnerships and not expect too much in return. As you learn to give of yourself, you will gain greater inner happiness. Virgo here is a fine placement for a career in the military service. Be sure to blend both Mercury and Neptune to determine the right kind of partner for you. *Pianist Oscar Levant, singer-actor Jerry Reed, photographer Anthony Armstrong-Jones.*

Virgo ♍ on the Cusp of the Eighth House   (Partner's assets, support from others, sex, taxes, death, regeneration, inheritance). You are very practical when it comes to handling other people's money; thus you'd do well in the banking or accounting fields, especially if Capricorn or Pisces is on the Ascendant. You need much convincing before you can become interested in the psychic or the occult; you need to have things proven to you before you will accept them. Any difficulties in your sex life will be due to your being overly critical, analytical, and demanding of your partner. With Aquarius rising, you may have Gemini on the cusp of the 5th house. This combination of Aquarius-Gemini-Virgo leads to a desire for change in the love life, yet you are afraid to reveal your deep sexual needs. This results in many, but not too fulfilling, sexual experiences, unless Mercury is in a fixed sign. With Virgo on the cusp, this house is probably best unoccupied. In delineating this placement, pay particular attention to all aspects to Mercury. *Magician Harry Houdini, psychoanalyst Karl Jung, former First Lady Pat Nixon.*

Virgo ♍ on the Cusp of the Ninth House   (Law, religion and philosophy, foreign travels, import and export). You particularly need to understand life through the heart as well as through the mind. Diplomacy is strong in your makeup, and you take a practical approach to religion and philosophy. You may travel in connection with your work; if Sagittarius rises, travel and broadening your mind is the key to your well-being. With Capricorn on the Ascendant, you will desire a college education and should achieve this easily. You are tactful and astute and should do well in the service of another, often in such capacity as manager, valet or agent. *Author Erich Remarque, conductor Arturo Toscanini, Chief Justice Earl Warren.*

Virgo ♍ on the Cusp of the Tenth House   (Profession, ego, prestige, status, one of the parents, reputation). You may have more than one profession in your lifetime, and one may well be teaching. To work hard in order to achieve a certain amount of status is important to you. If Scorpio or Capricorn is on the Ascendant, you are keenly critical of yourself as well as others. You dislike being proven wrong. With Sagittarius rising, you should have excellent coordination (unless Mercury is challenged). If Mercury is well placed, success is promised in almost any field of endeavor, but especially one where organization, mobility, challenges and tactful handling of the public are necessary. *Composer George Gershwin, athlete Bob Mathias, educator Maria Montessori.*

Virgo ♍ on the Cusp of the Eleventh House   (Friends, hopes and wishes, large organizations, unforseen circumstances). You are basically shy and shun large groups of people, but you are sympathetic, understanding, and always willing to help out the underdog. Thus, you may do well in any humanitarian undertaking. You are vulnerable and thus should beware of being victimized by fair-weather friends. If Sagittarius rises, and Mercury and Jupiter are in aspect to each other, you love animals and would make a good veterinarian, animal groomer or trainer. With Scorpio rising, you like to lead in your own very special way, which may include group work. With Libra rising, you usually work best on a one-to-one basis, whether it is with friends or in organizational work. *Scientist Louis Pasteur, feminine activist Gloria Steinem, writer Faith Baldwin.*

Virgo ⍐ on the Cusp of the Twelfth House   (Hidden talents and resources, research, behind-the-scenes activity). Critical of yourself as well as others, you prefer to nit-pick at surface trivia, rather than face yourself honestly. With Virgo or Scorpio rising, you may be attracted to institutional work and problems. You are interested in, and try to understand the nature of health and disease, but you must guard against hypochondria. Any sort of work that requires attention to details and the ability to work behind the scenes appeals to you, but there may be some difficulties in employment security and marital affairs if Mercury has challenging aspects. If there are any planets in the 12th house, you may be interested in some of the psychological or counselling fields. *Actor James Dean, guru Maharaj Ji, Indian leader Mahatma Gandhi.*

Libra ♎ on the House Cusps

Always blend the interpretation with the ruler - Venus ♀

Libra ♎ on the Cusp of the First House   (Personality, identity, the physical body, early childhood). Tactful and peace-loving, you have a talent for conciliation and the development of relationships with others. To truly achieve, you need companionship. You can see both sides of a question and have a hard time taking a stand; thus, you appear indecisive. Charming, and usually good looking, you want to be liked and are always trying to balance things out mentally and emotionally, but it is rare that you achieve either unless Venus is well placed. You may have weight problems after middle age. *Actress Debbie Reynolds, Princess Grace of Monaco, basketball great Kareem Abdul-Jabbar.*

Libra ♎ on the Cusp of the Second House   (Finances, possessions, assets, self-worth, earning ability). Your money is often bound up in partnerships, and you are overly cautious in your desire to maintain financial equilibrium. You prefer a job where you do not get dirty, since you are neat and like to do things systematically. Innately refined, especially if you also have Libra rising, you do well in any field that requires good taste and appreciation of art and beauty. You are attracted to fine possessions (jewelry, furs, fine paintings) and usually take good care of them, unless Venus is very afflicted. If Leo rises, you may spend more than you should, especially if Venus has challenging aspects to Jupiter. *Writer Thomas Mann, composer Igor Stravinsky, baseball player Warren Spahn.*

Libra ♎ on the Cusp of the Third House   (Siblings, communication, short trips, immediate environment, the conscious mind). You love justice and like to cooperate with those around you, so you usually have good rapport with siblings. Your great versatility of mind, unless it finds an outlet where specialization is not required, may lead to dilettantism. Musical, artistic and literary you can, when motivated, be the life of the party. Your ability to see both sides of a question leads others to call upon you for advice. You have a pleasant way of communicating and are rarely drawn into argument or discussion, unless Venus is poorly placed. With Leo rising, you could easily combine your dramatic personality with some artistic talent or hobby. If Virgo or Cancer is on the Ascendant, you may communicate in a quieter and less showy way. *Composer-conductor Leonard Bernstein, singer Tom Jones, commentator John Barbour.*

Libra ♎ on the Cusp of the Fourth House   (Home and parents, foundations, real estate, the end of life). With Cancer rising, you need roots, you love your home, and must have it for emotional stability; if you are to be truly comfortable, your surroundings should be beautiful and artistic. You are restless and it is difficult for you to stay in one place. If Leo or Gemini rises, until you determine your higher values, you will find little peace, pleasure or prosperity in your waning years for you can find yourself on a social merry-go-round going nowhere. *Entertainer Rosemarie Guy, actor Robert Stack, singer Paul Simon.*

Libra ♎ on the Cusp of the Fifth House   (Love and romance, children, creativity, avocation, fun and games, speculation). Musical and artistic interests are paramount to your sense of well-being. Friends, romance and involvement with others are very important to you, especially if Gemini or Cancer is rising. Usually, you taste life early and marry late. You may be regarded by others as being pleasure oriented and happy-go-lucky because of your light and airy approach to life. Mercury in Libra here strengthens the mental faculties. If Taurus is rising, you will be less playful but still quite sense-oriented and the position of Venus in your chart then becomes all-important. *Actors Ryan O'Neal and Desi Arnaz, designer Don Loper.*

Libra ♎ on the Cusp of the Sixth House   (Health and nutrition, work, employees, service given, pets). Unless there is harmony in your working environment, you can be quite antagonistic in spite of the fact that you like to give and receive service. If you like your work you are a perfectionist in all you do, but you need constant variety, especially if Gemini or Aries is on the Ascendant. With a well-aspected Venus, you will do well in the personnel field or any place where you can use your artistic talents. With Taurus rising, you are persevering, and if Venus is well placed, this could express in some artistic field such as writing or painting. Kidney problems are a possibility unless you pay close attention to your health and diet. *Writer Taylor Caldwell, golfer Lee Trevino, labor leader Walter Reuther.*

Libra ♎ on the Cusp of the Seventh House   (Partnerships, marital and business, public relations, legal affairs). This is Libra's natural house position in the flat chart, and to have Libra here you *must* have Aries rising. Partners, and learning to reach out and be with others become a natural need. You come across as quite demanding and arbitrary, so you need a pleasant and poised marriage partner. You often won't exert yourself much in partnership relations unless Venus and Mars are well aspected to each other. Sentimental and artistic, in spite of your somewhat demanding personality, you need to find someone who will accept you as you are. What you want is a partner who has looks, savoir faire, and who can make you proud. Being very socially-oriented, you can be a social arbiter and a leader of society. *Princess Caroline of Monaco, singer Helen Reddy, baseball pitcher Sandy Koufax.*

Libra ♎ on the Cusp of the Eighth House   (Partner's assets, inheritance, taxes, sex, regeneration). With Pisces on the Ascendant, you may marry for money or in anticipation of an inheritance only to be disappointed, unless Venus is very well placed. Sometimes, an early deception in love will promote better judgment the second time around. Avoid overindulgence in alcohol as there is a tendency to kidney problems. Learning to compromise in financial matters promotes maturity. Libra here is often the judge, the banker or the manager of other people's affairs. If Aries is rising, your ardent nature can be quite sex-oriented, and one affair may not suffice. Your wish to explore all alternatives may lead you to much variety but few meaningful involvements. *Actress Carole Lombard, writer George Sand, flyer Billy Mitchell.*

Libra ♎ on the Cusp of the Ninth House   (Philosophy and religion, higher education, long trips, in-laws, foreign dealings). You are fervently idealistic, quite liberal in your outlook and devoted to peace and justice, often taking the part of the underdog (especially if you have Aquarius rising.) If Pisces rises, your ambitions may lack realism but you are most likely artistically gifted. Good taste is paramount in your approach to life; you find crass and boorish behavior offensive. You are not overly fond of travel unless it is first class, the only way to go as far as you are concerned. If you have Capricorn rising, you will seek practical philosophies that will help you in life-ones that are concrete and useable. By contrast, if Aquarius rises, you may prefer more outre areas, astrology might be right up your alley, especially now as it gains social acceptibility. *Opera star Leontyne Price, actors Spencer Tracy and Charles Boyer.*

Libra ♎ on the Cusp of the Tenth House   (Profession, reputation, ego, one of the parents, honor, career). You are tactful in your dealings with the public, much more so than you are with those at home. With Capricorn on the Ascendant, you have a strong sense of form and structure (♄) with an eye for beauty (♀); therefore, architecture and similar professions are appealing to you. Feminine interests are strong in your life if Venus is well aspected, and men with Libra here do well in careers catering to women. You are often the incurable romantic who will give up everything for love. Success is most likely after age thirty, when you have learned and matured from your first Saturn return (especially if you have Capricorn rising). With Sagittarius or Aquarius rising, success comes a bit easier. Law is a good profession since you can see both sides of a matter and are just in your appraisals. *Artist Leonardo DaVinci, architect Frank Lloyd Wright, golfer Johnny Miller.*

Libra ♎ on the Cusp of the Eleventh House　(Aims and objectives, friends, unforseen circumstances, money earned through profession). Friends are very important to you, and you often choose them from the artistic and musical fields. If Venus has challenging aspects, care should be exercised in your choice of associates as you may be drawn to undependable types who can lead you down the garden path. If Scorpio or Capricorn rises, you need to define your goals clearly to yourself, early in life, or the balancing act of Libra may result in a wasted life partying, playing and having fun, rather than doing anything productive. *Ballplayer Stan Musial, violinist Jascha Heifetz, band leader Vincent Lopez.*

Libra ♎ on the Cusp of the Twelfth House　(Hidden strengths, behind-the-scenes activities, institutions, retreat). You can face your troubles in a very philosophical way, but you need to face yourself without self-pity and see others as they are and not as you wish them to be. Otherwise you'll tend to blame others for your problems and never learn to truly deal with life as it is. There can be a secret marriage or love affair, especially with Scorpio rising. Your artistic and literary sense is usually well developed, particularly if Venus is well placed. If Libra also rises, you will have difficulty in keeping your private life and secrets concealed; they have a way of eventually becoming public knowledge. *Musician Jose Feliciano, comedian Red Skelton, actress Ginger Rogers.*

Scorpio ♏ on the House Cusps

Always blend the interpretation with the ruler - Pluto ♀ and the co-ruler Mars. ♂

Scorpio ♏ on the Cusp of the First House　(Personality, identity, self-expression, the physical body). It is not easy to know you for much lies hidden beneath the surface. You often appear to have a very placid countenance while underneath you are indeed a complicated human being with much more sensitivity than you show. You have great strength and reserve, you command respect from others, and you tend to see things through to the bitter end, particularly if Mars and Pluto are well aspected. However, you must be on constant guard against a sarcastic tongue, which can turn others away from you. *Actress Bette Davis, writer Upton Sinclair, artist Paul Cezanne.*

Scorpio ♏ on the Cusp of the Second House   (Finances, possessions, self-worth, talents and resources, assets). Often there is financial strain, but your resourcefulness enables you to learn from adversity and to profit from it, especially if Scorpio also rises. You are sober, thrifty, and a good organizer, but you are apt to take on more than you can handle efficiently due to your feelings of having to constantly prove yourself to yourself and others. Politics and scientific fields may prove rewarding to you. You also have a talent and a good mind for business, especially where big money is concerned. You tend to keep your financial dealings private, and if Pluto has challenging aspects, you may have an inflated idea of your own self-worth. *Politician Tom Dewey, Presidents Franklin D. Roosevelt and James Garfield.*

Scorpio ♏ on the Cusp of the Third House   (Communications, the conscious mind, short trips, siblings, immediate environment). You are a shrewd observer and can be either secretive and suspicious or mystical and occult. You select your words carefully and can use them as weapons. If Libra rises, you weigh and consider things carefully before commiting yourself. You are not verbally very communicative and your fixity of ideas can at times promote harsh judgments of others, especially if either Mars or Pluto has challenging aspects. But, if Mercury is strong, Scorpio here will make you communicate in a most sharp and witty way. If Virgo is rising, you are analytical with a quick grasp of knowledge and a good memory. Your incisive mind makes you a good literary or artistic critic. *Comedian Groucho Marx, White House Chief of Staff H. R. Haldeman, mystery writer Agatha Christie.*

Scorpio ♏ on the Cusp of the Fourth House (The home, one of the parents, real estate, foundations, the end of life). Your feelings are deep and strong, and you have a great need to prove yourself. Unless your parents were very intuitive, your rebellious attitude in youth may have led to an unhappy home life and thus an early leavetaking. If Leo is on the Ascendant, you have the urge to succeed in life by your own efforts and may turn your back on help from others. Having great inner strength, you are both loyal and persistent. With Cancer rising, you are intuitive and very sensitive, but unless the Moon has a great deal of flow this is not always apparent to others. An inheritance often comes late in life. *Seer Edgar Cayce, writer Zelda Fitzgerald, actress Marilyn Monroe.*

Scorpio ♏ on the Cusp of the Fifth House (Love and romance, creativity, children, amusements, avocation). You either have tremendous self-control or none, depending upon your Mars and Pluto aspects. You have a great interest in sex, but often out of curiosity rather than passion, especially if Gemini is rising. You may excel in the sports field but you are also fond of mental pursuits, many times involving yourself in the scientific or research fields. If you can, you love deeply and passionately. You may have secret love affairs and you can be jealous, particularly if Mars or Pluto is in a fixed sign. If you choose to channel your energies into creative pursuits you can be a dynamo, never giving up. *Actress Polly Bergen, chairman Nikita Khrushchev, diplomat Henry Cabot Lodge.*

Scorpio ♏ on the Cusp of the Sixth House (Health and nutrition, habits, wardrobe, service given, pets, employees). You dislike routine and confinement in your work. You have great professional integrity and you pride yourself on your conscientiousness and your resistence to fatigue. You are thus a tireless worker when you like your work. If Gemini or Cancer is on the Ascendant, your nervous system is in high gear and the health may be affected until you learn to slow down and do things in moderation, not an easy lesson for you to learn. You are not always the easiest person to get along with, especially if Taurus rises, because you lack flexibility in your habits and attitude. Scorpio here is often a potential indicator of health problems that involve the sex organs and the rectum, especially when there are challenging aspects to Pluto or Mars. *Actress Loretta Young, ballplayer Ted Williams, astronomer Johannes Kepler.*

Scorpio ♏ on the Cusp of the Seventh House (Partners, marital and business, legal affairs, dealings with the public). With Scorpio here, Taurus *must* be on the Ascendant. You are very stable, fixed, and quite set in your ways, so that with a partner of compatible temperament your basic loyalty causes you to stick to marriage for a long time, sometimes too long! If Pluto or Mars has challenging aspects, there may be jealousy and sexual problems; your health could thus suffer from an unsatisfactory partnership. Your partner's intense devotion attracts you; in fact, it remains a vital need if you are to remain loyal, for you demand loyalty and devotion. With Venus well aspected to Pluto or Mars, your choice of partner is usually a wise one. *Murderer Charles Manson, actress Liza Minelli, composer Giacomo Puccini.*

Scorpio ♏ on the Cusp of the Eighth House (Partnership assets, taxes, sex, inheritance, occult matters, regeneration). This is the natural house position for Scorpio in the flat chart, and thus all 8th house matters are accepted as innately so. While you love life, you can also accept death objectively. With Aries rising, you may have an inferiority complex, and to prove yourself you will take risks and run the possibility of an accident. With Pisces or Taurus rising, the tendency is to prove yourself through sex, in a rather lusty and possessive way. You are a good money handler, know its value, and thus you might do well in banking, accounting and related careers. Sometimes, there is a morbid preoccupation with death, if Mars or Pluto has difficult aspects and you have not found sufficient creative outlets. You cling to objective realities and generally sidestep the intangibles, unless Pisces rises and Neptune is strong in the horoscope. *Actor Ramon Novarro, entertainer Barbra Streisand, dancer Margot Fonteyn.*

Scorpio ♏ on the Cusp of the Ninth House (Religion and philosophy, ethics, foreign dealings, higher education, in-laws). You seek the meaning of life with emotional intensity, not orthodoxy, but rather through the occult and mystical. You travel all of your life, if not physically, then through travels of the mind. You are often slow to act and over-prudent, unless Aries rises. This is a good placement for medical doctors, teachers, and publishers, because of your innate and tacit understanding of life. With challenging aspects to Pluto, you could be a religious fanatic. With Aquarius rising, you are not likely to adopt the religion of your parents, but rather seek out a philosophy of life and religion that suits your particular life-style and beliefs. *Psychoanalyst Karl Jung, actor Vincent Price, religious leader Krishnamurti.*

Scorpio ♏ on the Cusp of the Tenth House (Reputation and community standing, profession, one of the parents, career). Though you may feel unappreciated, you have tremendous drive and will work hard to achieve, especially if you have Capricorn or Pisces rising. When Aquarius rises, this is a good placement for government work, research, the medical field, or secret pursuits like the CIA. You are versatile and reliant, and you'll do well when given responsibility early. With Pluto or Mars angular, or if they are in challenging aspect to the Sun or Moon, you may have an overpowering parent who stifled your initiative. *President Thomas Jefferson, actor Dustin Hoffman, impresario Rudolf Bing.*

Scorpio ♏ on the Cusp of the Eleventh House (Friendships, aims and objectives, large organizations, unexpected occurrences). You must learn greater tolerance and refrain from judging your friends. Your initiative and self-assurance impress others, but your leadership may be shortlived due to a lack of tact, especially if either Sagittarius or Aquarius rises. You can be rather fatalistic. If Capricorn rises and Mercury has challenging aspects, pessimism must be overcome. You may be well advised to study the philosophy of Dale Carnegie, since winning friends and influencing people does not come easily to you. Yet, once you become a friend to those chosen few, you are a true friend who will go out of your way to keep the friendship intact. *Poet Robert Browning, dancer Fred Astaire, composer Robert Schumann.*

Scorpio ♏ on the Cusp of the Twelfth House (Hidden strengths, secret affairs, institutions, the unconscious mind). This placement can be the powerhouse that lights the way to the unconscious mind, or it can be completely destructive; the choice is yours. You may seem to have secret enemies, but most of the time you are your own worst enemy because of an inability to face up to yourself, especially if Scorpio is rising. You need to learn regeneration, but you can only achieve it through your own efforts. If Sagittarius rises, your choice always seems to be serve or suffer, and you may have to work hard to uproot the tendency to resentment; but once you've looked deep within and accept yourself your inner strength knows no limits. *Attempted assassin Arthur Bremer, Nazi Field Marshal Hermann Goering, evangelist Billy Graham.*

Sagittarius ♐ on the House Cusps

In your delineation, be sure to consider the ruler - Jupiter ♃

Sagittarius ♐ on the Cusp of the First House (Personality, identity, the physical body). Your keyword is freedom—of thought, speech, and action. Breezy, friendly, and optimistic, you probably experienced great restlessness in your early life, particularly if Jupiter is in a Mutable sign, or has challenging aspects. But being intuitive and idealistic you often become interested in spiritual horizons in your later years and then settle down. Generous and courageous, quite talkative and excitable, with an attention-getting laugh, you are one of those people who rarely pass unnoticed in a crowd. *Artist Leonardo DaVinci, actress Joan Crawford, writer Erich Remarque.*

Sagittarius ♐ on the Cusp of the Second House (Earning power, self-worth, possessions, talents, values). Usually there is financial good luck, unless Jupiter is heavily afflicted. You are liberal, fond of gambling, and you usually win. Generous and willing to share, you can be spiritually and psychologically gifted, especially with the 2nd decanate on the cusp. Money can come through travel or the education field. If Jupiter is too well aspected, there may be a genuine lack of concern for material things and a tendency to be lackadaisical, or over confident in financial dealings. *Ice skater Sonja Henie, President Ronald Reagan, actor Clint Eastwood.*

Sagittarius ♐ on the Cusp of the Third House (Communication, siblings, short trips, local environment, the conscious mind). You are adaptable to circumstances, unless Scorpio rises and Jupiter is in a fixed sign. With Libra on the Ascendant you have natural charm and good manners. You are imaginative, possess a good legal and executive mind and can be prophetic or religious. If literary ability runs in your family your writing talents may be accented especially if Scorpio rises, bestowing a quick, dry wit. You are fond of travel. Sagittarius here promotes good relationships with siblings if Jupiter is well aspected. When Jupiter has difficult aspects, there is often an interruption in the education or there may be an early separation from family members. *Ventriloquist Shari Lewis, President John F. Kennedy, emcee Johnny Carson.*

Sagittarius ♐ on the Cusp of the Fourth House (Home and one of the parents, private life, real property, the latter years of life). You definitely need to be treated as an individual, and you should be exposed early in life to literature and given the opportunity to engage in mental activities, especially if Virgo rises. Your parents tried to give you a good background, based upon solid religious or philosophical standards, yet you take it for granted and just accept it as your due if Virgo rises and Jupiter is unstable. Even though you may spend some of your life traveling in foreign countries, you still take great pride in your own native land and region, your family home, and loved ones. At some time in your life you may share your home with your in-laws. You prefer to live in a home that is as large and spacious as your pocketbook will afford. Your latter years may find you developing an interest in law or religion. Especially when Leo rises, you enjoy entertaining in your home and take increased pride in its furnishing and appearance. *Actress Julie Andrews, heiress Patty Hearst, singer Jaye P. Morgan.*

Sagittarius ♐ on the Cusp of the Fifth House   (Love and romance, children, creativity, speculation, avocation). If Leo rises, your optimistic and ambitious spirit may lead to recklessness and foolhardiness; often this is the sign of a born gambler whose luck depends upon how well aspected Jupiter is in the chart. However, your strong personality and sunny disposition provide you with many admirers, and this pleases you. You have marked self-esteem. Lucky, generous, and idealistic in love, you are often in love with love. You may very well benefit through your children, the field of sports or speculation. If Jupiter is not well placed in your chart, these same areas may cause problems. If Virgo is on the Ascendant, you will be more prudent and less likely to jump into affairs of the heart prefering the safer outlets of love of children, sports, needlework and handicrafts. *Actor Jack Nicholson, swimmer Mark Spitz, Indian Prime Minister Indira Gandhi.*

Sagittarius ♐ on the Cusp of the Sixth House   (Health and nutrition, service given, habits, pets, work, employees). You take pride in your work, but you need a strongly aspected and prominent Mars to really work hard; otherwise, you tend to be rather lazy and need a lot of sleep. You like a job where you can move around - and even better, travel, especially if Gemini or Cancer are on the Ascendant. You are neat and tidy, but dislike routine. With Leo rising, you seek work that will permit you to expand and grow. If Jupiter has difficult aspects, unless you curb a tendency to overindulge yourself, you are prone to liver problems and tumors. Problems with the hips, upper legs, and sciatic nerve are also possible with Sagittarius here. *Artist Vincent Van Gogh, boxer Jack Dempsey, inventor Guglielmo Marconi.*

Sagittarius ♐ on the Cusp of the Seventh House   (Partners, marital and business, legal affairs, dealings with the public). With Sagittarius here, Gemini *must* be rising. You are so curious, congenial, and self-expressive that you like many people and thus find it difficult to love just one person. Don't fence me in is your motto! The more liberty you have in marriage, the happier you will be and the longer it will last. More than one marriage is distinctly indicated, especially if Jupiter and Mercury have challenging aspects or are in cardinal or mutable signs. You want companionship more than love or sex, and the partner who understands this will command your respect. If you find the right partner and don't rush into an early marriage, you will idealize your mate and try very hard to please. *Actress Shirley Temple, writers George Bernard Shaw and John Steinbeck.*

Sagittarius ♐ on the Cusp of the Eighth House   (Partnership assets, sex, death, regeneration, occult matters, legacies). If Aries or Gemini is rising, this is a very good placement for scientific research. Inventive and subtle, you have a strong interest in religious philosophies and life after death. With Taurus rising, benefits may come through partnerships, and there is a chance of inheritance. While sex is of great interest to you, this interest is often more mental than physical. You are very fortunate in receiving support from other people, and you can be quite successful in the political arena. *Senator Charles Percy, publisher William Randolph Hearst, writer Jean Cocteau.*

Sagittarius ♐on the Cusp of the Ninth House   (The higher mind, higher education, distant travel, ethics, religion and philosophy). This is the natural house for Sagittarius in the flat chart, and therefore, unless Jupiter is very challenged, all philosophical and higher mind matters are of prime interest to you. You have great ideology of spirit; you like to be involved in social work and the general cause of humanity. With Aries rising and difficult aspects to Mars, imprudent and rash actions may give serious difficulties with the law. Usually though, especially if Pisces rises, you are a devout, religious, and law-abiding citizen. Fond of travel and interested in foreign matters, you seek constantly to expand your horizons. Success and a good reputation are especially important to you, so you usually take whatever steps are necessary to achieve them. *President Dwight D. Eisenhower, General Douglas MacArthur, artist Maurice Utrillo.*

Sagittarius ♐on the Cusp of the Tenth House   (Profession, one of the parents, reputation, ego, career, employers). You are cheerful, friendly, and outgoing, especially if you have Aquarius rising; adversity and the struggle for success stimulate you. If Pisces is rising, and Jupiter has very difficult aspects to it, you may find that others seem to stand in the way of your achievement. However, with a flowing Jupiter, you may seek to reach for the stars and achieve in professions like preaching, flying, or dancing. You also make a good leader, manager and executive, and you are well able to sell your ideas to the public through the written or spoken word. If Aries is on the Ascendant, and Mars is well placed, you can pioneer new ideas and new fields. If Jupiter is well aspected to Saturn, superiors will give you a helping hand up the ladder to success. *Comedian Shelley Berman, pilot Billy Mitchell, adventuress Osa Johnson.*

Sagittarius ♐on the Cusp of the Eleventh House   (Hopes and wishes, friends, social activities, unforseen circumstances). Your superior intelligence usually allows you to take a direct and impersonal approach to life. You can be a leader in humanitarian movements, but you resent any encroachment on your personal life, especially if Aquarius rises. By making few demands upon them, you keep your many loyal friends over great distances and for long periods of time. If Jupiter has challenging aspects, others may try to take advantage of your good nature, and if Neptune is involved in those aspects, you can be easily led astray by fair weather friends. You are known for your generous giving of yourself, especially if Pisces rises. However, if you have

Capricorn rising, you may have more goals to reach for and at times may use or abuse your friends. *Actor Desi Arnaz, Jr., actress Kim Novak, Governor George Wallace.*

Sagittarius ♐ on the Cusp of the Twelfth House   (Hidden strengths, the unconscious, confinement, secret affairs, institutions). You generally maintain an optimistic faith in life, and your tolerance and kindliness can bring growth and deep understanding, especially if Jupiter is positively placed in the chart. With Sagittarius or Aquarius on the Ascendant, you are better able to look within and intuitively use your inner resources. With Capricorn rising, you need vision and must learn compassion, for you feel that you and your work often go unappreciated. Jupiter's influence here can be rewarding in a subtle and hidden way; it gives you protection when it is least expected. *Authors Hermann Hesse and Joseph Wambaugh, ballplayer Maury Wills.*

Capricorn ♑ on the House Cusps

In your delineation, be sure to consider the ruler - Saturn ♄

Capricorn ♑ on the Cusp of the First House   (Personality, identity, the physical body). You were prone to delicate health early in life, but this improves with Saturn's help as the years go by. You're a hard worker and very ambitious to succeed; it is important for you to achieve on the material level and prove yourself. You need to see tangible results for your efforts. Dignified, patient and persistent, you can be too one-sided, nearly over-disciplined, taking everything very seriously, and so you may appear to be reserved and cold. Childhood can be a difficult time for you; you never seem really young, never the giggly teenager. But, by the same token, you age gracefully and won't appear as old as your years. *Actors Spencer Tracy and Sean Connery, Chief Justice Earl Warren.*

Capricorn ♑ on the Cusp of the Second House   (Possessions, earning power, values, self-worth, talents). Ambitious for money with a desire to save, you can be generous with yourself but are rarely so with your possessions. What is yours belongs to you, and you guard and preserve it. Capricorn here does not deny money, but it does indicate the necessity to earn it. Sometimes, inheritance comes through the father but it may have strings attached to it if Saturn has challenging aspects. With Sagittarius rising, your breezy outer behavior belies the fact that you are really quite practical and prudent, and you could have a talent for real estate or anything having to do with land and investments. With Scorpio or Capricorn rising, it becomes quite important that your value and self-worth are not solely based on material things, else you will have only outer security. *Actor Jackie Cooper, Los Angeles mayor Tom Bradley, writer Emile Zola.*

Capricorn ♑ on the Cusp of the Third House   (Communication, the conscious mind, short trips, siblings, early environment and education). If

Scorpio is rising, you are reflective, cautious, suspicious, and serious minded because your early environment was likely not very happy or lighthearted. You may feel misunderstood and have trouble expressing your true feelings, hiding them beneath a facade, especially if Libra or Sagittarius rises. You tend to take life very seriously unless Saturn has flowing aspects to it. This placement may indicate difficulty with siblings, and often, that you must take responsibility for younger brothers and sisters. Sometimes, you are denied an early education, if Saturn is afflicted by the ruler of the Ascendant. *Comedian Lennie Bruce, industrialist Henry Ford, author Victor Hugo.*

Capricorn ♑ on the Cusp of the Fourth House   (Home and parents, real property, closing years of life, your roots). In spite of parental restriction, or a rather rigid and traditional upbringing, you take lots of interest in the home, and there is generally always a strong link with the mother. You may cling to the family home too long. If Saturn is in a fixed sign, you like to put down roots and not move too often. Having great pride in your ancestry, you can become a pillar of your community. You tend to feel lonely at times, even when in the bosom of your family. If Virgo or Scorpio is on the Ascendant, you may have to take responsibility for family members, because they sense that they can depend upon you, personally and financially. If Libra rises, you may supplement your mate's income by working from the home or dealing in real estate. *President John Quincy Adams, tennis star Arthur Ashe, actress Debbie Reynolds.*

Capricorn ♑ on the Cusp of the Fifth House   (Love and romance, children, creativity, speculation, sports, risk and hazard). Though you may show a cold exterior in love, particularly if Virgo is rising, you are often very highly sexed but more in a lusty than sensuous way; your fear of rejection forces you to put up a cold front. You are very trustworthy, unless Saturn has difficult aspects, then you seem capricious. A good teacher, though a stern disciplinarian, you are not a giver by nature and can build a wall to keep others out. You feel that you work hard for everything you get, and thus it is well deserved. Generally you have few children, but feel great responsibility for them. Often, those with Capricorn here are gifted musicians, especially if Leo or Libra rises. You are not prone to speculate or take many risks; rather, you put your efforts into sure things that bring tangible results. *Composer Franz Liszt, poet Emily Dickinson, band leader Guy Lombardo.*

Capricorn ♑ on the Cusp of the Sixth House   (Work, service given, health and nutrition, habits, pets, employees). A great organizer, possibly an efficiency expert, especially with Cancer or Virgo rising, you often work for the government or other large organizations. Since you are the hardest worker of the zodiac, you need a permanent and stable occupation in which you can achieve status and respect. If Leo rises, you may have chronic health difficulties with your spine, bones or heart, especially if you are unable to find work that appeals to you. If Cancer rises and Saturn is afflicted, especially by

Venus, there is potential for skin problems. If Saturn has difficult aspects, you may get trapped into a dull, boring and routine job, particuarly if Virgo rises. Wherever we find Capricorn or Saturn, there is a tendency to overcompensate; if we do not use this energy in work or service, or if we refuse to accept responsibility in this area of life, the health may be adversely affected. *Scientist Thomas Huxley, astronomer Galileo, actress Betty White.*

Capricorn ♑ on the Cusp of the Seventh House   (Partners, business and marital, dealings with the public, legal matters). With Capricorn on this house cusp, you *must* have Cancer rising. Cancer's nurturing nature seeks a mature partner, someone who makes you feel secure. Yet, you don't wear your heart on your sleeve; you want affection but are suspicious of it when it is offered, so you bottle up your feelings and recoil within yourself when affected by sentiment, unless the Moon (ruling your Ascendant) has a great deal of flow. You neither give nor take easily. Capricorn here may delay marriage or you may be seeking a settled mate, a "father-image" type, or if your protective nature is strong, you may marry a younger person. You have a tendency to limit your partner in some way, or the reverse may also be true whereby you feel restricted by any serious commitment. *Singer Kate Smith, pianist Van Cliburn, artist Salvador Dali.*

Capricorn ♑ on the Cusp in the Eighth House   (Legacies and wills, death, regeneration, partnership assets, sex, taxes). Capricorn here promises a long life and rarely a sudden death; however, you dread growing old and are afraid of dying. If Taurus rises, you are very careful with joint finances but may still have difficulty with your partner's assets. With Gemini rising, your mind has an innate understanding of economics; thus, you are often found in a place of responsibility for the financial affairs of others. Unless the rest of the chart should deny it, this is practically the signature of a banker. If Saturn has difficult aspects to it, you need to adjust your values. You have great courage and can stand strong in the face of adversity. *Secretary of State Henry Kissinger, General George Patton, Prime Minister Harold Wilson.*

Capricorn ♑ on the Cusp of the Ninth House   (Higher education, law, religion and philosophy, foreign dealings, ethics). You have a good legal mind, and though skeptical by nature you are willing to be shown. Unless Saturn is well aspected, you are not especially fond of travel unless it is in connection with your work; you suspect foreigners. There is a conflict here between materialism and spirituality unless Taurus rises, which makes you more dogmatic. If Aries or Taurus rises, you are a good organizer and manager with much common sense and an appreciation of all that is tangible. If you have had a college education, it is likely you earned it largely through your own efforts. *Naturalist John Audubon, writer Arthur Conan Doyle, chef Julia Child.*

Capricorn ♑ on the Cusp of the Tenth House   (Profession, career, one of the parents, reputation). This is the natural house of Capricorn in the flat chart. You aim high and seek a career or profession that will bring you prestige and recognition. One of the parents, usually the father, played an important role in your life; to prove yourself to this parent is a strong motivating force in your life. You show great perseverance in the pursuit of your aspirations; neither opposition nor obstacles can deter you, especially if you have Aries rising. With Taurus or Pisces rising, though not a coward, you are conservative in any matter that might hurt your reputation; you prefer to sidestep trouble at all costs. Your strong sense of responsibility and organization often leads you into a career as an executive or in some branch of government service. *Playwright Tennessee Williams, entertainer Bette Midler, senator Joseph McCarthy.*

Capricorn ♑ on the Cusp of the Eleventh House   (Friends, hopes and wishes, social organizations, unforseen circumstances). Since you don't seek people out, you don't have too many friends, but a few close ones are all that you require. Older people seem to play an important role in your life, and you may have strong ties with your grandparents. With Aquarius or Aries rising, you usually achieve your goals because you are so willing to work hard for them. If Saturn is poorly placed, Capricorn here can make you quite suspicious of others and unwilling to involve yourself in any joint endeavors. If Pisces rises, you may feel that you always give more than you receive in return; as the result, you prefer to be a loner, rather than feel alone in a crowd. *Actor David Carradine, Princess Margaret of England, writer Henry Miller.*

Capricorn ♑ on the Cusp of the Twelfth House   (Hidden strengths, behind-the-scenes activities, the unconscious mind). Inherent selfishness needs to be overcome with Capricorn here, especially if Capricorn is also on the Ascendant. Unless you can learn to serve others, there can be much sorrow in the area of life shown by Saturn's placement in the chart. There is a tendency to arthritis and the crystalization of attitudes because you place too much importance on ego and prestige. True humility is an important lesson you must learn. You like to work alone, and usually have a hobby that you work on in solitude. Yet with Aquarius rising, Capricorn here can give you the solidity and the inner strength so necessary if you want to utilize the best Aquarius has to give and not be an eccentric - up today and down tomorrow. *Photographer Anthony Armstrong-Jones, President Warren G. Harding, writer Sylvia Plath.*

Aquarius ♒ on the House Cusps

In your delineation, be sure to consider the ruler - Uranus ♅ and in certain cases, especially young children, blend in Saturn ♄

Aquarius ♒ on the Cusp of the First House   (Physical body, personality, identity). You appear quite self-confident, and especially as you mature, exude an air of "if you like me, fine - if you don't that's fine too".

But you don't really mean it. You enjoy being different, and you even pride yourself on your individualism, but to be liked is as important to you as the next person. If you have Uranus prominently located, you could be a rebel-but always *with* a cause. *Your* cause! You are quite set in your ways—unless Uranus is in a mutable sign. You have sufficient personal magnetism to draw other people to you, and they will often accept behavior from you that they might not tolerate in others. If Saturn is very strong in your horoscope, you may hold on to certain traditions; if Uranus is stronger than Saturn, you will do all that you can to change the status quo. Physical exercise daily of some type is important; you tend to have sluggish circulation. *Writer F. Scott Fitzgerald, labor leader James Hoffa, journalist Bill Moyers.*

Aquarius ♒ on the Cusp of the Second House   (Possessions, earning power, inner talents and resources) If Capricorn is rising, you may surprise those around you by not being as serious about money and possessions as your rather ambitious personality might suggest. In fact, there might be quite a few monetary ups and downs in your life which will affect you deeply only if Uranus has many difficult aspects; otherwise, you will rise to the occasion and willingly start all over again. Your personal value system, and especially your personal freedom, are of utmost importance to you; if Aquarius or Sagittarius rises, you will establish these values at a relatively early age in life. With Capricorn rising, you may tend to the material side first and only later realize that true freedom is not found in money or goods. However, whatever rises in your chart, you do enjoy unusual possessions, like collecting old cars, antique furniture, or rare and unusual books. *Entertainers Liberace and Mike Douglas, consumer advocate Ralph Nader.*

Aquarius ♒ on the Cusp of the Third House   (Communications, short trips, siblings, early education, the conscious mind). You are highly motivated to communicate and express yourself. You are happiest when you can do this in a unique and really individualistic way; you even pride yourself when people consider you different. You are particularly vocal about causes that you espouse. Areas that involve your mind are very important to you, especially if there are aspects linking Uranus with Mercury, which would also give you a talent for speaking foreign languages and mathematics. If Sagittarius is rising, you may tend to scatter your intellectual energies in too many directions, or you may be a non-stop talker. If Scorpio or Capricorn rises, you will talk less but your mind will be just as active. Unless Uranus has very difficult aspects to it, you are an avid and easy learner with a great love of books and reading. Your relatives and siblings may not understand you or what makes you tick, and some may even consider you to be the black sheep of the family, but they will tolerate your difference unless Uranus has difficult aspects. At some point in your life, maybe for no better reason than boredom, you may decide not to continue your education. *Astronaut John Glenn, actor Keenan Wynn, opera star Patrice Munsel.*

Aquarius ♒ on the Cusp of the Fourth House   (The home, family, one of the parents, real property, the latter years of life). Your family life may not be run of the mill, or you may have considered your parental home to be different than that of your peers. If Uranus has difficult aspects, especially to the ruler of the Ascendant, Sun or Moon, your parents may have separated or divorced. You may have felt your home life unsettled, either because of many moves or constant ups and downs; as a result, you'll look for a more harmonious and quieter type of life, especially in your later years. In the home *you* establish, you wish to be at liberty to do as you please, which may not be too easy for you if Libra rises and you have chosen an Aries-type partner. If Saturn is very prominent in your chart, you are happiest around older people, especially during your younger years, but if Uranus is stronger than Saturn, a more bohemian circle appeals to you, especially when Sagittarius rises. With Scorpio rising, you are quite set in your ways and tend to be too demanding of your loved ones at home. Since you are also rather high-strung, you need to learn at an early age to curb your irritability and learn the art of compromise. *Philosopher Friedrich Nietzsche, actor Charlie Chaplin, singer Glen Campbell.*

Aquarius ♒ on the Cusp of the Fifth House   (Love and romance, children, creativity, sports, avocation, speculation). With Libra or Scorpio rising, you tend to be very exploratory in matters of love and romance; nothing seems too far-fetched. You feel that if it exists, why not try it? Children are important to you, especially when they are old enough to communicate, and you could be an excellent teacher since you love to shape their minds and have the ability to take them as they are; to talk to them on their own level. You can be quite intuitive, and if your chart shows any talent for art, you could be creative in a most unusual even inventive way. If Virgo rises, you may have some problems expressing as individualistically as you may wish to since Virgo prefers to be rather proper and not do wildly different things. Unless Uranus is well aspected, this is not a good position for gambling or speculation. *Actor Omar Sharif, Robert Ripley of "Believe It Or Not", President Richard Nixon.*

Aquarius ♒ on the Cusp of the Sixth House   (Health and nutrition, work, employees, service given, pets, habits). If Virgo is rising, you take great pride in working harder than anyone else, but you are not necessarily well organized; in fact, you may feel like a nervous wreck time and time again, since you wish to do so much and the day never seems to have enough hours in which to accomplish everything you set out to do. To do well in your work is very important to you, and you can be a born reformer. You like a job where you can give service at some kind, to the underdog, to humanity, and you'll do it willingly - even for free. If your efforts are not directed into work and service, you may tend to hypochondria or somehow put greater emphasis on your health and nutrition. Since you have a rather active nervous system, especially if Virgo rises, you are better advised to direct your energies into more positive areas. If Cancer rises, you may be very interested in all kinds of fad diets, and organic foods, as well as a job in the medical fields. *Gossip columnist Rona Barrett, singer Doris Day, actress Helen Hayes.*

Aquarius ♒ on the Cusp of the Seventh House   (Partnerships, marital and business, dealing with the public, legal affairs). With Aquarius here, you *must* have Leo Rising. You seek partners who will stimulate you intellectually, who can be a real *friend* to you as well as a partner, who will not be afraid to act independently and look or behave in a most individualistic way. Yet, with Leo rising, you are a strong and dominant personality in your own right, and once you have what you thought you wanted you may try to change your mate over to suit you, to domineer - the usual result is marital ups and downs, and sometimes even divorce. If you do find a mate who will go along with your demands, he or she will become your best friend and the most important person in your life. *Entertainer Maurice Chevalier, actor Richard Burton, President Lyndon B. Johnson.*

Aquarius ♒ on the Cusp of the Eighth House   (Partner's resources, sex, regeneration, death, taxes). With Aquarius here, you enjoy sex as a game, exploring all phases in a detached and sometimes unconventional way, especially with Leo or Gemini on the ascendant. With Cancer rising, your basic insecurities might be stronger than your curiosity, so you talk a good game - but that's all! You are highly intuitive, even psychic if you wish to go in that direction and if the rest of the chart supports this. But beware of schemes! You can also be quite gullible, especially when Uranus has challenging aspects. The occult appeals to you, regardless of what sign is rising, and you like to do unconventional things - unconventional to others, not you. If Uranus or Saturn are very challenged, you may tend to get depressed very easily, especially if Cancer is rising. If Gemini rises, you may have difficulties in handling the resources and money of others; learn to balance your own checkbook first. Whatever sign rises, with Aquarius here you tend to be a free-thinker when it comes to matters relating to death. *Secretary of Navy James Forrestal, actress Jane Russell.*

Aquarius ♒ on the Cusp of the Ninth House   (Religion and philosophy, ideals, ethics, higher education, foreign dealings, in-laws). You have a very vivid imagination. If Gemini is rising, you could be a writer or inventor of some kind. Your mind is highly active. Higher education is important to you; if for some reason you are unable to go to college you will continue to study and learn throughout your life attending adult classes or anything that may be offered. Curious about life, you will seek your own answers through some philosophy or religion totally your own. With either Gemini or Cancer rising, travel and foreign cultures fascinate you. Unless Uranus is weak in the chart, your ideas and ideals will be unorthodox. *Madam Xaviera Hollander, physicist Albert Einstein, emcee David Frost.*

Aquarius ♒ on the Cusp of the Tenth House   (Profession and career, one of the parents, reputation, ego, status). With Taurus rising, your need to succeed and stand with both feet on the ground may be stronger than your great idealism and impossible dreams, and only the entire chart and position of Uranus can indicate in which direction you will go. With Aries or Gemini rising, you want a profession or career that is different and not run-of-the-mill, and you don't mind being known as an odd-ball. If Uranus has many challenging aspects, you'll need to watch yourself - you may provoke scandals or bring much disappointment upon yourself. If the rest of your chart supports it, this is a good position for work in large organizations, even government or politics, since people will be attracted to you and admire you for daring to be yourself. With a well-placed Uranus, friends will often help you in your career. This is also an excellent placement for the astrological field as well as work in electronics and with computers. *Psychic Peter Hurkos, writer Herman Melville, actress Celeste Holm.*

Aquarius ♒ on the Cusp of the Eleventh House   (Hopes and wishes, friends, large organizations, unexpected occurrences). This is the natural house position for Aquarius in the flat chart, and thus all 11th house matters should work well for you unless Uranus is very poorly placed in your horoscope. With Aries rising, you have many friends. However, with your rather blunt approach and tendency to get bored easily, this is not indicative of long-lasting friendships unless Mars and Uranus are in passive signs. The humanitarian instinct is innate in your basic nature, and you'll likely be happiest when involved with groups that work to better mankind in some way. With Taurus rising, you could be very successful in politics, especially if Uranus is prominent and Venus is well placed in the chart. You work well in large organizations and are ambitious to succeed. With Pisces rising, your imagination may be too good and your story-telling and dramatic ability such that you have trouble sticking to the truth. Socially you are quite popular and very helpful to one and all - as long as it is on your terms. *Senator Robert Kennedy, writer Percy Shelley, actor Jason Robards.*

Aquarius ♒ on the Cusp of the Twelfth House   (Hidden strengths, the subconscious, behind-the-scenes activity). Uranus is known as the "Awakener", thus with Aquarius on the cusp of the house of subconscious mind, your inner awakening becomes more important than anything else. Uranus is a transcendental planet and most people do not react to its far-removed and rather abstract influence until later in life; therefore, you may feel an inner turmoil and unrest that you cannot really explain until well after Saturn has made its first return at about age 29. This is especially true if Aries is rising in your chart. With Aquarius rising, you will greatly resent any kind of restraint, but being more used to the Uranian feelings you learn to cope with your emotions quite well, unless Uranus is very challenged in the horoscope. With Pisces rising, your intuition is usually quite well developed, you feel empathy for the underdog and all those in need. This Aquarius-Pisces combination makes you the happiest when you are giving service of some kind or working with the underprivileged; also, it makes you a very private person, one who will always show a different face to the world, a mask hiding your true self. It is a good placement for actors. With a weak chart, the tendency can be to escape through alcohol or drugs. *Actress Carole Lombard, actor Warren Beatty, governor John Connally.*

Pisces ⩊ on the House Cusps

In your delineation, be sure to blend in the ruler Neptune ♆ and sub-ruler Jupiter ♃

♈ **Pisces ⩊ on the Cusp of the First House** (Personality, identity, the physical body). You may not have great physical energy and stamina unless Mars is strong in your chart. Pisces is a dual sign and there are two different types. The first type is the doer and server who draws energy from higher sources and has good intuition, who goes quietly about his work in a compassionate and detached manner. The other type is the drifter and dreamer who cannot face failure and thus will not try to succeed. Easily discouraged and not very practical, you are absentminded at times. Music plays an important role in the lives of both types; it eases their moodiness. Whichever type you are, you react with great emotion to life. *Conductor Leopold Stokowski, Vice President Walter Mondale, director Alfred Hitchcock.*

Pisces ⩊ on the Cusp of the Second House (Personal finances, possessions, values, resources and talents). If Capricorn is rising, you have financial difficulties until you free yourself from the purely material and realize that the security you seek cannot be bought, but needs to come from the inside out. With a Pisces or Aquarius Ascendant, you are emotional regarding most 2nd house areas; yet tangible things don't always mean that much and you may even be careless with your belongings. If Neptune is afflicted, study all documents well before you sign them. You may earn through investment in Neptune related fields - films, acting, photography, music, oil, shipping. *White House aide John Dean, illusionist Harry Houdini, actor Errol Flynn.*

Pisces ⩊ on the Cusp of the Third House (Communications, siblings, short trips, early education, the conscious mind). You are musical, intuitive, imaginative, and usually good at creative writing, but with Aquarius or Sagittarius rising you must learn how to concentrate or studying can be arduous. If Neptune has difficult aspects, there may be trouble and sorrow through siblings; there may even be a separation from them. With Sagittarius or Capricorn rising, you are quite socially oriented and like to keep up with the Joneses. The sensitivity of Pisces on the house of communications can enhance your love for poetry, both reading and writing it, but it does not mean that you will be sensitive in the way you express yourself—in fact, you can be quite blunt at times. *Actress Clara Bow, actor Dustin Hoffman, writer James Joyce.*

Pisces ✕ on the Cusp of the Fourth House   (Home, one of the parents, the latter part of life, real property). Your strong, emotional family attachment often causes you to render service to family members, especially in your latter years. With either Scorpio or Capricorn rising, you seem to be plagued with obligations that must be met, which is not always easy for you. Pisces here can sometimes indicate some skeleton in the closet, such as an alcoholic parent. Sometimes secret sorrow and spiritual aloneness have to be handled. Your own home will be very important to you; it will serve as a retreat from the world where you can periodically recharge your batteries. *Actress Mary Astor, handicapped worker Helen Keller, President Abraham Lincoln.*

Pisces ✕ on the Cusp of the Fifth House   (Love and romance, children, creativity, avocation, amusement, sports). Dual and impressionable in love, you are a true romantic. If Neptune has challenging aspects, your over-idealism can bring sorrow through loved ones or children. Wherever Pisces is located, there we often find some sense of frustration or the self-sacrifice syndrome, and here in the 5th house it may mean that there is never enough time or money to develop your considerable creative potential. You may neglect your family in the pursuit of pleasure, or you may devote too much time to your children - tying them to you with a silver cord. Your children can be home angels and neighborhood or school devils, but it is hard for you to see their devilish side. If Neptune is afflicted, you should avoid gambling and speculative ventures that promise a quick payoff. *Writer Pierre Salinger, actress Ginger Rogers, singer Glen Campbell.*

Pisces ✕ on the Cusp of the Sixth House   (Health and nutrition, habits, work, service given, pets). If either Virgo or Scorpio rises, you may not be too strong physically, and if your emotions are allowed to run free, ulcers may be the result. When Neptune is afflicted, there is often decreased resistence to disease, and diagnosis of health problems is difficult. You'll do well in Piscean vocations, such as art, music, or photography, otherwise professional worries are indicated as well as unreliable employees. Cultivate some creative hobby to relieve mental tension. Uproot the tendency to worry about little things. With Libra rising, your need to balance and weigh everything can make you quite demanding of yourself and others at work; yet, you are also intuitive enough to know when to stop, and thus you can make a good boss. *Rock star Alice Cooper, writer Anais Nin, President Woodrow Wilson.*

Pisces ✕ on the Cusp of the Seventh House   (Partnerships, marital and business, dealings with the public, legal matters). With Pisces here, you *must* have Virgo on your Ascendant. You tend to seek an impractical, idealistic partner, one to whom you can give sympathy and support—even an alcoholic or one who is handicapped—so you can experience sorrow through marriage. Or, you may seek the knight in shining armor on his white horse, and no one else will do. With Pisces here and Virgo rising, the inclination to be critical and nit-picking can cause difficulties in dealing with others in a face-to-face situation. Good, balanced judgment is an asset in helping you to deal with a certain amount of gullibility as far as other people are concerned. Blend the placements of Neptune and Mercury to determine the kind of partner you will be drawn to. *Comedian Groucho Marx, Beatle Ringo Starr, President Richard Nixon.*

Pisces ⋉ on the Cusp of the Eighth House   (Resources of the partner, sex, taxes, death matters, regeneration). If Cancer is rising, you are very sensitive, and once you have developed compassion you are able to direct your intuitive ability very positively. You should learn to work with or help others, especially if Leo rises, or you will find that experience is a quick teacher. There can sometimes be deception in terms of partnership assets. You are highly sensitive to any criticism of your sexual abilities. If Neptune has difficult aspects, use great care in the use of drugs and anesthetics, and always get a second opinion when any surgical procedure is indicated. With Cancer or Virgo rising, sex may not be very important to you, or you may just relegate it to what you consider more meaningful, such as a deep relationship. *Football great O. J. Simpson, seer Edgar Cayce, chess champion Bobby Fischer.*

Pisces ⋉ on the Cusp of the Ninth House   (Philosophy and religion, higher education, foreign affairs, ehtics, long trips). You take a mystical approach to religion and are more devotional than intellectual if you have Cancer on your Ascendant. With Gemini rising, you seek a philosophy of life rather than a religion. With Leo rising, you can be very spiritual. Tenderness and compassion make you a good nurse, and you can develop a helpful healing capacity. You enjoy travel by water, and you find it very relaxing to vacation where there are lakes and streams. You may spend much of your life in foreign countries if Neptune has a prominent place in the chart. *Duchess of Windsor, actress Ava Gardner, Prince Charles of England.*

Pisces ⋉ on the Cusp of the Tenth House   (Profession and career, reputation, one of the parents, ego, status, authority). You can be an executive with great vision, but you are not always practical unless Taurus rises and Venus and Neptune are in good aspect. With either Gemini or Cancer rising, you may have two jobs or professions as you have difficulty in really knowing what you want; you will always wonder whether you've picked the right career. If Neptune is well aspected, this is a very good placement for success in music, writing, or the acting field. In a female chart, this often indicates the woman who is happy as a homemaker with a hobby to keep her busy. *Tenor Enrico Caruso, writer William Faulkner, The Duke of Windsor.*

Pisces ⋉ on the Cusp of the Eleventh House   (Hopes and wishes, friendships, large organizations, unexpected events). You draw some of your friends from the psychic and occult fields while others hail from the literary and acting groups. Beware of deception from friends and acquaintances if

Neptune has challenging aspects. What others say about you means a lot to you, and deep hurt and resentment ensue when you feel you have been slighted. You are most generous with those whom you cherish, but you must overcome a tendency to be too thin-skinned where others are concerned. With Gemini rising, you enjoy gossiping with your friends. *Queen Victoria, commentator Tom Snyder, heiress Christina Onassis.*

Pisces ⊁ on the Cusp of the Twelfth House (Hidden strengths, limitations, the subconscious mind, frustration, self-undoing). This is the natural house of Pisces in the flat chart, and consequently you should handle 12th house matters well unless Neptune is badly aspected in the horoscope. With Taurus or Pisces rising, you have a strong sense of personal service and are always ready to help the underdog. Unless Neptune is well placed, there can be considerable loneliness and disappointment in your life because you so often underestimate or misunderstand others; you also have trouble seeing yourself honestly. You require solitude at times in order to recharge your batteries. But, you must also guard against hiding from others or playing the role of the martyr. With Aries on the Ascendant, you come on quite forcefully as if to hide the sensitivity and vulnerability you really feel subconsciously and deep inside. If the ruler of the Ascendant is placed in the 12th house you will be able to look at yourself much more objectively, and such fields as psychology or counselling can be very good for you. *Senator Robert Kennedy, composer Johannes Brahms, actor Sal Mineo.*

How to Delineate the Cusps of the Houses

In the introduction to Lesson 13, we briefly delineated Walt Disney's 2nd house cusp. To illustrate some more, let's now look at his 6th house. Aquarius is on the cusp, the ruler - Uranus - is in Sagittarius in the 3rd house. According to our notes, he should take pride in hard work, yet he may not necessarily be well organized and try to do more than time permits and as the result, be quite nervous. To do well is important to him, and he can be a reformer. How much of this should we apply to Walt Disney?

With a Capricorn stellium, work was definitely very important to him, and ruler Uranus conjunct the Sun added even more emphasis to the 6th house. Uranus in his 3rd house indicates that communication of some kind played an important role in the type of work that he did. Being in Sagittarius, it might entail some type of reform, or at least something that will enable him to reach high, involving some idealistic goal, which definitely includes some form of humanitarian service. In Disney's case, the rest of the chart shows us that creativity and film making were his ways of working and giving service. Was he disorganized, and very nervous? There is too much earth here for him to really be disorganized but enough mutability to thrive on nervous energy, and probably occasional irritability since there are plenty of squares in his chart to produce all kinds of tension and challenges. With the ruler of the 6th house in the 3rd, the possibility of working with a relative is emphasized. Walt's brother, Roy, was his right hand all through his life.

To give you one more example, let's look at Walt Disney's 10th house for career, his standing in the community, and one of the parents. Gemini is on the cusp with its ruler, Mercury, in Scorpio in the 3rd house. The first thing that strikes us is that the ruler of his 6th house of work and the ruler of his 10th house of career are both in the 3rd house of communications. This again confirms that communicating of some kind is very important to Disney. Remember, we always need confirmation in delineating. Our notes state that Disney should enjoy working with others; this is really neither confirmed nor denied in his chart. We know that in his work he had to deal with many people, but how much he enjoyed it we don't know. A Sagittarius Sun likes to be with people, but Mercury in Scorpio can just as easily enjoy solitude.

Our notes indicate that there may be some career changes. In Disney's case, he started out as a cartoonist and then became a producer; he expanded into television and finally founded his famous amusement parks Disneyland and Disney World, definitely showing more than one career. We also state that Gemini on the 10th house cusp can be an excellent speaker or teacher. With ruler Mercury in Scorpio involved in a yod to the Midheaven (see Lesson 6) and his 5th house, we see that his ability to express is more along artistic lines than in the speaking or teaching fields.

After you have looked at the cusps and its ruler, be sure to realize that Neptune is in the 10th house, and it will thus color his career. Neptune is the highest planet in the chart. It is the finger or apex of the yod. It is at 0° (see Lesson 18). It is retrograde (see Lesson 7), and it is one of the most important planets in Disney's horoscope. You should also keep in mind that Mercury, ruler of the 10th house, is in mutual reception with Pluto, ruler of the 3rd where Mercury is placed, bringing both houses and both planets together in a very harmonious way, and enabling Disney to use the most positive attributes of these planets and houses.

Review Question: Delineate Walt Disney's 5th house. You'll find our delineation in the Appendix on page 245.

Lesson 15
Aspects To The Ascendant And Midheaven

In Volume One of "The Only Way To... Learn Astrology" we devoted quite a number of pages to the different aspects made between the planets. We also gave you keywords to impress upon you not only how each aspect manifests, but also that you should always remember what you are aspecting. Aspects to the Sun will for example, stress the inner self, aspects to the Moon involve the emotions, whereas aspects to Mercury are mental, and so on for each planet. Each aspect has a certain feeling which can be expressed through a keyword. The conjunction gives emphasis; the opposition gives self-awareness; the square challenges you into action; the trine creates flow; and the sextile gives ease; whereas the inconjunct (quincunx) demands that you make certain adjustments. All of this is discussed in Lesson 7 of Volume One.

The Ascendant and the Midheaven are not planets; they are points in the horoscope, the two most important angles of the chart. The Ascendant describes you as you are born into this world and is predicated upon the exact birthtime and birthplace. The Ascendant shows your outer personality, your natural disposition, the way people see you and the way you would like them to see you; in other words, the way you package yourself. It also represents your physical body, it shows how you approach life, your appearance, bearing and behavior. Therefore, all aspects to the Ascendant will be personal and will affect your outlook and your deportment.

The Midheaven is the cusp of the 10th house, it is the highest or southern-most point, it follows logically that it is also the highest you can reach in a worldly sense. It is your reputation, your status and standing in the com-munity; it describes your profession or career, fame and promotion, your worldly achievements. It shows any and all authority, such as your boss or government. In childhood it represents parental authority; therefore, it portrays one of the parents, whichever one in your mind stood for authority (the 4th house describes the other parent). Since our inner feelings are always more important than outer manifestations, the most important facet of the 10th house is that it represents your ego and is therefore a driving force that propels or urges you on to be somebody and to achieve. Any aspects to the Midheaven will carry some of the ego drive with them. In early years, they will describe the career and the ease or challenges in pursuing it. The kind of profession suited for the individual in question will be described by the sign on the cusp, the planet ruling it, and any planets placed in the 10th house.

We have classified the aspects into three categories: 1) conjunctions to show where the greatest emphasis is placed. 2) trines and sextiles to demonstrate the easy and flowing relation to the angles and 3) squares, oppositions and inconjuncts to describe the challenges and tensions manifested.

In the next few pages of this lesson we give you some key phrases for aspects to the Ascendant and Midheaven. As always, we need to remind you that these words and phrases cannot be used without evaluating the rest of the horoscope. At the end of this lesson, we briefly delineate Walt Disney's aspects to his Ascendant and Midheaven to get you started.

Sun conjunct Ascendant   You feel the need to project your personality, to have others see you shine, and it goes without saying that others notice you; but whether in a positive or negative way depends upon the other aspects to this conjunction. In fire signs, there is a tendency to have a rather inflated opinion of your own abilities, but with proper application, this conjunction can be a positive expression of your individuality. You are a leader (after all, this is the Aries house combined with the power of the Sun), and it is sometimes difficult for you to handle and respect another's position of authority. You are generous, and usually outgoing, unless the Sun is in the 12th house. You tend to show off and want to be the center of attention; yet, you have great integrity and usually a zest for life and living. With many challenging aspects, you may be too egocentric. *Movie producer C. B. DeMille, conductor Leonard Bernstein.*

Sun trine / sextile Ascendant   These aspects usually promise good health, the ability and opportunity to project your personality in a very positive way, and a creative and philosophical outlook on life. Sociable and outgoing, you enjoy performing for others, and usually have a good self-image. Honest and direct in your approach, you may get bored if things don't go your way. You are well co-ordinated, and if the rest of the chart confirms, you could be interested in, and have an ability for, sports. The trine and sextile work particularly well if there are squares or oppositions to spur you into utilizing the opportunities available. *Boxer Max Baer.△, tennis pro Don Budge ∗.*

Sun square / opposition / inconjunct Ascendant   These aspects give an inordinate amount of personal drive, but achievement is reached by the trial-and-error method. Often there are health problems to be overcome (especially with the inconjunct), and sometimes there is a conflict-of-ego situation to be handled in regard to a male in the life, usually the father. In a woman's chart, it may be necessary to cope with difficulties in marriage or with business partners, particularly with the opposition. Often, you have difficulty getting along with people until you understand your own personality, but since you definitely need relationships with others, learning true cooperation is important for you. Your strong personality may need to be toned down so that others can find ways to interact with and understand you. *Composers Johann S. Bach □ , Frederic Chopin ☌ , writer Charles Dickens ⊼ .*

Sun conjunct Midheaven   It is important in the development of your ego that you learn to lead in a positive way. A career is very necessary to you; even if you don't work for money, you will make a profession of volunteering or find some way to shine in the community. Because of your dominant personality, others will follow you, so take care that your leadership commands respect. Admiration and success are very important to you, and with enough squares and oppositions to this conjunction, you can achieve great heights in any field. Though you are great at taking charge, it is difficult for you to play the subordinate role; therefore, you do best in a field where you can manage or shine as an individual. Often a male is an important influence in your life, especially in your youth. *Tenor Enrico Caruso, explorer Richard Byrd.*

Sun trine / sextile Midheaven   It is easy for you to be a leader, and with squares and oppositions operating with this aspect, you can become an outstanding executive, manager or administrator. Success in your chosen field comes easily, and as you pursue your goals, you rarely come into conflict with others. Your parents' influence has a good effect upon you, and you have learned to develop a sense of personal values. The problems here can be an inherent laziness; because success is so easily attainable, the drive to achieve is felt to be not worth the effort, and you may choose the path of least resistance. *Actress Mary Astor △ , writer Faith Baldwin ✳ .*

Sun square / opposition / inconjunct Midheaven   With any of these aspects, success is often fleeting or arrived at only at the cost of great effort and willpower. You need to get ahead in life and will assert yourself at all cost, but you must learn to compromise, and you may find it difficult to decide just what it is you want to do with your life. Very often, there is a conflict with parental authority—you feel the need to do your own thing and will not heed good and well meant help and advice. When you learn to handle your subjectivity and inner feeling of limitation, you can achieve your aspirations. *Composer George Friedrich Handel □ , author Truman Capote ☌ , artist Leonardo DaVinci ⊼ .*

* * * *

Moon conjunct Ascendant   Environmental is the word for you, and it is important that your environment is peaceful and stable. Home and family-oriented, you have an innate nurturing instinct and love to take care of others. Yet, you know what appeals to the public and could be a good salesman. In childhood, your mother played an important role in your life, and you will always maintain an inherent understanding of women and their needs, because of this relationship. You are very emotional, and everyone knows it, because you make no effort to hide your feelings, unless your Moon is in the 12th house. Though others respond to your compassionate and caring nature they are also often baffled by your eternally changing moods. Emotionally vulnerable, it is hard for you to handle criticism, and when so confronted, you will withdraw much like a Cancer. If the Moon is in the 12th house, the sign on the Ascendant will make all the difference in how much or how little you will show of your emotions, but they are still there and even more vulnerable when bottled up and kept hidden. *Actor Charles Chaplin, politician Thomas E. Dewey.*

Moon trine / sextile Ascendant   It is very easy for you to show your feelings, and because of your charm and outgoing personality, you draw others to you. Your mother is an important factor in your life, and you enjoy a supportive and loving relationship with her. Since it is very easy for you to communicate and be friendly, and since you also enjoy working in groups, you may do well in acting or the political arena. Music is often a dominant factor in your life; in fact, you may have a pleasant singing voice. Usually easygoing, you are quite imaginative and creative. You enjoy fun and good times with friends and family. Should the Moon be in the 9th house, travel will help expand your horizons. *Singer Deanna Durbin △ , actor Roddy McDowall ✳ .*

Moon square / opposition / inconjunct Ascendant   Overly sensitive to the point of being touchy, your ability to get along with others is directly dependent upon your ability to sublimate your feelings and emotions. In youth, you may have had a hot temper and sarcastic tongue, but with maturity you usually realize that these are traits to be replaced with understanding and compassion for others. Often it is hard for you to handle anger without giving way to your emotions; this trait may persist into maturity. Your feelings influence all of your relationships so you find it difficult to relate to others, except on the emotional level, and you always feel you are somewhat at the mercy of others when it comes to partnership (opposition), work (inconjunct) or home (square) situations. Because of your vulnerability, you need much support from others. Often your relationship with your mother is challenging, and you seek maternal support from those you feel rapport with. *Statesman Benjamin Disraeli □ , entertainer Mike Douglas ♂ , comedian Jack Benny ⊼ .*

Moon conjunct Midheaven   Your feelings and emotions are directly tied to your ego, so if you achieve status, honor and prestige, your personality functions well. If, however, you are thwarted in your ambitions, you may feel emotionally unappreciated and thus, inhibited. You have a natural knack for knowing what appeals to the public, and so you do well in public relations or in the sales field. Women, in general, may be helpful to your career; undoubtedly your mother had a strong influence on you in the choice of your life's work. If the Moon is in the 10th house, you may have regarded your mother as the authority during your childhood; in a male's chart, unless the Sun, Mars or Saturn is very strong, your male image may be weak and you'll need a lot of confirmation in order to feel secure. *Singer Nelson Eddy and commentator Lowell Thomas.*

Moon trine / sextile Midheaven   Some type of public career is where you'll do best because of your innate understanding of the wants and needs of people in general. Since you are considerate and compassionate, people will have confidence in your judgment, and your sensitivity to others' needs makes it easy for you to succeed. You learn through your emotions, so it is important that you trust your feelings and your hunches. You may be attracted to the old and traditional, the tried and true, but this does not prevent you from tuning in to new trends which the public will accept. You could succeed in a career where you deal in real estate, farming, mining, or the sale of commodities. Should the Moon be in the 6th house, you may try quite a few jobs before you settle on a permanent career. *Chef Julia Child △ , singer Johnny Cash * .*

Moon square / opposition / inconjunct Midheaven   Since you wear your feelings and your emotions on your sleeve, people are well advised to give you a wide birth or learn to handle you with kid gloves. Your feelings tend to conflict with the needs and desires of others, and it is hard for you to choose whether to heed your own needs and emotional requirements or to listen to the advice and promptings of others. You often seem to be at the mercy of your emotions, and you may have to resolve partnership and business problems at some time in your life. Though strongly attached to home and family, especially when the Moon is in the 5th house, you will turn your back on them in order to assert yourself and establish your own security. If the Moon has many other challenging aspects, popularity is difficult for you to attain; sometimes, recognition is achieved through notoriety or for all of the wrong reasons. *Murderer William Heirens □ , artist Paul Cezanne ♂ , actor James Dean ⊼ .*

* * * *

Mercury conjunct Ascendant   Mercury rules communication and the Ascendant represents your personality, so you need to express yourself graphically and openly. Never at a loss for words describes you perfectly. However, if this conjunction has challenging aspects to it, they may occasionally be the wrong words at the wrong time. Intellectually impulsive, bright and witty, you are not afraid to speak up and tend to dominate any conversation. Mentally restless, you are an inveterate question-asker; this restlessness may also show in constant physical activity - the compulsive worker, for instance, especially if Mercury is in a mutable sign. If there is a Uranus aspect involved, you may be a nail-biter, hair-twister, nose-twitcher. Usually, Mercury here indicates an avid reader, particularly if it is behind the Ascendant in the 12th house. If Mercury is in the 1st house, you have a strong need to deal with other people in all areas of your life and are often drawn to the younger generation, for example in teaching. *Commentator Tom Snyder, ventriloquist Edgar Bergen.*

Mercury trine / sextile Ascendant   This can be an aspect of the creative nature. There is a need to express and communicate through the literary, artistic or musical fields, especially if Mercury is in the 3rd or 5th houses. Self-expression is easy for you; you have great interest in everything and everyone around you. Mental activities and games attract you, and both your mind and hands should be kept busy, because if they are not, you are easily bored. Affable, friendly, and outgoing, social activity is a necessity, and you are a congenial companion who is always sought out for parties, fun and games. Curious by nature, you may be the eternal student, especially if Mercury is in the 9th house. *Dress designer Gilbert Adrian △ , consumer advocate Ralph Nader ＊.*

Mercury square / opposition / inconjunct Ascendant   Though you have a need to communicate, you can be ego-oriented to the point that others resent your authoritarian attitudes and you must learn the art of conversational compromise so as not to turn others off. Often, you are a non-stop talker who needs the center of the stage to feel secure in a social or business situation. You want the stimulation of give-and-take with other people, but be sure that it is not all give and no take! You like to work with your hands and your mind, and may be a good writer. Nervousness may have to be handled, especially with the inconjunct. You are easily caught up in rumor and gossip, often without realizing it, and may find that you alienate others with your critical remarks even though you do not mean them hurtfully. Most of all, you want to be noticed for your mental acuity. *Lt. William Calley of Mi Lai □ , authors Hermann Hesse ℰ , and Charles Dickens ㅈ .*

Mercury conjunct Midheaven   Your sense of ego develops in direct proportion to your ability to communicate your thoughts and ideas to the world at large. A natural actor, teacher or politician, unless Mercury has very challenging aspects, it is easy for you to stand up and make yourself heard. Mentally attuned to the public and its needs, you naturally do well in any field that involves communicating your ideas and opinions. Unless Mercury is in one of the Earth signs, you must learn to cultivate stick-to-it-iveness or with your mercurial approach to so many subjects you may come across as shallow and vacillating. Often there is a pronounced sense of humor that you have a need to share with others. *Comedians Lenny Bruce and Red Skelton.*

Mercury trine / sextile Midheaven   There is an ease and flow to your conversational abilities and work habits that draws others to you. Often, your advice is sought after and heeded, because you seem to know and understand what motivates others. You are usually attracted to your life's work early and find it easy to get the proper education to see it through. The relationship with your parents is almost always harmonious, and they help you in your efforts to establish yourself in your professional field, whatever it is—law, politics, writing, art, crafts. Study comes easily to you and you enjoy learning, books and any mental challenge. *Senator Charles Percy △ , writer Maurice Maeterlinck ✳ .*

Mercury square / opposition / inconjunct Midheaven These aspects do not detract from your mental ability, but you may at times find it difficult to put your thoughts into words, at least words that others understand. There is a tendency to get so wrapped up in your own thoughts, words and ideas that you forget that others need to express themselves also. You can't have a good argument if you won't let the other fellow get a word in edgewise. With the square, there is often an inherent shyness in front of the public; you're plenty vocal in private but have trouble when in the limelight. However, this is usually overcome with maturity and you go on to function very well on stage. Nervous tension often causes you to blurt things out without thinking them out first - especially with the inconjunct. Tact and diplomacy have to be actively worked on; they are not second nature to you. *Singer Pearl Bailey □ , labor leader John L. Lewis ♂ , trumpeter Louis Armstrong ⊼ .*

* * * *

Venus conjunct Ascendant Venus here usually adds charm, sociability, and good looks, but it can also bring self-indulgence which may cause health problems if it has challenging aspects, especially aspects involving Jupiter, Uranus and Pluto. Witty, with an everpresent sense of humor, you are able to attract and influence other people because you are so pleasant, such a good conversationalist, and so sincere in your approach. Often you have dimples, a cleft in your chin, and a sweet tooth. You are noted for your good taste in dress and can be known as a dandy or a clothes horse. Sociable and outgoing, you are the life of any party, and probably the most popular person around. If Venus is in your 12th house, you could be a bit shy, but usually your need for social give-and-take takes precedence and you come across as friendly, accommodating and personable. *Writer Jean Cocteau, actor Ronald Colman.*

Venus trine / sextile Ascendant You are talented, creative, and perhaps musical. Your friends, siblings and children mean a lot to you, and you are on good terms with most of the people in your sphere. Charming and friendly, you are a good host - one who goes way out for your guests. Agreeable and pleasure-loving, you'd rather play than work. You like to make a good impression on others, and this usually comes easily to you, as do most other things in life. All of this ease and affability may cause you to be a bit lazy, which is the curse of all good Venus aspects. Artistic musical talent abounds with this aspect, especially if Venus is in the 3rd or 5th house. *UN secretary Trygve Lie △ , Beatle/musician Paul McCartney *.*

Venus square / opposition / inconjunct Ascendant These aspects seem to give grace, agility and an ease of movement that serves you well in any sporting endeavors. You may have an indulgent parent if Venus squares from the 4th or 10th house. If it opposes from the 6th, or if it inconjuncts, there may be health problems centering in the kidney area or excessive weight could present a challenge. You make a good impression on others and are at your best working with people. You tend to win others over by turning on the charm, yet this isn't really necessary since when you are your natural self, people are drawn to you like a magnet. Partnership is important to you, and unless Venus has very challenging aspects, marriage should prove happy and rewarding. You tend to attract people to you who want to take care of you, and if improperly used, these aspects could make you too dependent upon others. Like all Venus aspects, these give creative, artistic and musical talent. *Actor Rory Calhoun □ , boxer Max Baer ♂ , baseball star Henry Aaron π .*

Venus conjunct Midheaven Your ego is directly tied to your appearance, and it is important to you to appear successful and attractive to the public. If Venus is in the 10th house, you are probably involved in a career where art, acting, or beauty are paramount. There can be a Pollyanna attitude that accompanies this Venus aspect—the idea that life is beautiful, life is wonderful, and that one doesn't have to work to succeed. This is especially true if Venus has many trines and sextiles. Yet, you want to be somebody, you like people, and generally get along well with them. Thus, you could do well in public relations or the entertainment field. *Actress Loretta Young, blind musician Jose Feliciano.*

Venus trine / sextile Midheaven Since you are affable, social and appealing, others are drawn to you, and you have many pleasant and friendly relationships. You go out of your way to be agreeable, and avoid conflict with others; you are well thought of in all community and career contacts, and usually have little trouble in getting ahead in life. Your parents are supportive, as are any brothers and sisters, and you have a harmonious home and business life. If other areas of your chart indicate it, this can be an aspect of artistic ability. Beauty, in and of itself, is very important to you. *Composer Anton Bruckner △ , drug experimenter Timothy Leary *.*

Venus square / opposition / inconjunct Midheaven: Giving and receiving love is so vital to you that you are liable to compromise your own innate sense of propriety for the sake of popularity. You are warm and loving, and you have a strong artistic and creative drive, but often fear that others won't accept you for yourself. Thus, you go out of your way to be helpful and supportive to others to gain the recognition that is so important to you. You have a warm and loving relationship with your family and partner, and your home is tastefully decorated and furnished. Social acceptance is necessary to your well being and is usually assured unless Venus is poorly placed. If Venus is inconjunct from the 5th house, there may be a career change - from one creative field to another. *Psychic Peter Hurkos* □ , *actor James Dean* ℰ , *scientist Louis Pasteur* ⊼ .

* * * *

Mars conjunct Ascendant Self-reliant, daring and adventurous, you rush in where angels fear to tread and willingly take on any challenge. Unless Mars is in a passive sign (such as Cancer or Pisces) and has few challenging aspects, nothing daunts you, and you are capable of great physical effort. With or without challenging aspects, and regardless of sign, you have a quick tongue and a big mouth. If these qualities are put to positive use, you'll do well in any field requiring glibness and ease of expression, such as law, acting, politics or the ministry. Strongly self-oriented, you find cooperation with others difficult, if not downright impossible. So, naturally you work by yourself and have to learn to master irritability and quarrelsomeness. Sports should attract you, and if you are not actively engaged in some sports career, you are an avid fan and Sunday participant. If Mars is in the 12th house, some of the above-mentioned qualities are hidden or inner-directed in your early years, but sooner or later you will express them outwardly. *Evangelist Billy Sunday, actor Derek Jacobi.*

Mars trine / sextile Ascendant Strong willed, independent and self-assertive, you are not afraid to let your voice be heard, and you express your ideas and thoughts positively. Your creativity finds outlets in travel (especially with Mars in the 3rd or 9th houses) or sports (with Mars in the 5th house), and you can be quite innovative in these areas. Never one to turn down a challenge, you throw yourself wholeheartedly into all your affairs. Your friends are predominantly male and you enjoy creating a macho image even if you're a woman. You do not like others to make demands on you, but will willingly give of yourself in most situations. *Athlete Bob Mathias* △ , *actress Mary Martin* ✳ .

Mars square / opposition / inconjunct Ascendant These are among the zodiac's most driving aspects. But you must learn to channel the drive into productive areas and not scatter your energies to the winds. Sometimes, your intensity can cause physical problems, such as a nervous stomach or ulcers, especially if Mars is in the 4th or 6th houses. Often there is a hot temper to be handled with Mars placed in the 3rd or 10th houses. When properly used, Mars here makes you capable of great output, both physically and mentally, and you can work longer hours with less rest than most people. Frequently though, you sacrifice tact and diplomacy for disputes and disagreements as you are very competitive and always willing to rise to any challenge. You often attract people who will give you a bad time, but that's all right with you because these are the only people you respect. It is important for you to learn the art of compromise so that you can put your energy together with the energy of others and accomplish great goals. *Composer George Bizet*□, *transsexual Christine Jorgenson* ♂ , *entertainer Sammy Davis, Jr.* ⊼ .

Mars conjunct Midheaven   Your drive and energy ideally are career oriented. You strive for recognition of your achievements and yours is a do or die effort. Determined, you know exactly what you want to accomplish and you approach your goals with direct action. As you forge ahead, you brook no interference, and if confronted, it is not easy for you to back down gracefully. Yours is a domineering and forceful personality, and it would be nice (but highly unlikely unless Mars has some trines and sextiles) if you learned to deal with others graciously and without anger. You focus on a career where you can gain a position of leadership or authority, and you often succeed in your own business. *Industrialist Henry Ford, General Douglas MacArthur.*

Mars trine / sextile Midheaven   You have a gift of gab and can usually talk yourself into or out of any situation. Your drive and energy are productively channeled and you are capable of a prodigious amount of effort. Strong-willed and individualistic, you throw yourself into things with wholehearted enthusiasm. You state your ideas very positively, and generally others accept your leadership with a minimum of static. Independent and outgoing, you are easy to get along with as long as others understand and respect your enthusiastic and exuberant approach to life. *Actor Errol Flynn* △, *financier Bernard Baruch* ✳ .

Mars square / opposition / inconjunct Midheaven   Forceful and dominant, you achieve your goals at any cost, overcoming obstacles, even enjoying pitting yourself against great odds. Nothing stops you in your efforts to get ahead, at least not for long. Undaunted is a good word for you. If Mars is in the 7th house, you may be controversial, but you seem to thrive on adversity, so this seldom bothers you. People may turn away from you because you come on so strong, and it would be wise for you to try to implement a little tact and diplomacy in your dealings with others. One area of difficulty is your attitude toward authority; this could stem from a childhood where you felt that a parent tried to dominate you. Once your security has been established, the strong need to override others and their ideas is more easily handled and you become mellower. *Chancellor Konrad Adenauer* □ , *writer Jack Kerouac* ♂ , *nutritionist Adelle Davis* ⊼ .

* * * *

Jupiter conjunct Ascendant   You are outgoing, friendly and generous, at least on the surface. Religion or philosophy plays a large role in your life, and you are usually quite broadminded and willing to give others the benefit of the doubt. However, if Jupiter has challenging aspects, you may be quite vocally opinionated and even bigoted. Often the sports field attracts you, and you excel in anything that requires physical prowess. You are helpful to others and very tolerant as long as people respect your moral and ethical standards.

Fond of travel and the outdoors, you try to be open to any suggestions and ideas that will broaden your horizon. If Jupiter is in the 12th house, you are not quite as outgoing, but you are very fortunate and always seem to be looked upon by others as lucky. Sometimes, Jupiter in the 1st house can give a weight problem. *Sports announcer Howard Cosell, director Dino DeLaurentiis.*

Jupiter trine / sextile Ascendant   People are important to you, and with your charm and outgoing personality, you have no trouble attracting them. Friends play an important role in your life and often help you to achieve your goals. Humorous, fun-loving and gregarious, you enjoy life to the fullest and are often the life of the party. Take care not to be too glib and surface-skimming, enjoying only the fun and games and never realizing your potential for religion, law, philosophy and other fields of learning. Your motto might well be "Don't fence me in", as travel is your keyword; you like to be constantly on the move. Often, you have great success in a foreign country. *Emcee David Frost △ , actress Julie Andrews * .*

Jupiter square / opposition / inconjunct Ascendant   You have a tendency to dramatize and enlarge on everyday occurrences; properly channeled, you can use this ability to write or act. Other people are important in your life scheme, but you have a need to dominate in partnership and social situations. You will find that in order to mature in relationships, you will have to learn the art of compromise and the need to see more than your own viewpoint. Your parents play a vital role in shaping your moral and ethical outlook and it is likely that you try hard to live up to their image and expectations. You are a very restless person, both mentally and physically, and it is imperative that you have an adequate outlet that will channel this energy productively. *Actors Desi Arnaz, Jr. □ and Omar Sharif ♂ , writer Faith Baldwin ⊼ .*

Jupiter conjunct Midheaven   You come across as a very moral and upstanding citizen. Your public image is important to you, and even though you are ambitious and want to get ahead, you will never jeopardize your standing in the community in order to do so. Religion may play a crucial role in your life, and your career will undoubtedly involve travel and sports. If Jupiter is in the 9th house, you may find teaching or the legal field an excellent outlet for your interest in law, order and ethics. If Jupiter is in the 10th house, your career will be aided by friends or a parent. *Tennis star Arthur Ashe, senator Robert F. Kennedy.*

Jupiter trine / sextile Midheaven   Luck is your keyword, and friends and relatives are most supportive to you in all phases of your life. You get along easily with your fellow workers, superiors, and all authority figures because of your seemingly easy personality and willingness to learn. You never come across to others as being pushy or threatening. However, unless there are strong Saturn aspects, you may be a bit lazy in pursuing your ambitions and tend to coast along. Sports, social work, law, publishing and teaching are all fields that you find appealing, and success in your field, (whatever it is), comes readily to you. *Chief Justice Earl Warren* △ *, actor Ryan O'Neal* ✳ .

Jupiter square / opposition / inconjunct Midheaven   You are very ambitious for material reward and feel that a good day's work is worth a good day's pay. You are quite energetic and want to express yourself creatively. Thus you do well in the entertainment or sports fields as well as in the usual Jupiterian occupations. Politics may appeal to you, and you can achieve much popularity; however, you must watch that you do not alienate others with your outspoken and blunt approach and opinions. Home and family are precious to you, and if Jupiter is in the 4th house, your home will be large, sumptious, surrounded by a lot of land and may even be on a hill. You cannot stand to be hemmed in, physically or emotionally, and you may tend to avoid close relationships because of this feeling. *Actor Marlon Brando* □ *, President Abe Lincoln* ♂ *, singer Cher* ⊼ .

* * * *

Saturn conjunct Ascendant   Saturn here adds a note of gravity to the personality. Somewhat somber and often slow to smile or laugh (especially as a youngster), you are a responsible and dependable type of person whom others know to be stable and steady. You have good bone structure, are often photogenic, and this placement may make you quite petite, slender or rawboned. Wherever Saturn is, it limits, and when near the Ascendant it may limit your physical size. With challenging aspects, your health may be problematical and your early childhood even perilous. But once the first seven years are past, your health improves and you look forward to a long life. Unless Venus, Mercury or the Sun is well placed, you may be quite pessimistic, seeing only the dark side of things and feeling that life is difficult and your path is to work hard. Serious, you are older than your years when young, but with flowing aspects, you learn to relax, enjoy life, and appear to grow younger as you get older. *Writer Albert Camus, haut couture designer Coco Chanel.*

Saturn trine/sextile Ascendant   Steady and dedicated, you are a hard worker. Serious in outlook, you handle responsibility well, and others look to you for leadership. Loyal and reliable, other people know that they can depend on your sense of realism to get things done. Mainly attracted to anything that is useful and disciplined, you are good at mathematics and music. You tend to disdain anything trivial or purely decorative. Your friends are important to you, especially if Saturn is in the 3rd or 11th houses, but you are choosy and prefer to have one or two good friends rather than dealing with groups. You have a tendency to be pedantic and stick too much to the tried and true, rather than venture into the new and different. This is somewhat alleviated if Uranus is strong. *Singer Glen Campbell* △ *, evangelist Billy Graham* ✳ .

Saturn square / opposition / inconjunct Ascendant   "Life is serious; life is earnest" could well be your motto. It is not easy for you to relax and enjoy, to reach out to others, to love and be loved. This is not to say that you do not experience emotion - you do, but you feel so guilty in doing so that you cover up and appear quite withdrawn, cool and even haughty. An achiever, work is very important to you and it comes first in your scheme of things. When given a great deal of emotional support, you can overcome your deep-seated tendency to hide your feelings. It is important that you learn to like yourself so that you will know that you are worthy of being loved by others. You often cover your feelings of insecurity by coming on as a clown or comedian, poking fun at yourself. This placement may indicate health problems that can be handled by paying attention to proper diet and a healthy mental attitude. You are drawn to older people, especially with the opposition, as you feel more comfortable with them. Relationships at best are not easy for you, and with very challenging aspects to Saturn you could be a recluse, shunning all types of contact with others. *Actor Charles Bronson □ , scientist Rachel Carson ♂ , rock star Mick Jagger ⚹ .*

Saturn conjunct Midheaven   Ambition is your keyword; you take on responsibility at an early age and tend to thrive on it. Discipline seems to come from within; early in life you learn how to pace yourself. Whether you succeed or fail stems largely from how you learn to handle success or failure as a young person. At your first Saturn return (at approximately age 29), the events it brings and how you handle them will be a strong indicator of how you will react to life's experiences from then on. You must learn to deal with authority. Before you can lead successfully, you must learn to follow. Whatever you do, others will be watching you; like it or not, you will serve as an example to them - for good or bad. *Musician Henry Mancini, Governor Jerry Brown.*

Saturn trine / sextile Midheaven   Patient and painstaking, you do things in a systematic way, taking good care of your possessions and proceeding through life with method and organization. If Saturn is in the 3rd or 11th houses, you may be somewhat of a loner because you are so dedicated to achieving your goals that you don't have much time for social activity. You know inherently that success comes with hard work, and you are more than willing to do your share. Indefatigable, you are a true seeker. It is more important to you to be right than popular. Always respectful of authority, because of your dependable and mature attitudes, you can become a figure of authority yourself. *Scientist Thomas Huxley △ , impresario Rudolf Bing ⚹ .*

Saturn square / opposition / inconjunct Midheaven   You have a tendency to withdraw from others; cooperation, especially on a one-to-one basis, doesn't come easily to you. You prefer to do only your own thing. There is a morose side to your nature; you feel that no one cares about you and that life is difficult, and at times, not even worthwhile. You must learn that these feelings come from within yourself and are not generated by outside circumstances. It may be that you have a very dominating parent (square) or partner (opposition), but this can be dealt with when you approach the problem with maturity and common sense. It is difficult for you to give and receive love unless Saturn has some flowing aspects to it; often you must deal with loneliness and depression. However, support comes from older people, and as you learn to deal with your inner conflicts, with poise and equanimity, you build up your ego and function well in any position where high standards, morality and diligence are needed and admired. *Director Federico Fellini □ , Secretary of Navy James Forrestal ☍ , actor David Carradine ⋊ .*

* * * *

Uranus conjunct Ascendant   You always feel different from everyone else, or at least you want to be unique in some special way. All of your life you will feel that you march to the beat of a different drummer. Always a little ahead of your time, you are interested in anything the least bit avant garde or unconventional. Restless and sometimes nervous (depending upon the aspects to Uranus), as a youngster you were the class clown and cut-up; anything to avoid the humdrum of everyday life. You feel a need to always be on the go. Try to channel your electric energy into productive areas; inattention to details and carelessness will lead you into unsatisfactory behavior patterns. Though this aspect makes you rebellious, it also gives a strong creative and inventive streak, which when positively applied borders on genius. *Composer George Gershwin, actor John Travolta.*

Uranus trine / sextile Ascendant   These aspects make it easy for you to stand out in your field, to be head and shoulders above your competitors. Independent and excitable, at an early age you demanded the right to be yourself, to follow your own dictates, and when given this opportunity, you can be extraordinarily successful. You can be so outspoken that you offend others, but because of your agile mind, unique ideas and an ability for leadership, they don't stay angry with you for long. You are drawn to original and unusual friends and acquaintances, and you constantly need change. In fact, life would seem boring to you if you did not frequently find it in an uproar. *Writer Truman Capote △ , football player O.J. Simpson ✳ .*

Uranus   square / opposition / inconjunct   Ascendant   You are rebellious and confident that you can go your own way, do your own thing and still be accepted by the world around you. When Uranus or the Ascendant has some helpful aspects, this is often true, and you are regarded as a leader in your sphere. Because you are so freedom-loving, almost to the point of eccentricity, you find it difficult to relate to other people; all of your relationships are challenging, to say the least. If others choose not to accept and follow you, you (a leader in every sense of the word) go blithely on your way doing your own thing anyway. The square manifests as rebellion against parents and the status quo of your youth, and you frequently leave home early to pursue your own dreams. The opposition brings difficulties with partners (marital or business) and challenges you to learn the lesson of cooperation, if Uranus is in the 7th house. If it is in the 6th house, the energies will manifest in health and work situations. The inconjunct brings great physical and emotional strain and needs to be channeled into a truly creative or inventive endeavor or the physical body will suffer. *Boxing great Muhammad Ali □ , actress Lucille Ball ♂ , Princess Caroline of Monaco ⊼ .*

Uranus conjunct Midheaven   This aspect usually brings you before the public in an unusual way. You are viewed as the total individualist and you rarely heed any pressures to conform to society's demands. Often you choose an out-of-the-ordinary career field, but if you do choose a mundane one, your approach to it is novel and unique. Sometimes you have a parent whom you feel to be different, and as a child you find this a difficult situation to handle. However, you grew up knowing that you can break the rules and get away with it because of the example you have before you. You are often attracted to a career field in the media, electronics or computers. *Writer Vance Packard, comedian Tom Smothers.*

Uranus trine / sextile Midheaven   You'll tend to choose a progressive field when seeking a career - something out of the ordinary, scientific, or technical in which you can demonstrate your qualities of leadership and inventiveness. Never one to observe or be held back by tradition, you may well develop an interest in the occult, astrology or some strange "ism" or philosophy. You find your own company stimulating, and though you relate well to others, often you like to go off by yourself and enjoy life at your own pace in your own way. Rarely are you tied to material possessions as you feel these bind you to a conventional life style (and this is certainly not for you). You thrive on excitement and are constantly in pursuit of the new and different. *Composer Anton Bruckner △ , writer Victor Hugo * .*

Uranus   square / opposition / inconjunct   Midheaven   Eccentric, individualistic and very excitable, you can create a stir wherever you go. You are happiest when you can keep those around you off balance and wondering what unusual thing you will do next. Your method of communication is erratic, to say the least, and you enjoy shocking others with unacceptable language and insulting remarks. Some of your outrageous behavior may be due to a difficult relationship with one or both of your parents (especially with the opposition). Your total disregard for convention and public acceptance may cause you to be very rebellious, going your own way without regard for what others say or think. Because of your waywardness, it will not be easy for you to get and keep a job until you learn to channel Uranus' erratic energy into productive areas that encompass the scientific, technical, occult or astrological fields. *White House Chief of Staff H. R. Haldeman □ , writer Ernest Hemingway ♂, heiress Christina Onassis ⊼ .*

* * * *

Neptune conjunct Ascendant You view life idealistically and romantically, almost to the point of being unrealistic, especially if the conjunction has only flowing aspects. With squares and oppositions to it, you are still aesthetic in your approach and willing to see only the best in others; however, you are also somewhat more realistic and down to earth. Often musical, artistic and creative, you need to develop an outlet for these talents or you tend to drift aimlessly and dreamily through life, eternally seeking your own utopia where everyone is as they appear and life makes no challenges or demands. You depend a great deal on other people's reactions to you; you rarely act until you can see how your actions will affect those around you. At your best, you are perceptive and intuitive; at your worst, deceptive and unreliable. *Activist Jerry Rubin, musician Cat Stevens.*

Neptune trine / sextile Ascendant You are able to weave a web of illusion; therefore, acting, writing, politics and law are all areas where you can excel. Your sensitivity serves you well in dealing with others, and you are often able to tune in to their needs and expectations. Intuitive and perceptive, you instinctively know what the public will accept, so you do well in any field relating to sales or public relations. Your imagination is always active and you are very creative, if not in the arts then surely in handicrafts. You should rely heavily on your hunches because they come from a powerful source within your subconscious; when you've learned to listen to your still, small voice, you will know that you are on the right track. *Writer James Joyce △ , feminist Gloria Steinem ✳ .*

Neptune square / opposition / inconjunct Ascendant These aspects give just as much creative and inspirational ability as do the trines and sextiles; they just require a little more effort on your part to make them productive. You must learn to be direct and straightforward, rather than evasive and manipulative. When you proceed directly to your point, others listen and are charmed by your way with words and inspirational approach. However, if you fantasize, exaggerate and blow things out of proportion, you alienate those around you and have difficulty in all relationships because others find it hard to believe in and trust you. With the inconjunct, you should be very careful with drugs and alcohol; you are very susceptible to any foreign substances that you may take into your body. With the opposition, you are often easily deceived and misled and must learn not to take on other's problems. This tendency, along with a deep-seated need to be needed can make you an easy mark for anyone who is looking for someone to unload all their problems on. You must take care not to be victimized while at the same time you must avoid victimizing others. *Magician Harry Houdini □ , writer Erich Remarque ♂ , singer Johnny Cash ⋌ .*

Neptune conjunct Midheaven Glamor is your keyword. Others see you as compelling, charismatic. A career in films, TV, photography, oil or shipping would be in keeping with your image. Sensitive to everything around you, you soak up experience like a sponge, and often your sensitivity to impressions leads you to a career in the writing field. You must avoid becoming depressed when things do not go your way. You may try many vocations before settling down in one that brings the spiritual rewards which are so important to you. Often you have psychic or intuitive ability, and if you do not use this in a public career at least it serves as a private guide. *Predictor Criswell, actor Tyrone Power.*

Neptune trine / sextile Midheaven   Passive and peaceloving, you are idealistic in your view of the world, and also very generous and sharing in your relationships with others. Animals and people in need attract you; there is nothing you won't do to help your fellow man. Creed, color, race and religion mean nothing to you in your dealings with the public; you are truly a world citizen. However, you do take on the feelings and vibrations of those you associate with, so it is important that you try to surround yourself with positive and outgoing, rather than negative and depressed, companions. Your feelings, somewhat shy and retiring until you know you can trust someone, are easily hurt. You are often the victim of unintentional slights. *Princess Margaret of England △ , President Harry Truman ✶ .*

Neptune square / opposition / inconjunct Midheaven   It is hard for you to face up to your mistakes because of your insecurity and self doubt. Your early years may have been undermined by a poor relationship with one or both of your parents who may have been ill, weak or alcoholic. You must always work to build up your own self-image; until you can see something in yourself to love, others will find it difficult, if not impossible, to find you worthy of attention and affection. You tend to scatter yourself in many directions and need early in life to define your career aims or you may flounder around indefinitely and never really establish yourself in a job field. Perceptive and intuitive, and even religious if your background indicates it, you may find great peace of mind in the pursuit of an idealistic philosophy. *Attorney General John Mitchell □ , composer Frederic Chopin ♂ , actress Judy Garland ⊼ .*

* * * *

Pluto conjunct Ascendant   This is a powerful aspect for good or bad, giving intense powers of concentration and a need to exercise your will and power over others. Unless you use this aspect positively, it can cause you problems because it is hard for you to take life lightly. You throw yourself headlong into everything you do and suffer the consequences later. Intensely emotional, you dramatize anything that happens to you, sometimes out of all proportion, and when so involved, you can be irritable, touchy, and even irrational. When positively used, this aspect gives great physical stamina, the drive to see things through, and the ability to control almost any situation. Your competitiveness causes you to automatically dominate most relationships and so you tend to attract rather weak people to you or face those with strong personalities in head-to-head competition and confrontation. *Actors Jack Nicholson and Christopher Reeve.*

Pluto trine / sextile Ascendant   You enter into all relationships with great intensity, and many of your friendships have a lasting influence on your life. People are drawn to you because of your strength and positive attitude. You are most curious about what makes other people tick and are always involved in psychological probing. You take life seriously, are a leader and promoter, and once your mind is made up about anything, you rarely change your viewpoint. You need to reform and regenerate those around you, and most of the time this is done in a positive and productive way. Others look to you for guidance and direction and you rarely let them down. *EST founder Werner Erhardt △ , entertainer Maurice Chevalier * .*

Pluto   square / opposition / inconjunct   Ascendant   A powerful personality, you have much to give and much to share, but you must find a positive way to do it. Your tendency is to run roughshod over others, to inflict your will on them whether or not they are receptive. Your life seems to be a series of crises (especially with the inconjunct), but you enjoy the stimulation of excitement and eventually learn to roll with the punches, so that when things go too smoothly you become bored and go out of your way to stir things up, often by trying to manipulate others for your own ends. Generally, when you can't get along with other people, instead of seeing that you are partly to blame, you feel that everything is their fault and that they are not making an effort to see your side of things. Compulsive behavior must constantly be dealt with; you should avoid acquaintances who will lead you down the garden path. *Astronomer Johannes Kepler □ , blind writer Helen Keller ☌ , scientist Louis Pasteur ⊼ .*

Pluto conjunct Midheaven   You need to be a leader. It is imperative to you that you be out in front of the parade. Not one to take a backseat to anyone, even if no one follows, you go your own way - never looking back and rarely compromising. One of your parents has a great deal of influence upon you, and the two of you have an intense relationship. This may be a good and but if the conjunction has challenging aspects often this parent will try to dominate you to your detriment. Sometime in your life there will be an important change of direction, often occurring when you are least aware of it and you are able to view it only in retrospect. *Actor Sidney Poitier, composer Igor Stravinsky.*

Pluto   trine / sextile   Midheaven   Again the leadership ability is apparent, but it is softer in effect and more easily accepted by those with whom you come into contact. You are ambitious with a desire to succeed and will do well in occupations where you can give guidance or advice. Usually you'll decide upon your career direction early in life and often there is help from a friend in this area. Since you are introspective and adept at financial manipulation, the practice of law and business management are the professions where you will feel comfortable and can establish a good reputation. Surprisingly, these aspects often signify success in the music fields. *Violin virtuoso Yehudi Menuhin △, musician Herb Alpert ＊.*

Pluto   square / opposition / inconjunct   Midheaven You are a powerful person in your field, but it takes time, energy and dedication for you to achieve the goals you have set your sights on. Often you meet defeat on your way to success, only to rise from the ashes, Phoenix-like, to continue on your way. You are not above a bit of subterfuge or manipulation to get your own way. Until you learn the art of compromise and giving in to others' wishes, you will find it difficult to maintain good give-and-take relationships. Your worst fault is riding roughshod over other people to get to where you are going and you may find that when you do get to the top it is not the comfortable pinnacle you expected. *Playboy founder Hugh Hefner □ , boxing champion Joe Louis ♂ , architect Frank Lloyd Wright ⊼ .*

＊ ＊ ＊ ＊

To illustrate the application of our keywords, let's look at Walt Disney's horoscope again. We are purposely staying with the same chart since by now you should have a pretty good idea of the important facets in his horoscope. You should be able to discriminate and judge as to which words can, and which ones cannot, apply. Walt Disney has an inconjunct from Mercury to the Midheaven. Look again at the complete text we've given for this aspect; "Difficulty in wording thoughts so that others can understand them . . .". We've heard that as a youth Walt Disney had a bit of this problem, which is one of the reasons he adored the fantasy world. But then he also has the inconjuct from Mercury to Neptune, which (being part of a yod) helped him express artistically through Neptune, making words or thoughts less important than the visual image. "Too wrapped up to let others talk or listen to them...", a stellium in Capricorn gives much discipline, and so does a Virgo Ascendant. Even if the tendency was there, he surely overcame it early. The same reasoning would apply to the statement: "Nervous tension makes you blurt out things."

How about the sextile of Mercury to the Ascendant? "Creative, a need to express artistically, especially with Mercury in the 3rd or 5th houses; self-expression is easy, interested in everything and everyone around". Most of this applies and gets double confirmation by Disney's Sun also in the 3rd house of expression and Neptune, highest in the chart at 0° (see Lesson 18 - Critical Degrees). "Mental activities and games attract, and mind and hands should be kept busy to avoid boredom." This chart is artistic and business-oriented as opposed to mental or intellectual; therefore, we would say that he will be happy when expressing artistically (using his hands of course), combining this with good business whenever possible, and using his idealism in a practical way, rather than engaging in mental games. (Don't forget the Capricorn stellium).

"Friendly, outgoing, socially liked, etc . . ." This applies also, but again within reason. Disney equates to a Capricorn signature. He does have a Virgo Ascendant and quite a few squares to his Moon in the 1st house. Moon in Libra in the 1st house confirms someone who can be socially adept, and whose company others will enjoy. However, all the squares may challenge him to do more than just be sociable; they have to produce some results. He may act charming but not always feel like it or indeed really enjoy it. Therefore, whatever the sextile to the Ascendant may indicate the rest of the horoscope has to be kept in mind too!

Review Question: Delineate Walt Disney's Venus trine the Ascendant, and his Neptune and Pluto conjunct the Midheaven. You'll find our delineation in the Appendix on page 246.

QUIZ FOR PART TWO

ANSWER EACH QUESTION TRUE ("T") OR FALSE ("F"). Circle the correct letter. Then check your answers in the Appendix on page 247.

1. Chart patterns are the most important part of delineation.   T   F

2. A bowl pattern has all ten planets within 180°.   T   F

3. A locomotive Pattern must have at least an empty square   T   F

4. If there is a mutual reception, you can have a final dispositor.   T   F

5. A retrograde planet acts in a harmful or debilitating way.   T   F

6. The Sun and Moon never appear to be retrograde.   T   F

7. An interception can occur in any horoscope.   T   F

8. If one house has an intercepted sign, so does the opposite house.   T   F

9. The activities of the two houses that share the same sign are linked together in some way.   T   F

10. The North Node is known as "The Dragon's Tail".   T   F

11. The South Node is where we "give out".   T   F

12. If Venus is in Libra, and Mars is in Aries, these planets are said to be in mutual reception.   T   F

13. A planet that is a final dispositor must be dignified.   T   F

14. 22° Taurus is in the second decanate.   T   F

15. 12° Virgo is in the Capricorn dwad.   T   F

16. If the chart ruler is in the 9th house, there is an interest in friends and social activities.   T   F

17. If the element air is missing in the chart, this person may have a totally different way of communicating.   T   F

18. If the fixed quality is missing, this person has the ability to see things through and is steady and stable.   T   F

19. A person having no planets in angular houses is like a person with no mutable planets.   T   F

20. An unaspected planet is one with no major aspects to it.   T   F

21. Signs on the house cusps are a clue to how this person reacts to the activities of that particular house.   T   F

Part Three

Introduction

Steps to Give You Further Insight

In this part of the book we will introduce you to what are often referred to as goodies, and in a way, that is what they are—certain points, concepts and degrees that are not truly necessary in order to interpret a chart; however, all of them will help to give you further insight into the person you are dealing with. As you progress in Astrology, you will read about many other ways to gain insight. Some may be valid, some helpful, while others may prove to be a waste of time. However, don't discard them before you've tried them.

Astrology is a very personal approach to the individual's psyche, personality and makeup. You, the astrologer, are doing the interpreting, and therefore what works for you, and what helps you, is the only important point.

Once you have learned the basic ABC's of Astrology, which we have taught you in both Volume One and in the first two parts of this book, the rest becomes the icing on the cake—you can do an excellent job without this icing, but never turn down an additional tool that might help you to tune in to some of the hidden or subconscious areas of a human being.

Over the last sixteen years we have tried hundreds of so-called new approaches. Most of them are old and are being recycled. Usually, we get terribly excited over them at first. Then, as we put them into practice, we calm down, and after a year or so of experimentation we decide that we can do as well and sometimes better without them. But, once in awhile, we come across something truly valuable, and that, of course, we retain and incorporate into our teaching and utilize with our clients.

This same attitude should be used as you study Part Three. What we shall give you here are some very basic goodies used by many astrologers. Try them all. Use them for a year, and then if you find you don't need them—discard them.

Lesson 16
Planets in Oriental Appearance, the Prenatal Eclipse, the Vertex

Planets in Oriental Appearance

Any planet that rises before the Sun is said to be in oriental appearance—the word orient signifying East or rising. If, for example, your Sun is at 15° Gemini, the planet just rising before that degree in Gemini, or even Taurus, would be in oriental appearance, having risen or ascended on your birth date just prior to the Sun.

Here again, we are not talking of an interpretive must, but of an additional blend or nuance that gives us insight into some of the psychological or motivational needs of an individual. This is a method handed down to us by the ancients, and it should not be discontinued or ignored because it is old. It's easy enough to find in any horoscope. In Hermann Hesse's chart on page 31 for example, the Sun is at 10° Cancer 52', and the first planet that rose before his Sun was Mercury at 22° Gemini 40' in the 7th house.

A planet in oriental appearance is considered to be stronger than it might appear at first glance, as if the rays of the Sun soon to rise are already illuminating it and giving it strength and light. The occidental planet, which rises *after* the Sun, does not get that extra strength and light; it is following the Sun and, of course, the rising Sun sheds more light than the setting Sun. This is similar to the principle applied in aspecting—is the aspect approaching or separating? The approaching aspect always carries more strength than the separating aspect.

Since in Hermann Hesse's horoscope Mercury has risen before the Sun, all

Mercurial principles are very important to Hesse. These prime motivators are clear thinking, writing ability, the need to use his mind, curiosity concerning what stimulates him and others from Mercury in Gemini's position in the 7th house.

In Walt Disney's horoscope on page 236 Mercury has also risen just prior to the Sun and is said to be in oriental appearance. His prime motivation would be based on all that Mercury stands for. Reason, logic and rational thinking would be important, as would also the need to communicate in a rather probing way (Mercury in Scorpio). In Disney's case this is quite significant since it brings his elevated Neptune out of the clouds onto solid ground. In other words, the Mercurial principle will be strong, regardless of how and where Mercury is placed within the chart.

Since nothing stands by itself in a delineation, be sure to determine carefully if other factors confirm this tendency - in which case the emphasis is that much stronger. If other factors deny this, then you will have to start blending, adding a nuance here and softening something there in order to understand the total picture.

Review Question: Please delineate Joan Sutherland's planet in oriental appearance. Our analysis can be found in the Appendix on page 247.

Eclipses

Astronomically speaking, there are two kinds of eclipses—solar and lunar. The lunar eclipse occurs when the Earth passes between the Sun and Moon and thereby deprives the Moon of its illumination temporarily; the solar eclipse puts the Moon between the Earth and the Sun, which cuts off the light of the Sun from the Earth, so that for a time we cannot see the Sun at all. A lunar eclipse can occur only at the time of a full Moon; a solar eclipse can occur only at the time of a new Moon. Both types of eclipses can occur only when the Sun and Moon are close to one or both of the lunar Nodes.

As you progress in Astrology, you will learn about the effects of eclipses as they occur every year in the heavens and how they affect your natal and progressed horoscope. At this point, however, we prefer that you find the eclipse that took place just prior to your birth—your pre-natal eclipse. It makes no difference whether it was a lunar or solar eclipse. For your information we have included a Table of Eclipses from the year 1900 to 2000. See page 211. Eclipses prior to 1900 can be found in most ephemerides for the years in question.

We suggest that you mark the degree of your pre-natal eclipse somewhere in your natal chart for future reference. In Farrah Fawcett's horoscope it took place in December 1946 at 16° Gemini, which falls in her 12th house. This degree, though not a planet, will always remain a sensitive point, and even more importantly, the house where this eclipse falls will be accentuated throughout the lifetime of the individual.

Some astrologers feel that if the eclipse is closer to the natal North Node, the life will be easier, if closer to the South Node, the person faces greater difficulties. We have tried to test and document this, but we cannot categorically state that we agree. We suggest you observe for yourself, and then draw your own conclusions. Robert Janksy's book "Interpreting the Eclipses" explores this subject in depth.

Hermann Hesse's pre-natal eclipse point is at 25° Pisces in his 3rd house, which emphasizes communication of any kind. Now you might say that with a stellium of planets in the 3rd house that is obvious anyway - and you are right, but this gives added confirmation, which we always look for. 25° Pisces also becomes a sensitive degree in Hesse's horoscope when touched off by the transits in the sky. This will be a subject for discussion in our intermediate lessons in another book.

Review Question: Find the pre-natal eclipse point in the charts of Walt Disney and Joan Sutherland. Briefly delineate the pre-natal eclipse point in Joan Sutherland's chart. Our answer will be found on Appendix page 248.

Solar and Lunar Eclipses

1900	MAY 28	14:57	S	06♊47
	JUN 13	3:28	L	21♐33
	NOV 22	7:22	S	29♏34
	DEC 6	10:26	L	13♊46
1901	MAY 3	18:30	L	12♏42
	MAY 18	5:28	S	26♉34
	OCT 27	15:15	L	03♉36
	NOV 11	7:18	S	18♏13
1902	APR 8	14:5	S	17♈48
	APR 22	18:52	L	01♏43
	MAY 7	22:34	S	16♉25
	OCT 17	6:3	L	22♈57
	OCT 31	7:60	S	06♏58
1903	MAR 29	2:5	S	07♈13
	APR 12	0:13	L	20♎53
	SEP 21	5:10	S	27♍02
	OCT 6	15:17	L	12♈08
1904	MAR 2	3:3	L	11♍16
	MAR 17	5:46	S	26♓13
	MAR 31	12:32	L	10♎15
	SEP 9	20:49	S	16♍43
	SEP 24	17:35	L	01♈07
1905	FEB 19	19:0	L	00♍34
	MAR 6	4:52	S	14♓58
	AUG 15	3:41	L	21♒42
	AUG 30	12:50	S	06♍27
1906	FEB 9	7:47	L	19♌41
	FEB 23	7:43	S	03♓48
	JUL 21	13:14	S	27♋50
	AUG 4	13:0	L	11♒13
	AUG 20	1:13	S	26♌06
1907	JAN 14	6:12	S	22♑57
	JAN 29	13:38	L	08♌28
	JUL 10	15:27	S	17♋12
	JUL 25	4:23	L	01♒01
1908	JAN 3	21:45	S	12♑08
	JAN 18	13:22	L	26♋58
	JUN 14	14:6	L	23♐11
	JUN 28	16:31	S	06♋32
	JUL 13	21:34	L	20♑54
	DEC 7	21:55	L	15♊32
	DEC 23	11:49	S	01♑17
1909	JUN 4	1:29	L	12♐49
	JUN 17	23:31	S	26♊05
	NOV 27	8:54	L	04♊31
	DEC 12	19:44	S	20♐11
1910	MAY 9	5:3	S	17♉41
	MAY 24	5:34	L	02♐08
	NOV 2	2:8	S	08♏47
	NOV 17	0:21	L	23♉45
1911	APR 28	22:16	S	07♉30
	MAY 13	5:56	L	21♏15
	OCT 22	3:54	S	27♎38
	NOV 6	15:36	L	13♉00
1912	APR 1	22:14	L	11♎54
	APR 17	12:3	S	27♈06
	SEP 26	11:45	L	03♈06
	OCT 10	14:0	S	16♎53
1913	MAR 22	11:58	L	01♎17
	APR 6	17:33	S	16♈19
	AUG 31	20:52	S	07♍49
	SEP 15	12:48	L	22♓05
	SEP 30	4:46	S	06♎25
1914	FEB 25	23:56	S	06♓33
	MAR 12	4:13	L	20♍42
	AUG 21	11:55	S	27♌34
	SEP 4	13:55	L	11♓08
1915	JAN 31	4:58	L	10♌24
	FEB 14	4:23	S	24♒24
	MAR 1	18:20	L	09♍59
	JUL 26	12:25	L	02♒34
	AUG 10	22:52	S	17♌12

	AUG	24	21:27	L	00♓30	1929	MAY	9	5:58	S	18♉07
1916	JAN	20	8:40	L	29♋04		MAY	23	12:37	L	01♐47
	FEB	3	16:22	S	13♒32		NOV	1	11:47	S	08♏35
	JUL	15	4:46	L	22♑24		NOV	17	0: 3	L	24♉04
	JUL	30	2:40	S	06♌35	1930	APR	13	5:59	L	22♎41
	DEC	24	20:46	S	02♑45		APR	28	19:27	S	07♉46
1917	JAN	8	7:45	L	17♋31		OCT	7	19: 7	L	13♈53
	JAN	23	7:29	S	02♒45		OCT	21	22: 4	S	27♎47
	JUN	19	13:16	S	27♏39	1931	APR	2	20:10	L	12♎10
	JUL	4	21:39	L	12♑17		APR	18	0:46	S	27♈02
	JUL	19	2:43	S	25♋51		SEP	12	4:41	S	18♍28
	DEC	14	9:23	S	21♐50		SEP	26	19:48	L	02♈47
	DEC	28	9:47	L	06♋05		OCT	11	12:56	S	17♎15
1918	JUN	8	22: 8	S	17♊16	1932	MAR	7	6:54	S	16♓30
	JUN	24	10:28	L	02♑00		MAR	22	12:33	L	01♎38
	DEC	3	15:23	S	10♐40		AUG	31	19:17	S	08♍08
	DEC	17	19: 6	L	24♊57		SEP	14	21: 1	L	21♓46
1919	MAY	15	1:14	L	23♏16	1933	FEB	10	13:18	L	21♌31
	MAY	29	13: 7	S	07♊06		FEB	24	12:34	S	05♓28
	NOV	7	23:44	L	14♉37		MAR	12	2:33	L	20♍58
	NOV	22	15: 8	S	29♏16		AUG	5	19:46	L	13♒02
1920	MAY	3	1:51	L	12♏21		AUG	21	5:44	S	27♌42
	MAY	18	6:15	S	26♉59		SEP	4	4:52	L	11♓05
	OCT	27	14:11	L	03♉53	1934	JAN	30	16:43	L	10♌13
	NOV	10	15:52	S	17♏58		FEB	14	1: 3	S	24♒46
1921	APR	8	9:56	S	18♈01		JUL	26	12:16	L	02♒53
	APR	22	7:44	L	01♏35		AUG	10	9:13	S	17♌03
	OCT	1	12:10	S	07♎46	1935	JAN	5	5:36	S	13♑58
	OCT	16	22:54	L	22♈59		JAN	19	15:48	L	28♋41
1922	MAR	13	11:14	L	22♍06		FEB	3	16:17	S	13♒55
	MAR	28	13:12	S	07♈05		JUN	30	20: 0	S	08♋05
	APR	11	20:32	L	21♎03		JUL	16	5: 0	L	22♑44
	SEP	21	4:47	S	27♍25		JUL	30	9:17	S	06♌17
	OCT	6	0:44	L	11♈53		DEC	25	17:47	S	03♑01
1923	MAR	3	3:32	L	11♍38	1936	JAN	8	18:10	L	17♋16
	MAR	17	12:24	S	25♓54		JUN	19	5:16	S	27♊44
	AUG	26	10:40	L	02♓15		JUL	4	17:26	L	12♑27
	SEP	10	20:31	S	17♍05		DEC	13	23:27	S	21♐49
1924	FEB	20	16: 9	L	00♍47		DEC	28	3:49	L	06♋09
	MAR	5	15:44	S	14♓49	1937	MAY	25	7:51	L	03♐47
	JUL	31	19:59	S	08♌17		JUN	8	20:41	S	17♊36
	AUG	14	20:21	L	21♒45		NOV	18	8:19	L	25♉41
	AUG	30	8:23	S	06♍40		DEC	2	23: 3	S	10♐22
1925	JAN	24	15: 7	S	04♒09	1938	MAY	14	8:44	L	22♏56
	FEB	8	21:42	L	19♌36		MAY	29	13:43	S	07♊31
	JUL	20	21:57	S	27♋37		NOV	7	22:27	L	14♉54
	AUG	4	11:53	L	11♒30		NOV	21	23:52	S	29♏01
1926	JAN	14	6:39	S	23♑21	1939	APR	19	17:14	S	28♈45
	JAN	28	21:20	L	08♌07		MAY	3	15:12	L	12♏16
	JUN	25	21:25	L	03♑39		OCT	12	21:11	S	18♎38
	JUL	9	23: 6	S	16♋57		OCT	28	6:37	L	03♉54
	JUL	25	5: 0	L	01♒22	1940	MAR	23	19:48	L	03♎11
	DEC	19	6:20	L	26♊42		APR	7	20:29	S	17♈52
1927	JAN	3	20:23	S	12♑29		APR	22	4:26	L	01♏47
	JUN	15	8:24	L	23♐17		OCT	1	12:21	S	08♎10
	JUN	29	6:28	S	06♋31		OCT	16	8: 1	L	22♈42
	DEC	8	17:35	L	15♊40	1941	MAR	13	11:56	L	22♍37
	DEC	24	4: 0	S	01♑21		MAR	27	19:49	S	06♈45
1928	MAY	19	12:49	S	28♉16		SEP	5	17:47	L	12♓51
	JUN	3	12:10	L	12♐37		SEP	21	4:18	S	27♍47
	JUN	17	20:27	S	26♊21	1942	MAR	3	0:22	L	11♍49
	NOV	12	9:48	S	19♏47		MAR	16	23:37	S	25♓45
	NOV	27	9: 1	L	04♊51		AUG	12	2:45	S	18♌46

	AUG	26	3:48	L	02♓18	1956	MAY	24	15:32	L	03♐28
	SEP	10	15:39	S	17♍17		JUN	8	21:21	S	18♊01
1943	FEB	4	23:57	S	15♒18		NOV	18	6:48	L	25♉57
	FEB	20	5:38	L	00♍40		DEC	2	8: 1	S	10♐08
	AUG	1	4:32	S	08♌04	1957	APR	29	1:38	S	08♉29
	AUG	15	19:29	L	22♒02		MAY	13	22:31	L	22♏51
1944	JAN	25	15:30	S	04♒33		OCT	23	4:54	S	29♎31
	FEB	9	5:15	L	19♌14		NOV	7	14:27	L	14♉53
	JUL	6	4:40	L	14♑06	1958	APR	4	4: 0	L	14♎02
	JUL	20	5:44	S	27♋22		APR	19	3:36	S	28♈35
	AUG	4	12:27	L	11♒51		MAY	3	12:13	L	12♏27
	DEC	29	14:50	L	07♋54		OCT	12	21: 4	S	19♎02
1945	JAN	14	4:58	S	23♑41		OCT	27	15:28	L	03♉37
	JUN	25	15:14	L	03♑43	1959	MAR	24	20:12	L	03♎32
	JUL	9	13:26	S	16♋57		APR	8	3: 8	S	17♈33
	DEC	19	2:21	L	26♊52		SEP	17	1: 4	L	23♓30
1946	JAN	3	12:16	S	12♑32		OCT	2	12:13	S	08♎33
	MAY	30	21: 0	S	08♊49	1960	MAR	13	8:28	L	22♍48
	JUN	14	18:39	L	23♐03		MAR	27	7:25	S	06♈38
	JUN	29	3:52	S	06♋48		SEP	5	11:22	L	12♓55
	NOV	23	17:37	S	00♋50		SEP	20	22:60	S	27♍58
	DEC	8	17:48	L	16♐01	1961	FEB	15	8:43	L	26♒27
1947	MAY	20	13:35	S	28♉42		MAR	2	13:26	L	11♍40
	JUN	3	19:15	L	12♐16		AUG	11	11:10	S	18♌32
	NOV	12	19:49	S	19♏35		AUG	26	3: 9	L	02♓36
	NOV	28	8:34	L	05♊10	1962	FEB	5	0:17	S	15♒43
1948	APR	23	13:39	L	03♏24		FEB	19	13: 4	L	00♍18
	MAY	9	2:44	S	18♉23		JUL	17	11:55	L	24♑33
	OCT	18	2:36	L	24♈43		JUL	31	12:28	S	07♌49
	NOV	1	6:16	S	08♏44		AUG	15	19:57	L	22♒22
1949	APR	13	4:11	L	22♏56	1963	JAN	9	23:20	L	19♋05
	APR	28	7:49	S	07♉42		JAN	25	13:30	S	04♒52
	OCT	7	2:57	L	13♈33		JUL	6	22: 3	L	14♑10
	OCT	21	21:12	S	28♎08		JUL	20	20:29	S	27♋24
1950	MAR	18	14:27	S	27♓26		DEC	30	11: 7	L	08♋03
	APR	2	20:45	L	12♎30	1964	JAN	14	20:30	S	23♑43
	SEP	12	2:46	S	18♏47		JUN	10	4:34	S	19♊19
	SEP	26	4:17	L	02♈29		JUN	25	1: 7	L	03♑30
1951	FEB	21	21:30	L	02♏36		JUL	9	11:18	S	17♋15
	MAR	7	20:39	S	16♓28		DEC	4	1:32	L	11♐56
	MAR	23	10:37	L	01♎53		DEC	19	2:38	L	27♊12
	AUG	17	3:15	L	23♒34	1965	MAY	30	21: 6	S	09♊13
	SEP	1	12:43	S	08♍16		JUN	14	1:49	L	22♐43
	SEP	15	12:27	L	21♓45		NOV	23	4: 1	S	00♐39
1952	FEB	11	0:40	L	21♌20		DEC	8	17:10	L	16♊19
	FEB	25	9:37	S	05♓44	1966	MAY	4	21:12	L	14♏03
	AUG	5	19:48	L	13♒22		MAY	20	9:51	S	28♉56
	AUG	20	15:49	S	27♌32		OCT	29	10:13	L	05♏39
1953	JAN	29	23:48	L	09♌50		NOV	12	14:37	S	19♏46
	FEB	14	0:60	S	25♒03	1967	APR	24	12: 7	L	03♏39
	JUL	11	2:44	S	18♋30		MAY	9	14:43	S	18♉17
	JUL	26	12:22	L	03♒13		OCT	18	10:16	L	24♈23
	AUG	9	15:55	S	16♑45		NOV	2	6:24	S	09♏08
1954	JAN	5	2:11	S	14♑13	1968	MAR	28	23: 0	L	08♈20
	JAN	19	2:32	L	28♋27		APR	13	4:48	L	23♎17
	JUN	30	12:23	S	08♋10		SEP	22	10:22	S	29♍28
	JUL	16	0:21	L	22♑53		OCT	6	11:42	L	13♈15
	DEC	25	7:33	S	02♑59	1969	MAR	18	4:38	S	27♓25
1955	JAN	8	12:34	L	17♋22		APR	2	18:33	L	12♎44
	JUN	5	14:23	L	14♐16		AUG	27	10:48	L	04♓08
	JUN	20	4:12	S	28♊05		SEP	11	19:45	S	18♍53
	NOV	29	16:60	L	06♊48		SEP	25	20:10	L	02♈29
	DEC	14	7: 4	S	21♐31	1970	FEB	21	8:31	L	02♍24

	MAR	7	18: 4	S	16♓45		DEC	20	1:50	L	27♊30
	AUG	17	3:24	L	23♒54	1984	MAY	15	4:41	L	24♏39
	AUG	31	22:29	S	08♍05		MAY	30	16:53	S	09♊26
	SEP	15	10: 0	L	21♓28		JUN	13	14:26	L	22♐36
1971	FEB	10	7:45	L	20♌57		NOV	8	17:56	L	16♉37
	FEB	25	9:48	S	06♓09		NOV	22	23: 5	S	00♐50
	JUL	22	9:32	S	28♋56	1985	MAY	4	19:57	L	14♏19
	AUG	6	19:44	L	13♒42		MAY	19	21:30	S	28♉50
	AUG	20	22:40	S	27♌15		OCT	28	17:43	L	05♉17
1972	JAN	16	10:34	S	25♑24		NOV	12	14:50	S	20♏10
	JAN	30	10:54	L	09♌37	1986	APR	9	6:21	S	19♈07
	JUL	10	19:30	S	18♋36		APR	24	12:43	L	04♏01
	JUL	26	7:17	L	03♒20		OCT	3	18:21	S	10♎15
1973	JAN	4	15:40	S	14♑10		OCT	17	19:19	L	24♈06
	JAN	18	21:18	L	28♋34	1987	MAR	29	12:31	S	08♈17
	JUN	15	20:50	L	24♐42		APR	14	2:20	L	23♎31
	JUN	30	11:41	S	08♋32		SEP	23	2:54	S	29♍33
	JUL	15	11:40	L	22♑43		OCT	7	4: 2	L	13♈16
	DEC	10	1:45	L	17♊58	1988	MAR	3	16:14	L	13♍24
	DEC	24	15: 3	S	02♑40		MAR	18	2:23	S	27♓43
1974	JUN	4	22:17	L	13♐58		AUG	27	11: 6	L	04♑29
	JUN	20	4:56	S	28♊30		SEP	11	5:15	S	18♍41
	NOV	29	15:14	L	07♊03	1989	FEB	20	15:36	L	02♍01
	DEC	13	16:13	S	21♐16		MAR	7	18: 9	S	17♓09
1975	MAY	11	7:17	S	20♉00		AUG	17	3: 9	L	24♒13
	MAY	25	5:49	L	03♐24		AUG	31	5:32	S	07♍48
	NOV	3	13:16	S	10♏30	1990	JAN	26	18:53	S	06♒34
	NOV	18	22:24	L	25♉55		FEB	9	19:12	L	20♌45
1976	APR	29	10:33	S	09♉14		JUL	22	2:38	S	29♋03
	MAY	13	19:55	L	23♏04		AUG	6	14:13	L	13♒48
	OCT	23	5:22	S	29♎56	1991	JAN	15	23:45	S	25♑20
	NOV	6	23: 2	L	14♉34		JAN	30	5:60	L	09♌45
1977	APR	4	4:19	L	14♎23		JUN	27	3:16	L	05♑08
	APR	18	10:19	S	28♈16		JUL	11	19: 8	S	18♋59
	SEP	27	8:30	L	04♈14		JUL	26	18: 9	L	03♒09
	OCT	12	20:15	S	19♎23		DEC	21	10:34	L	29♊09
1978	MAR	24	16:23	L	03♎42	1992	JAN	4	23:16	S	13♑51
	APR	7	15: 4	S	17♈26		JUN	15	4:58	L	24♐24
	SEP	16	19: 5	L	23♓36		JUN	30	12:25	S	08♋57
	OCT	2	6:28	S	08♎43		DEC	9	23:45	L	18♊13
1979	FEB	26	17:22	S	07♓31		DEC	24	0:32	S	02♑27
	MAR	13	21: 9	L	22♍39	1993	MAY	21	14:20	S	00♊32
	AUG	22	17:53	S	29♌02		JUN	4	13: 1	L	13♐54
	SEP	6	10:55	L	13♓13		NOV	13	21:46	S	21♏32
1980	FEB	16	9: 0	S	26♒51		NOV	29	6:27	L	07♊01
	MAR	1	20:46	L	11♍20	1994	MAY	10	17:21	S	19♉49
	JUL	27	19: 9	L	05♒01		MAY	25	3:31	L	03♐38
	AUG	10	19:17	S	18♌17		NOV	3	13:48	S	10♏55
	AUG	26	3:31	L	02♓56		NOV	18	6:45	L	25♉36
1981	JAN	20	7:51	L	00♌17	1995	APR	15	12:19	L	25♎10
	FEB	4	21:58	S	16♒01		APR	29	17:24	S	08♉56
	JUL	17	4:48	L	24♑36		OCT	8	16: 5	L	15♈01
	JUL	31	3:36	S	07♌51		OCT	24	4:23	S	00♏17
1982	JAN	9	19:57	L	19♋17	1996	APR	4	0:11	L	14♎33
	JAN	25	4:43	S	04♒53		APR	17	22:38	S	28♈11
	JUN	21	12: 4	S	29♊47		SEP	27	2:55	L	04♈19
	JUL	6	7:32	L	13♑55		OCT	12	14: 3	S	19♎31
	JUL	20	18:45	S	27♋43	1997	MAR	9	1:55	S	18♓32
	DEC	15	9:32	S	23♐05		MAR	24	4:40	L	03♎33
	DEC	30	11:29	L	08♋24		SEP	2	0: 5	S	09♍34
1983	JUN	11	4:34	S	19♊43		SEP	16	18:48	L	23♓54
	JUN	25	8:23	L	03♑10	1998	FEB	26	17:37	S	07♓55
	DEC	4	12:20	S	11♐46		MAR	13	4:21	L	22♍17

	AUG	8	2:26	L	15♒31		AUG	11	10:53	S	18♌21
	AUG	22	2:15	S	28♌48	2000	JAN	21	4:45	L	00♌29
	SEP	6	11:11	L	13♓34		FEB	5	12:50	S	16♒01
1999	JAN	31	16:19	L	11♌27		JUL	1	19:34	S	10♋15
	FEB	16	6:22	S	27♒07		JUL	16	13:57	L	24♑20
	JUL	28	11:35	L	05♒03		JUL	31	2:14	S	08♌11
							DEC	25	17:36	S	04♑15

The Vertex Point

In recent years, astrologer Charles Jayne has done some very interesting research on the vertex point in the natal horoscope. Other astrologers have been using it with rather good results.

The vertex and anti-vertex (its opposite point) are the third *imaginary* angles of the horoscope (the other two being the Ascendant-Descendant and M.C.-I.C.). We say imaginary because to transpose any three-dimensional factor onto a two-dimensional, flat piece of paper results in imaginary points or angles. We are all familiar with the Ascendant-Descendant angle symbolizing the dissection of the globe by latitude between South and North, or the equator, and representing the horizon. We are also familiar with the second set of angles, the Midheaven (Medium Coeli) or M.C. and the Imum Coeli, which symbolizes the division of the globe by longitude. The vertex-anti-vertex would be the third axis symbolizing the up-and-down dimension existing in any three-dimensional sphere. Charles Jayne has given the following formula to calculate this axis:

> Subtract the latitude of the birth place from 90° in order to obtain the co-latitude. Use the I.C. (4th house cusp) as if it were the M.C., find that degree in your Table of Houses and go down to the co-latitude that you've just figured. Whatever is listed there for the Ascendant becomes the Vertex point. The opposite point (180° away) is the anti-vertex.

Using the horoscope of Hermann Hesse as an example: his I.C. is 20° Aries 30'. On Page 15 of the Table of Houses (Koch) we find 20° Aries. Hesse's birth latitude is 48° N 01', and by subtracting this from 90° we arrive at a co-latitude of 41° N 59', or approximately 42°, which lists 4° Leo 23' as the Ascendant in this column. Thus, 4° Leo 23' becomes Hesse's vertex point, and 4° Aquarius 23' his anti-vertex point.

According to Jayne, the nature of the vertex point is other-people oriented. It has more of a Western side of the chart flavor, where you are not always totally in control but subject to whims and wishes of others. In other words, the vertex point should be considered *re-active,* rather than active, *responsive,* rather than initiating. If astrologically speaking the Ascendant represents the personal consciousness and the Midheaven the social consciousness, then the vertex point might be said to represent the *group consciousness.* Or, to put it more simply, if we take personal action through our Ascendant, or social (career, profession, status,) action through our Midheaven, the vertex point is the reflection or reaction point to whatever we have initiated. Delphine Jay in an article on the vertex in "Astrology Now" puts it very well. "At the Ascendant *we are,* at the Midheaven *we do,* and at the vertex is reflected the earned growth path which can stimulate future openings.''

In our research, we have found that the vertex reflects many of these qualities. We have also found it to be helpful in doing comparison charts. Why did John and Mary get together when they really don't have that much in common? Check their vertex points and often you will find one of Mary's planets conjunct John's vertex point, or vice-versa!

In a natal chart delineation, the vertex point should be expressed or released for future growth potential. The person might not be consciously aware of this, since it is not a planet, but again one of those sensitive points in the horoscope; however, subconsciously he will feel the need to express - perhaps without really knowing the reason.

Hermann Hesse, for example, has his vertex point in his 8th house of research, the occult, regeneration and sex, in the sign of Leo. Hesse needed to prove and research and regenerate from within, yet in a rather showy or dramatic fashion. We would not call this a very sexual chart in itself, though Uranus in the 8th house likes to be experimental. If the vertex shows future growth potential, then in the 8th house Hesse needs the support of other people to find release. This would also be confirmed by a 7th house Sun, which needs to understand and relate to others.

Since the vertex point is a comparatively new tool in Astrology, we urge you to research it for yourself, and do let us know if you come up with some interesting results. Our own research seems to indicate that the vertex point is more important than the anti-vertex point, but here too—try it for yourself and see what you find.

Review Question: Calculate the vertex point for Walt Disney. Our answer will be found in the Appendix on page 248.

Lesson 17
Arabian Parts

The Arabian Parts (or The Arabian Points)

As the name implies, these parts or points were used in Arabian Astrology and have been in great favor, and subsequent disfavor, throughout the history of Astrology. Hindu Astrology still uses many of these parts, whereas the Western nations use mainly the Part of Fortune or Fortuna (⊗).

It is important that you remember that these Parts or Points are exactly what the name implies; namely, a sensitive point in the horoscope - NOT A PLANET - therefore, they are not a basic necessity in interpreting a horoscope. Yet, many astrologers still find them quite useful because they seem to show sensitive areas on a subconscious level, a level of which the person himself might not even be aware.

There are hundreds of Arabian Parts, and for your informaton, we are including a list of just under fifty of them. As you will see, you can make up your own parts once you understand the logic involved.

Nearly all Arabian Parts are based on the Ascendant as a starting point, and the formula usually reads: Ascendant + Planet X – Planet Y = The Part. The "Part of Father", for example, would be given as: Ascendant + The Sun – Saturn (Sun and Saturn both representing the father in astrology). The "Part of Mother", on the other hand, would be: Ascendant + Moon – Venus (Moon and Venus representing the mother).

In order to interpret any of the Parts you may decide to use or experiment with, it is important that you understand the procedure involved. First, *you need an accurate birth time* to know the exact degree and sign on the Ascendant. You also need to know what the Ascendant really stands for; it represents your outer personality, the body with which you were born into this world, the face you show to the world, your physical reality in this life.

Using the Part of Fortune, the most popular of all of the Parts, the formula is: Ascendant + Moon − Sun. The Ascendant is the starting point in the reality of the here and now to which is added the Moon. The Moon is your emotional personality, and since emotions are not based upon reasoning or sense but on feelings, most of our emotions are conditioned by what has gone before—our past experience, our upbringing, our memories. When we react emotionally, it is nearly always a reflex due to some past event which ticks off our memory bank. From this combination of physical reality and emotional personality, we subtract the Sun. The Sun is our inner personality, the life giver, the heart of the chart—but it also reflects the growth potential innate in the fiery outreach of Leo, and the creativity of the 5th house. Subtract this outreach, or growth potential, and we are logically left with what is deeply ingrained within our nature. Therefore, always keep in mind the planets you are dealing with, which one is to be added, and which one to be subtracted, in order to come up with a reasonable delineation.

Remember that by using the Sun, Moon, and Ascendant, the resulting part is connected to these three bodies; and if the Part makes an aspect to any of them, it will show the ability to integrate all three. We recommend that the orb of aspect to any Part be limited to ± 3° maximum. Every astrologer will have to experiment and see if he wishes to use any Parts, some Parts, or many Parts. Some astrologers even make up Parts as the situation arises. All career questions could start with the Midheaven, instead of the Ascendant; questions involving children could use the fifth house cusp as a starting point, and so on *ad infinitum.*

When we do an in-depth delineation, we prefer to use only two Parts: the Part of Fortune, as previously discussed, and the Part of Spirit (⊕). The Part of Spirit is the exact reverse of the Part of Fortune; Ascendant + Sun − Moon. We add the growth potential of the Sun and subtract the past (the Moon); therefore, we are left with the inner or subconscious growth potential of the individual.

To Calculate the Part of Fortune:

We shall use as an example the horoscope of Joan Sutherland.

		S.	D.	M.				
Ascendant	= 3° Taurus 00' or	1ˢ	03°	00'				
+ Moon	= 4° Sag 06' or	+ 8ˢ	04°	06'		S.	D.	M.
		9ˢ	07°	06'	to borrow	8ˢ	36°	66'
− Sun	= 14° Scorpio 08' or	− 7ˢ	14°	08'		− 7ˢ	14°	08'
					Result:	1ˢ	22°	58'
					or:		22° Taurus	58'

Explanation of Formula:

The zodiac has twelve signs. Aries is the first sign, therefore 3° Aries would equal 0 signs 3°. 3° Taurus becomes 1 full sign (namely Aries) and 3° of Taurus, or 1^S (S = Sign) 3°. 3° Gemini reads 2^S 03° and so on through the zodiac, until you reach 3° Pisces, which would read 11^S 03°.

Some people prefer to convert into whole numbers, rather than signs. In that case, 3° Aries would read 03, 3° Taurus would be 33, 3° Gemini would be 63, and 3° Pisces would be 333. Use whichever method seems easier to you. Keep in mind that when borrowing you are dealing with 60 minutes, 30 degrees, and 12 signs. In our illustration, we borrow 60 minutes in order to subtract, therefore our degrees are reduced to 6° which in turn is not enough from which to subtract 14°. We therefore have to borrow one whole sign, or 30°, leaving only 8 full signs instead of 9. This of course is run-of-the-mill math, but you have to remember that you are not dealing in decimals, but instead minutes, degrees and signs.

Should you decide to use the latter method, the formula will look as follows:

Ascendant	= 33° 00'		
+ Moon	= 244° 06'		
	277° 06'	convert to borrow:	276° 66'
		Sun position:	− 224° 08'
			52° 58' or
			22° Taurus 58'

If you decide to use this system, remember that you would borrow 360 full degrees if your top figure is less than the bottom one.

To check yourself for correct results: Realize that the Part of Fortune has to be the same distance from the Ascendant as the Moon is from the Sun. In the case of Joan Sutherland, the Sun is 19° 58' removed from the Moon. At 22° Taurus 58' the Part of Fortune is also 19° 58' away from the Ascendant, and thus correct.

To interpret Joan Sutherland's Part of Fortune, we would say that she is very much a product of her upbringing, past memories, frustrations and hang-ups. But since this Part falls in the 1st house, she is used to handling this or coping with it in a fairly practical and down-to-earth way (Taurus). Since all of the Parts operate on a subconscious or deep level, she might not even be aware of this fact. She just does without giving it too much thought, and therefore copes.

The Part of Spirit is figured exactly as the Part of Fortune, only the formula is reversed (Ascendant + Sun − Moon). In Sutherland's case, it is 13° Aries 02' and falls in the 12th house. We might say that for eventual evolvement or inner growth, Miss Sutherland will have to reach within, to get to know herself on the deepest and most private level in order to achieve true inner peace and enlightenment.

Review Question: Calculate the Part of Fortune and the Part of Spirit for Hermann Hesse, Walt Disney and Farrah Fawcett. Our answers appear in the Appendix on page 248.

Review Question: Calculate the Part of Fortune and the Part of Spirit for Hermann Hesse, Walt Disney and Farrah Fawcett. Our answers appear in the Appendix on page 248.

ARABIAN PARTS IN ASTROLOGY

Part	Formula
Assassination	MARS + Neptune - Uranus
Astrology	ASC + Mercury - Uranus
Bondage	ASC + Moon - Moon's dispositor
Brothers and sisters	ASC + Jupiter - Saturn
Catastrophe	ASC + Uranus - Saturn
Children (female)	ASC + Venus - Moon
Children (male)	ASC + Jupiter - Moon
Commerce	ASC + Mercury - Sun
Death	ASC + 8th cusp - Moon
Desire and sexual attraction	ASC + 5th cusp - ruler of 5th
Discord and controversy	ASC + Jupiter - Mars
Divorce	ASC + Venus -7th cusp (always opposition Venus)
Faith	ASC + Mercury - Moon
Father	ASC + Sun - Saturn
Fortune	ASC + Moon - Sun
Fortune in marriage of women	ASC + Saturn - Venus
Friends	ASC + Moon - Uranus
Goods	ASC + 2nd cusp - ruler of 2nd
Honor	ASC + 19° Aries - Sun
Imprisonment, sorrow	ASC + Part of Fortune - Neptune
Increase	ASC + Jupiter - Sun
Inheritance, possessions	ASC + Moon - Saturn
Life (female)	ASC + Moon - full Moon prior to birth
Life (male)	ASC + Moon - new Moon prior to birth
Love and marriage	ASC + Venus - Jupiter
Love and deception by women	ASC + Venus - Sun
Karma (fate)	ASC + Saturn - Sun
Marriage	ASC + 7th cusp - Venus
Mother	ASC + Moon - Venus
Organization	ASC + Pluto - Sun
Passion	ASC + Mars - Sun
Peril	ASC + Ruler of 8th - Saturn
Perversion	ASC + Venus - Uranus
Private enemies	ASC + 12th cusp - ruler of 12th
Public enemies	ASC + 7th cusp - ruler of 7th
Servants	ASC + Moon - Mercury
Sickness	ASC + Mars - Saturn
Spirit	ASC + Sun - Moon
Sudden advancement	ASC + Part of Fortune - Saturn
Surgery	ASC + Saturn - Mars
Travel by land	ASC + 9th cusp - ruler of 9th

Travel by air	ASC + Uranus - cusp of 9th
Travel by water	ASC + 15° Cancer - Saturn
Understanding	ASC + Moon - Venus or ASC + Mars -Mercury
Vocation	MC + Moon - Sun
Web	ASC + Neptune - Sun

Lesson 18
Fixed Stars and Critical Degrees

Fixed Stars

The term Fixed Stars was coined thousands of years ago in order to differentiate those bodies from what were called Wandering Stars, which we know today as the planets. The term fixed seems to apply even today, since the distance from Earth to the nearest one is so far that they seem to be immovable or fixed in their heavenly position. Actually, they do move, but no more than a minute or so each year, so that most of them need more than fifty years to change their position or advance by one degree.

By some of the ancient teachings Fixed Stars were credited with an influence of their own when conjunct a planet or the Ascendant or Midheaven. Their influence was less forceful when in opposition. The allowable orb should be held to ±1° maximum. Since we are talking of teachings handed down from approximately 150 A.D., all the qualities attributed to the different stars are fairly dire since the high priests kept power over people and kings through fear. Like everything else in Astrology, these dire keywords must be taken with a grain of salt and should be translated into today's language and imbued with today's more psychological and humanistic approach.

To give you a few illustrations which will explain what we mean *Caput Algol* at 25° Taurus 47' is known as the most malevolent of all Fixed Stars. Some of its keywords are: "The Evil One, violence, accidents to throat and neck, strangulation, beheading". That's pretty frightening language, to say the least! We know a child who was born when Mars was at 25° Taurus 10', or conjunct *Caput Algol*. During its birth the umbilical cord was wrapped around the baby's neck; the doctors noticed it immediately, made an incision, and delivered a hale and healthy child. Now in ancient times this child probably would have died of strangulation; in today's world, it would not. A man with 25° Taurus on his MC is known for figuratively loosing his head when he gets excited about a business deal.

Another rather dire sounding Fixed Star is the *Pleiades* (also known as the Weeping Sisters) at 29° Taurus 36'. We know quite a few people who have planets on this degree, yet none of them have been involved with "violence, blindness, or accidents" as the keywords portend, but we have noticed that many of them cry at the drop of a hat!

To go the other way, the fortunate Fixed Stars, such as *Betelgeuze, Spica* and *Arcturus,* promise honors, riches, fame and inspiration. This, too, is exaggerated. Of all the people we know who have one or more of these great and promising stars in their horoscope, none has attained fame, only one has riches, and only a handful are inspired. But, all of them seem to emerge unscathed from difficult situations or hardship. These fortunate stars seem to offer a certain kind of protection. Fixed Stars appear to emphasize qualities that are already evident in the chart; they do not change the basic meaning of the horoscope. They may strengthen or weaken, depending upon the nature of the particular star involved, that which already exists. You can read any chart without ever using a Fixed Star, but again, by using them you may gain some additional insight, add another nuance or blend to your delineation.

On page 225 is a list of the more prominent Fixed Stars. There are many more of course, and if you wish more information, these books will provide it: "Fixed Stars" by Vivian Robson; "Fixed Stars and Degrees of the Zodiac Analyzed" by E. C. Matthews; "The Power of Fixed Stars " by Joseph Rigor.

To illustrate how some of the Fixed Stars can work, in Walt Disney's horoscope we have the Fixed Stars *Bungula* conjunct Mercury, *Wega* conjunct Saturn, and *Altair* conjunct Venus. Remember that Disney was born in 1901 and the Fixed stars were 1° 10' less than they are now. The self-analysis and philosophical leanings of *Bungula* conjunct Mercury, also the reasoning ability, surely added to Disney's mental approach. His movies supposedly designed for children were full of morals and philosophies. The practicality and generousity of *Wega* conjunct Saturn (which rules his 5th house of creativity) also was rather obvious. Most certainly his creative efforts seen by Venus in the 5th house show the boldness and confidence given by *Altair.* Please remember, these are additional shadings and blendings, which unless shown in the natal delineation, have to be taken with a grain of salt. In Disney's case though, they serve to confirm factors that already are found natally.

Again let us stress, the Fixed Stars alone will not suffice for accidents or violence or honors or riches. But if this is evident in the natal horoscope, the Fixed Star will give additional confirmation— and, as you know, in Astrology everything should be confirmed more than once in order to be truly effective and meaningful.

Review Question: Please locate the important Fixed Stars in Joan Sutherland's and Farrah Fawcett's charts and then give your interpretation briefly. For our answer, please refer to the Appendix on page 249.

Important Fixed Stars

(Maximum Orb allowed: 1° - Positions are figured for 1972)

Name

Difda	Energy, self-destruction, nervousness	2° ♈ 11	Neutral
Alpheratz	Grace, popularity, independence, honors	13° ♈ 55	Lucky
Mirach	Good fortune through marriage, beauty, love, talent	0° ♉ '01	Lucky
Hamal	Violence, cruelty, brutality. Also the "Healer"	7° ♉ 16	Unlucky
Almach	Success in Venusian occupations, artistic ability	13° ♉ 50	Lucky
Caput Algol	Strangulation, beheading, danger to throat and neck, violence, the "Evil One"	25° ♉ 47	Unlucky
Pleiades	Accidents, blindness, violence, the "Weeping Sisters"	29° ♉ 36	Unlucky
Aldebaran	Eloquence, courage, war mongering, agitation	9° ♊ 24	Neutral
Rigel	Technical and artistic ability, inventiveness, humor	16° ♊ 26	Lucky
Bellatrix	Loquaciousness, accidents, sudden dishonor	20° ♊ 53	Unlucky
Capella	Inquisitiveness, open mindedness, powerful friends	21° ♊ 28	Lucky
Betelgeuze	Social aspirations, charm, culture	28° ♊ 22	Lucky
Alphena	Acute sensitivity, imagination, injuries to feet	8° ♋ 43	Neutral
Sirius	Ambition, pride, emotionality, wealth, fame	13° ♋ 42	Lucky
Castor	Sudden fame or loss, distinction, keen mind	19° ♋ 51	Neutral
Pollux	Contemplative speculation, audacity, the "Heartless Judge"	22° ♋ 50	Neutral
Procyon	Violence, sudden success then disaster, politics	25° ♋ 24	Unlucky
Regulus	Nobility, ambition, alertness, sudden downfall	29° ♌ 26	Neutral
Denebola	Criticism, perseverance, control, lack of imagination	21° ♍ 14	Neutral
Spica	Wealth, fame, honor glamor, the "Lucky One"	23° ♎ 27	Very Lucky
Arcturus	Inspiration, fame, honor, benefits through travel	23° ♎ 50	Very Lucky
Acrux	Interest in Astrology and religion, the "Femme Fatale"	11° ♏ 29	Occult
North Scale	Brilliant mind, the "Accursed Degree"	18° ♏ 59	Unlucky

Agena	Good health, high morals, disillusion through love	23°℔24	Lucky
Bungula	Occult and philosophical leanings, self-analysis	29°℔03	Lucky
Antares	Spirit of adventure, obstinacy, injuries to eyes	9°♐22	Unlucky
Wega	Luck in politics, generosity, practicality	14°♐56	Lucky
Altair	Sudden but ephemeral fortune, impulsiveness	1°♒23	Neutral
Fomalhaut	Congenital birth defects, faith, "Star of Alchemy"	3°♓28	Neutral
Achernar	Success in public office, religious benefits	14°♓54	Lucky
Markab	Violence, honors and riches, "Star of Sorrow"	23°♓06	Neutral
Scheat	Imprisonment, murder, suicide, drowning	28°♓29	Unlucky

Critical Degrees

This is another of those terms that has been handed down through the ages, and is not really to be taken in the way we understand the word critical. In Hindu Astrology, the zodiac of 360° is divided into 28 mansions, each representing the average daily travel of the Moon, or approximately 13°, starting from the 0° Aries point. If we divide the zodiac (360°) by 28, the result is 12° 51' 25'', or rounding it off, 13° Aries. Thus, by adding 12° 51' 25'' to that we have 25° 42' 50'', or roughly 26° Aries. Adding this increment once more, we reach 8°34' 15'' of Taurus, or nearly 9° Taurus. If you keep adding, you will realize that the mansions break down as follows:

CARDINAL SIGNS - 0°, 13° and 26°

FIXED SIGNS - 9° and 21°

MUTABLE SIGNS - 4° and 17°

In today's language, the term critical should be interpreted as giving additional emphasis or points of sensitivity.

Because these degrees are neither aspects nor planetary relationships, but merely points based upon an average lunar motion, the orb must be held within ±1°—in fact, we usually allow not more than ±45' of orb.

To illustrate: Joan Sutherland has the Moon at 4° Sagittarius 06', definitely on a so-called critical mutable degree. Her Moon is in a succedent house, it makes relatively few aspects (very public people usually have a prominent Moon), but it rules her 3rd house of communications, and somehow this degree gives her Moon additional sensitivity or emphasis - because communicate she does, with her glorious Taurean voice.

The term critical degree is also often used when referring to any planet, Ascendant or Midheaven at 0° or 29° of any sign. In this instance the word critical only indicates that the individual is just beginning or nearly ending some phase, the nature or type to be shown by sign, house or planet involved.

For example, Walt Disney had Neptune at 0° Cancer in his 10th house. This gave added emphasis to Neptune. Somehow he felt that little additional push, the need to try that new feeling innate in 0° which always indicates beginnings. Since it is the planet Neptune, the emphasis would be on a creative level, or, if the rest of the chart confirms, on a spiritual level. In Disney's case we know of course that it was creativity. He also had Venus at 29° Capricorn 42'. Here the emphasis is felt in a different way. Venus is ready to leave Capricorn and enter 0° Aquarius in a matter of 18', or very soon. There is a sense of urgency to quickly accomplish all that needs to be accomplished before Venus leaves Capricorn. In this case, Venus is in the 5th house, which again can mean creative effort, and in Capricorn, a well-planned and disciplined effort. Do not put too much emphasis upon these degrees, just keep them in mind for additional insight, blending, and feeling as to what may go on in the subconscious or deeper mind of the individual.

Review Questions: Briefly interpret the critical degrees in Hermann Hesse's horoscope. Refer to the Appendix on page 249 for our answers.

Lesson 19
Earth

Using the Position of the Earth in the Natal Horoscope

Astrologers have long been guilty of ignoring the position of the Earth in the natal horoscope. We feel that, since we are born on this planet, it should be recorded in every chart, just as we record the position of the Sun, Moon, and the other planets. If we happened to be born on Mars (and this may happen sooner than we might expect!) we wouldn't leave Mars out of the horoscope. So, then why omit the position of the Earth in our construction of the natal horoscope?

The Earth's position is found in the degree, sign, and house that is exactly opposite the position of the Sun. The symbol for the Earth is the cross of matter enclosed within the circle of infinity ($\oplus$), not to be confused with the arabic part of fortune ($\otimes$).

Even though we draw our horoscope in two dimensions, on a flat sheet of paper, we must realize that the chart has depth and takes into consideration the Earth's daily rotation as well as her yearly rotation around the Sun. Thus, when we say that the Sun is in Cancer, we mean that on Earth we are viewing the Sun against the zodiacal sign of Cancer. We would view the Earth against the backdrop of the sign of Capricorn if we were on the Sun at that moment in time. As long as we remain on the Earth, we see the Sun against the background of the sign that is opposite the one the Earth is in at any given time.

When you accept the need to plot the Earth's position in the horoscope, go a step further and consider it as the ruler of the sign Taurus. Venus, traditionally given as the ruler of Taurus, seems to light, airy, and gentle to have much relationship with practical, earthy, stable Taurus. True, Taureans have a great sense of beauty, and they are often creative and musical, but this could just as well be due to an affinity with the planet we live on. There are few Taureans who do not have their feet set firmly on the ground. They are consciously aware of the physical body, very concerned with their health; they are stolid, fixed, and usually present a placid face to the world. But, when subjected to stress, they can blow up or go on a destructive rampage, much as the Earth can when affected by adverse atmospheric conditions. The Earth shows our mission in life, where and how we meet the world on our own terms. Where the Earth is positioned in the chart shows where you can tap your greatest productive potential because if we accept it as the ruler of Taurus it rules the natural 2nd house of inborn talent and self-worth.

In Farrah Fawcett's chart, the Earth is in her 2nd house, in Leo and conjunct Pluto. It indicates her sudden dramatic (Leo) rise to stardom and the financial problems she is having along the way.

In Walt Disney's horoscope, the Earth is in his 9th house in Gemini, and it rules the 9th house (as the ruler of Taurus). This indicates his ability to turn fantasy into a concrete business by using his dreams (9th house) and his hands (Gemini).

There are quite a few theories on the importance of Earth in the natal horoscope. Some astrologers feel that the Earth rules Cancer, some agree with our theory of its rulership over Taurus. But, like any theory, until it has been experimented with for a long time, no definite conclusion can or should be drawn. We have observed Earth in the charts for quite a few years and feel that the rulership of Taurus explains many things and works very well. But please try it for yourself. In fact, we would appreciate it if you will put the Earth in the horoscopes you use, and then observe it in action and let us know your findings and your feelings about it. Much research is still needed, with many horoscopes with the Earth in each sign and ruling each house, before we can establish a better understanding of its meaning and importance of Astrology.

Lesson 20
Steps to Delineation

There comes a time in any learning process where you have to stop, pull it all together and then, before you are ready to go on to the next level, sit down and do it. By "do it" we mean—PRACTICE! Get the birthday of someone you know, erect the chart, and then DELINEATE it. Get another birthday, preferably of someone you don't know too well, calculate the chart and again DELINEATE it, either to that individual or to someone who knows that person very well. Get another birthday, this time of someone you do not know at all, but who is interested in Astrology and would like to have his or her horoscope interpreted. Set up the chart and then very carefully, giving yourself plenty of time, delineate that chart, step-by-step, checking all phases as we have outlined in this book and in Volume One. Next, using your notes, sit face-to-face with this individual and delineate the horoscope. Notice expecially where you were right and where you were wrong. Make yourself detailed notes of where you went wrong. That's where the learning process really comes in. But, also realize that people don't know themselves totally. You may mention some talent or ability and get a big "Me? No way!". At that point, probe a little deeper before you draw back and figure that you were wrong. This is especially true in dealing with a young person; they rarely know all of their potential.

To help you pull it all together, we will give you a list of steps to take in order not to overlook anything. Our students have found this list most helpful; we hope that you will too.

Step One—Overview

a. North/South, East/West emphasis. How many planets above/below the horizon, East/West of the Meridian?

b. Chart Pattern? (Bowl, Bucket, Locomotive, See-saw, Splay, Splash, Bundle, Fan, or no discernable pattern).

c. House emphasis. How many angular, succeedent or cadent planets? How many fall in the house of life, substance, relations, or endings?

d. Elements and qualities. Is there a predominance, and does that person have a certain signature (predominance of cardinal/fire would be an Aries signature, for example). Or, is a quality or an element missing?

e. Is there a final dispositor? Are there any mutual receptions? Which planet is the chart ruler?

f. How many planets are dignified? Exalted? In their detriment or fall?

g. As you aspect, make a note of any configurations (grand crosses, T-squares, grand trines, yods, and any others). Also, note if there is a stellium, of if one planet seems more important by being the highest one in the horoscope, or receiving the most aspects.

h. Blend the Sun, Moon and Ascendant to get a general feeling of whom you are dealing with.

i. For later use in delineation, note critical degrees, planet in oriental appearance, important Fixed Stars, the pre-natal eclipse point, any Arabic Parts you may decide to use, the vertex point if you wish to insert it and Earth (again only if you want to use them). Also note if there are any interceptions, or any retrograde planets.

Blend Steps (a) through (h) to get a feeling for the individual. As you now get ready to take the chart apart, always keep this overview in mind.

Step Two—Interpreting Each Area of the Chart

When reading any planet in the chart, keep the following in mind:

a. The basic nature of the planet (Moon = emotions, Mars = drive, etc.)

b. The sign that the planet is in (and for the Sun, Moon and Ascendant add the decanate)

c. The sign and house that the ruler is in (Mercury in Capricorn - what sign and house is Saturn in?). This gives an added nuance.

d. The house that the planet rules (Mercury rules two houses - those with Gemini and Virgo on the cusp)

e. The house that the planet is posited (located) in (Mercury in the 2nd will work differently than Mercury in the 4th)

f. All aspects that this planet makes.

g. Special considerations—Is the planet on a critical degree? Is it conjunct a Fixed Star? Is it intercepted, retrograde or stationary, elevated, dignified, exalted, in detriment or fall?

Since the Sun is the heart of the chart, we recommend that you start with the Sun as you follow the second step outlined above.

Next delineate the Moon, followed by the Ascendant.

Some astrologers will move on from this point and interpret Mercury next, since Mercury represents the mind and the reasoning ability which is important. Also note the planet in oriental appearance for additional motivation.

You now have a good understanding of the person you are dealing with, but you still have not seen the total picture. To find all of the potential and characteristics, you have to go around the whole chart, house by house and planet by planet.

If there are any planets in the 1st house, delineate them as suggested above. Then, go to the 2nd house. Look at the sign on the cusp, see where the ruler is located by house and sign. Blend the cusp and the ruler (use our cusp notes to help you). Interpret the values, financial affairs, earning power, and all else that the 2nd house stands for. If there are any planets in this house, delineate them. If you wish, you may also delineate the ruler of the 2nd house next.

Follow this procedure, house by house and planet by planet, until you have reached the 12th house and delineated all ten planets.

When reading any house, keep the following in mind:

a.   The basic nature of the house.

b.   The sign on the cusp of that house in relation to that basic nature.

c.   The planetary ruler of the sign on the cusp. You must blend the two signs and the two houses. (Aries on the 4th house - ruler Mars in Gemini in the 6th: Blend the Aries drive with the Gemini intellect and communicating ability. Ruler of the 4th in the 6th: you may work from the home).

d.   Any planets in the house that will color the emphasis on the house.

e.   Any interception which gives the house one more ruler or makes it the largest house in the chart.

Appendix

Horoscope Calculation for Part One - Math

WALT DISNEY
born 12/5/1901 at 12:30 AM CST
Chicago, Ill. 87W37 - 41N53
LMT correction   - add 9' 30''
EGMT - add 5^{h}50' 30''

	H.M.S.		
	00:30:00	AM	12/5/1901 CST
+	9:30		meridian corr. for Chicago
	00:39:30	AM	LMT 12/5/1901
+	12:00:00		to account for AM
	12:39:30		LMTI
+	2:07		LMTI correction
+	0:56		EGMT correction
+	16:50:25		S.T. 12/4/1901
	28:91:118		convert
	29:32:58		
	24:00:00		subtract one day
	5:32:58		T.C.S.T.

To find GMT

	00:39:30	AM	LMT 12/5/1901
+	5:50:30		EGMT for Chicago
	6:30:00	AM	GMT 12/5/1901

To find Constant Log:

	11:60		(noon in hrs. & min.)
−	6:30	AM	GMT
	5:30		Interval

Constant Log for 5° 30' = 6398

	Sun	Moon	Mercury	Venus	Mars
12/5	12°♐40'	11°♎53'	27°♏47'	29°♑56'	8°♑38'
12/4	− 11°♐39'	29°♍48'	26°♏17'	28°♑55'	7°♑52'
	1° 01'	12° 05'	1° 30'	1° 01'	46'
	1.3730 PLR	2980	1.2041	1.3730	1.4956
	+ 6398 CL	6398	6398	6398	6398
	2.0128	9378	1.8439	2.0128	2.1354
− (5th)	14'	2° 46'	21'	14'	11'
	12°♐26'	9°♎07'	27°♏26'	29°♑42'	8°♑27'

Name Walt Disney
Date December 5, 1901
Time 12:30 AM CST
Place Chicago, IL
Long. 87W37
Lat. 41N53

Source
DC Doane, Charles Jayne
and Jos Silverman confirm
the above data. Daughter
states 7:30 AM CST

DD

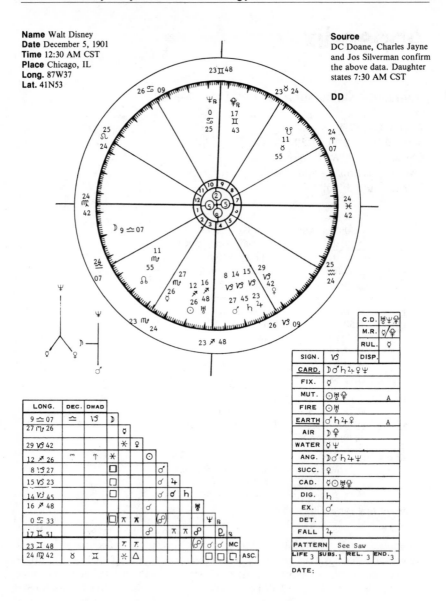

LONG.	DEC.	DWAD												
9 ♎ 07	♎	♑	☽											
27 ♏ 26				☿										
29 ♑ 42			✳	♀										
12 ♐ 26	♍	♈	✳		☉									
8 ♑ 27			□			♂								
15 ♑ 23			□			♂	♃							
14 ♑ 45			□			♂	♂	♄						
16 ♐ 48						♂			♅					
0 ♋ 33			□	ㅈ	ㅈ	(☍)				♆	℞			
17 ♊ 51					☍		ㅈ	ㅈ	☍		℞	℞		
23 ♊ 48			ㅈ	ㅈ		(☍)					♂	♂	MC	
24 ♍ 42	♉	♊	✳	△							□	□	□	ASC.

C.D.	♅♆♀
M.R.	♀/♀
RUL.	☿

SIGN.	♑	DISP.	
CARD.	☽♂♄♃♀♆		
FIX.	☿		
MUT.	☉♅♀		A
FIRE	☉♅		
EARTH	♂♄♃♀		A
AIR	☽♀		
WATER	☿♆		
ANG.	☽♂♄♃♆		
SUCC.	♀		
CAD.	☿☉♅♀		
DIG.	♄		
EX.	♂		
DET.			
FALL	♃		
PATTERN	See Saw		
LIFE 3	SUBS. 1	REL. 3	END. 3

DATE:

Horoscope Calculation for Part One - Math

FARRAH FAWCETT
born 2/2/1947 at 3:10 PM CST
Corpus Christi, TX. 97W24 - 27N47

LMT correction   - subtract 29'36"
EGMT - add $6^h29' 36"$

H.M.S.

	3:10:00	PM	2/2/1947 CST
−	29:36		meridian corr. for Corpus Christi
	2:40:24	PM	LMTI
+	0:27		LMTI correction
+	1:05		EGMT correction
+	20:47:20		S.T. 2/2/1947
	22:88:76		convert
	23:29:16		T.C.S.T.

	2:40:24	PM	LMT 2/2/1947
+	6:39:36		EGMT for Corpus Christi
	8:70:00		convert
	9:10:00	PM	GMT 2/2/1947

Constant Log for $9^h 10'$ = 4180

	Sun	Moon	Mercury	Venus	Mars
2/3	13°♒49'	13°♋48'	21°♒53'	27°♐06'	7°♒03'
2/2	−12°♒48'	28°♊59'	20°♒06'	26°♐04'	6°♒15'
	1° 01'	14° 49'	1° 47'	1° 02'	48'
	1.3730	2095	1.1290	1.3660	1.4771
	+ 4180 CL	4180	4180	4180	4180
	1.7910	6275	1.5470	1.7840	1.8951
+ (2nd)	+ 23'	5° 40'	41'	24'	18'
	13° ♒ 11'	4°♋39'	20°♒47'	26°♐28'	6°♒33'

Please note that 9:10 PM GMT is 9 hours or more than 1/3rd of 24 hours past the noon position of the planets, therefore all your corrections should be more than 1/3rd and less than half. This is a good way to check your math. The Moon, for example, has a motion of 14° 49', or nearly 15°, therefore the correction should be over 5°, which it is - at 5° 40'. The Sun has a motion of over 1°, therefore the correction should be more than 1/3rd of 60 minutes (20') which it is - at 23'.

This same eyeballing technique can of course be used to correct the slower planets that move no more than a few minutes each day. In Farrah's chart, for example, Jupiter moves from 25° 10' to 25° 18' from February 2 to 3. Taking your more than 1/3rd correction, you can add 3' to Jupiter's position of the

2nd place it in the chart at 25° 13'. Corrected Saturn would read 4° 49', the motion is 6 minutes *backwards* (retrograde), therefore you would subtract 2 minutes from Saturn's position on the 2nd.

Name Farrah Fawcett
Date February 2, 1947
Time 3:10 PM CST
Place Corpus Christi, TX
Long. 97W24
Lat. 27N47

Source
Birth Certificate

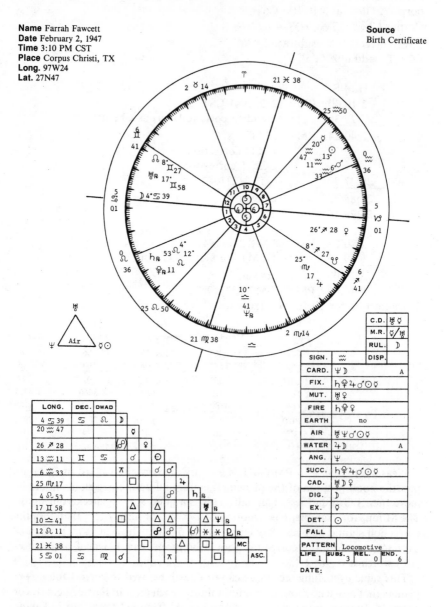

Answers to Quiz No. 1 · Part One

1.   Sidereal Time, Local Mean Time, Greenwich Mean Time, Prime Meridian, Constant Log, True Calculated Sidereal Time.
2.   1 minute, 60 minutes, 30 degrees, the entire zodiac.
3.   East to West. North to South.
4.   4°
5.   In an AM birth. When the TCST is over 24 hours. If DST or WT is in effect.
6.   5th.
7.   4 minutes.
8.   Added. Subtracted.
9.   Equivalent Greenwich Mean Time.
10. 6/14/52. 6/16/52 and 6/15/52.
11. 11° ≈ 21'.
12. 6:10 PM GMT.
13. The opposite of how you correct the other planets.
14. Subtract. Add.
15. You must use 0:00:00 PM for noon; 0:00:00 AM for midnight.
16. You must subtract GMT from noon to find the INTERVAL.
17. Subtract.
18. You must add 12 hours.
19. When the person is born in the PM.
20. Flat or Solar Equilibrium.

Answer to Review Question · Lesson 7

Retrogrades · Joan Sutherland: Joan Sutherland's Uranus is retrograde in the 11th house, in accidental dignity because the 11th house is the natural house position for Uranus and Aquarius in the flat chart. That fact, plus the trine to Saturn, gives Uranus additional strength. The need to be different and unique could be used in a disciplined and positive way rather quickly. The need to dominate is less emphasized in a succedent position than in an angular one, and with Mars retrograde in her 1st house, she learned to plan before acting and probably realizes that in order to achieve her goals, she needs to submit rather than dictate. With Mars ruling her 12th house, her subconscious, she probably does not even find it hard to go within before coming out. Since Uranus rules her 10th house of career and status, she knows that she is going to use her uniqueness in her profession. Therefore, the two retrograde planets are probably helpful to her.

Answer to Review Question · Lesson 8

Interceptions · Bob Dylan: Bob Dylan has Pisces intercepted in the 3rd house and Virgo intercepted in the 9th house. These two houses cover an arc of more than 53° each, which is quite large and will innately push Dylan in the direction of communication and religion, both keywords for the 3rd and 9th houses. Four planets are involved here: Uranus, ruler of the 3rd house cusp, Neptune, ruler of the interception, the Sun, ruler of the 9th house cusp, and Mercury, ruler of that interception. Uranus, the Sun and Mercury are part of a tight grouping of planets occupying the 5th house of creativity, the 6th house of work and the 7th house of partners and the public while Neptune not only rules an intercepted house, but is itself intercepted in the 9th house; it is also retrograde. This could show that some of his ideas and ideals and creative efforts may have seen delays and he may have felt much hesitancy in expressing his real thoughts openly, especially since Mars is intercepted in the 3rd house. But that same Mars also gives him the energy to work hard for success, particularly since it squares the Sun and therefore challenges him into action.

Dylan should use his 9th house in order to work out his tensions and frustrations, but since the chart emphasis is in the 5th and 6th houses (6 planets in those 2 houses), the energies will have to come from creativity, fun and games and romance and possibly children (5th house matters) and of course hard work (6th house). But work will never seem that hard to him with Jupiter, the Sun and Venus in that house.

Not only is the action in the 5th and 6th house because of the many planets involved, but also because these houses are linked together by the same sign Taurus - on the cusps. Dylan most certainly works in a creative field and he may eventually give service through his religious work to young people, as we suggest in our explanation of the linking of these two houses. Of course the 11th and 12th houses are also tied together with Scorpio on both cusps. Since Dylan found religion he has done much charitable work, and with Pluto, ruler of Scorpio, in the 8th house, he should continue to get public support for his endeavors, especially if he makes the necessary adjustments in the way he communicates to those whose support he is seeking (Pluto inconjunct Mars in the 3rd house).

Since the preceding interpretation needs confirmation, and the whole chart should be considered, make a few notes as you look at Bob Dylan's horoscope. Realize that Neptune is the highest planet in the chart, that it is retrograde, that there is a final dispositor, no cardinal planets, quite a few planets in critical degrees, some fixed stars, and other factors that make Bob Dylan the unique person he is.

Answer to Review Question - Lesson 9

Mutual Reception - Farrah Fawcett: Farrah Fawcett has a mutual reception between Mercury in Aquarius in the 8th house and Uranus in Gemini in the 12th house. Mercury is exalted in Aquarius. It is trine to Uranus which rules Mercury. Even without the mutual reception, the Mercury-Uranus relationship is rather benefic. Mercury functions well even without this added boon. Uranus, on the other hand, truly benefits through the mutual reception. In Gemini, Uranus tends to fly off in all directions. The person who has it is inclined to start too many things without finishing any of them. Uranus here is almost too mental. In the 12th house and retrograde, Uranus' energies can be too inner-oriented. Uranus trines the Sun and Mercury and gives a fantastic mind and indicates a truly intelligent, even an intellectual, person - but the 12th house Pisces overlay and the retrograde tend to put a veil over her real personality; "What you see is not at all what you get". Her mutual reception helps to bring out the most positive expression of Uranus. Instead of fleeing into a dream world, or refusing to see herself for what she is, she is using the veil by hiding behind a role. Farrah is an actress and the public sees her in whatever role she decides to play. But she does not have to hide from herself.

Final dispositor: Walt Disney's Sun is in Sagittarius, ruled by Jupiter in Capricorn ruled by Saturn in Capricorn. His Moon is in Libra, ruled by Venus in Capricorn, bringing us back to Saturn. His Mercury in Scorpio leads to Pluto in Gemini - a mutual reception - so we have no final dispositor. To briefly see what else happens in his chart, Neptune in Cancer is ruled by the Moon, which brings us back to Venus and Saturn. That takes care of all the planets and signs and shows us that Disney has Saturn in dignity and a mutual reception.

Joan Sutherland's Sun is in Scorpio, ruled by Pluto in Cancer, ruled by the Moon in Sagittarius, ruled by Jupiter in Aquarius, ruled by Uranus in Pisces, ruled by Neptune in Leo, taking us back to the Sun in Scorpio, and around and around without getting anywhere else. The only planet not accounted for is Mars, which is ruled by Venus in Scorpio, leading back into the unending circle. Result: No final dispositor.

Farrah Fawcett's Sun in Aquarius is ruled by Uranus in Gemini, leading to Mercury in Aquarius, a mutual reception, and back in a circle. Her Moon is dignified and stands by itself. The two Leo planets lead back to her Sun. Jupiter in Scorpio leads back to Pluto in Leo, back to her Sun. Neptune in Libra leads to Venus in Sagittarius, back to Jupiter and so on — no planet is a final dispositor.

The Chart Ruler - Walt Disney: Walt Disney has Virgo on the Ascendant; its ruler Mercury is in Scorpio in the 3rd house. The need to communicate is important, so are mental pursuits, but in Scorpio the thinking is deep and probing, the communication can be incisive, even sarcastic at times. Superimpose that feeling on analytical, and at times critical Virgo and you know that Disney said what he thought in no uncertain terms. But, the sextile to Venus made it bearable. People would not get too offended because he could charm his way into their hearts. The Moon in Libra in the 1st house confirms this. The Ruler of the Ascendant in the 3rd house often indicates more than average dealings with siblings. In Disney's case, his brother, Roy, played a most important role in Walt's life; Roy was the businessman behind the entire Disney organization, enabling Walt to express his creative and artistic talents while Roy took care of everything else.

Answer to Review Question · Lesson 10

Bundle Pattern · Jean-Claude Killy: As the name for this pattern implies, all of the planets are bundled or bunched together in the tight confines of a trine. In Killy's case, this is an exact trine from Mercury to Mars. Since Killy's chart is so tightly concentrated, there can be little integration with the many empty houses, no configurations, not even an opposition is possible with this type of chart. This lack of awareness, even the lack of needing others, results in a rather self-centered person, and all of the energies are concentrated in those areas where the planets are located. In Killy's case, we are talking of the 10th, 11th, 12th, 1st and 2nd houses.

We know that in Astrology we need something to push us into using a trine or sextile. If there is no opposition, we have to look for a strong stellium or some squares. The square closest in orb (Killy's chart has no real stellium) will be the planet that propels us to act - the trigger planet as Marc Edmund Jones calls it. Killy has a tight square (2° orb) between his Sun at 5° Virgo in the 1st house and Mars at 3° Gemini in the 10th house. To give Mars even more importance and challenge, it squares the Moon, is conjunct Uranus, and is the highest planet in Killy's horoscope. Mars is placed in the 10th house, which it rules. Therefore, we can see what pushes Killy to work as hard as he does, to be as ambitious as he is. We know that Leo rising likes to do things that are rather showy and dramatic, which skiing most certainly is, especially the way Killy zooms downhill.

The bundle pattern very often has another effect. As the native succeeds in doing whatever it is he has set out to do, the need to get out of the tight confines and explore the big wide world represented by the empty houses pulls him toward the affairs of these houses. But, since he sees the world only his way, instead of fitting himself into other people's ways and actions, he will inveigle others to see it his way, and therefore he will always be considered a leader - rarely a follower. Killy is still too young to have demonstrated what he will do with the rest of his life, and which course he will follow; he is a very good businessman too, quite money hungry, and he should do well in some area of show business. He has already appeared in several U.S. TV commercials.

At the risk of boring you and sounding very repetitious - the keywords and key sentences we give you for chart patterns (and for everything else for that matter) ARE GUIDELINES ONLY! THEY SHOULD NEVER BE USED WITHOUT TAKING THE ENTIRE HOROSCOPE INTO CONSIDERATION!

A Chart Pattern may be important, but *whatever shows has to also be confirmed somewhere else in the chart.* Please remember that as you delineate.

Answer to Review Question · Lesson 11

Chart Overview · Joan Sutherland: Four planets East and six planets West is basically no important division, but in this case the six planets West include her Sun, Moon, chart ruler (Venus), and Mercury; therefore, we know that relating to others and pleasing others is very important to Joan Sutherland. With seven planets above and only three planets below the horizon, we understand that the need to become somebody, to have a public career and elevate herself above her birth position is meaningful to her. This also shows the ability to be outgoing and objective. This last fact needs to be evaluated though, since Scorpio is not the most objective sign in the zodiac. Final judgment of this should be reserved until the chart has been delineated.

There is no obvious planetary pattern; it does not qualify as a true splash since there are too many conjunctions.

Her qualities show a definite trend to fixed; there is only one cardinal planet, but she does have six planets in angular houses. This well compensates for the cardinal lack. Not enough drive is *not* one of her problems. Mars in the 1st house would confirm this. The elements show a preponderance of water, with earth and air being rather scarce. The Air feeling is amply supplied by five planets in the houses of relationships, whereas the single Earth planet is compensated for by the Ascendant in Taurus. Therefore, despite an imbalance at first glance, upon more careful scrutiny we realize that Sutherland's elements are well distributed and she can use all four of them as needed. Her final signature is Scorpio (fixed-water), which shows rather obviously with three planets in this sign. There is no final dispositor, no mutual reception, and no interception.

Venus is the chart ruler. It is in the 7th house, thus, partners and the public become very important to her. With Venus conjunct the Sun she is able to shine with a partner and the public. Being in Scorpio, she would take it all quite seriously and feel very deeply. Venus is not terribly happy in Scorpio (the sign of its detriment), but Venus does feel very much at ease in the 7th house where it is accidentally dignified (Venus rules Libra). The blend of the detriment and accidental dignity, Venus' easy conjunction to the Sun and more difficult opposition to Mars all have to be taken into consideration when interpreting Joan's horoscope.

Joan Sutherland has no planets in dignity, exaltation, or in fall. Venus, Mercury and Mars are in their detriment. Just like Venus, Mars is also accidentally dignified by house position (1st house/Aries), which makes Mars' energy easier to handle. Mercury can become quite scattered in Sagittarius, but with so many fixed planets in her chart, Mercury is really more of a blessing than a detriment: it lightens the otherwise too serious and too sensitive traits, which is particularly helpful since Mercury rules her 5th house of love and creativity as well as her 2nd house of values.

She has a very important configuration, a T-square which involves Venus and the Sun, both opposing Mars, and all squaring Jupiter. First of all, this draws the 1st, 7th, and 10th houses together; secondly, it is even more important in her case since the 3 houses involved are all angular houses - the houses of action. Third, three personal planets are involved in this configuration, showing that she has to react to these aspects at a early age. The Sun, Venus, and Mars all have flowing aspects to Pluto, so this becomes the avenue through which she should use the energy generated by the T-square. Pluto rules her three Scorpio planets. It is placed in the 3rd house of communication and we would say that she uses these energies quite positively.

We have already discussed the retrograde Mars and Uranus in Lesson Six. Pluto retrograde does not add much to the general overview either.

The most exact aspect in Sutherland's chart is a square between Saturn and Neptune, giving her the ability to use all her creative talent in a most disciplined way and in a concrete manner. Also exact is the opposition from Venus to Mars, pulling her in two directions (self vs. others or partners), but also enabling her to become aware of her needs involving others. The inconjunct between Uranus and Neptune is also quite close; it forces her to make adjustments or compromises between her home and homelife and all 11th house matters, which probably included her friends at an earlier age, and large organizations (such as opera companies) in her later years.

Be sure to keep this overview in mind as you interpret each planet and house.

Answers to Review Questions · Lesson 12

Decanates · Hermann Hesse (Sun):   Hermann Hesse's Sun at 10° ♋ 52' is in the second or Scorpio decanate, ruled by Pluto in Taurus in the 5th house. To the feeling and rather sensitive Sun we now add a Scorpio overtone, making it deeper yet, more probing, and also more demanding. Pluto, ruler of the decanate, is in Taurus in the 5th house giving an overlay of values, practicality and the creativity innate in the 5th house. The 7th house (Libra) position of the Sun already has overtones of needing balance, needing to relate, so we are dealing with a rather complex inner person; all the sensitivities of the water elements (the Sun makes a very close trine to Mars in Pisces), yet the need to be approved of by others. Hesse is intense in his wish to create (Pluto in the 5th house), and the opportunity to do so (Sun sextile Neptune), yet often held back by his wish to please others or balance his needs to fit into the needs of partners (7th house Sun). By adding the Scorpio decanate to his Sun, we can now realize how important Pluto is in the chart, and we can understand the deep turmoil ever present in Hesse, yet mostly hidden behind a rather friendly, optimistic and idealistic Sagittarius mask.

Dwads · Farrah Fawcett (Moon):   Farrah Fawcett's Moon at 4° ♋ 39' is in the Leo dwad. This adds quite a bit of drama and showiness to her Cancer Moon. The Moon is happy in Cancer because it is dignified here. Emotionally, she is sensitive, and since the Moon sits just behind her Ascendant, or in the 12th house, she is also very intuitive. However, this position can make her rather passive, especially since the Moon does not have many aspects to it. The Leo dwad helps her to come out, it adds self-reliance and a romantic dash.

Farrah's Ascendant at 5°♋26' falls in the next dwad, namely Virgo. To the Cancer nature, ruled by the Moon in Cancer, we now add an overlay of practical, analytical Virgo, enabling her to put into practical use some of the attributes promised by the Ascendant.

Answer to Review Question · Lesson 13

The Moon's Nodes · Walt Disney: Walt Disney's Mean North Node is at 11° ♍ 56' his True North Node at 13° ♍ 20' in the 2nd house; the South Node is, of course, at 11°♉56' or 13°♉20' in opposition in the 8th house. Interpreting the houses in one way, you might say that Walt Disney was more at home in occult matters, or that sex was very important to him and he should strive to earn his own money. But you need to look at the entire chart before you make any such statement. Sex does not look like a subject that was uppermost in Disney's mind, nor was the occult. A better interpretation is that Disney probably relied on other people's resources until he finally realized that he could stand on his own feet, find his own set of values and act upon them—and as the result, he was able to make very good money and develop his self worth.

Answer to Review Question · Lesson 14

Walt Disney's 5th house cusp delineated: Since creativity seems to be so important in Walt Disney's chart, the 5th house should give us a good indication of it. With Capricorn on the cusp and its ruler, Saturn, dignified in Capricorn and placed in the 4th house, we know that 5th house matters are a most basic part of his nature, nearly a necessity. Since Saturn is conjunct Jupiter, which gives him the ability to expand, and also conjunct Mars, the planet of action and drive, we realize that all 5th house matters were most important from an early age. Saturn squares the Moon; he probably felt a lack of tenderness from the parents, particularly the mother (Venus is in Capricorn). It is quite common that this feeling of denial - and we say feeling because this is the way the child feels, not necessarily the way the parents really behave - leads to a double ambition to prove oneself, especially in a chart like Disney's where there is a stellium in Capricorn.

Apart from his creative ability and need to express it and succeed, which of the guidelines we indicated for Capricorn on the 5th house apply to this chart? A cold exterior in showing his love? Probably, but softened considerably by the ruler of the Ascendant in Scorpio and Sun in Sagittarius. Trustworthy? Yes. Stern disciplinarian and not a giver by nature? Pretty stern and quite demanding, but softened also by the same aspects cited above. Works hard for everything and feels that he deserves what he gets? Definitely. According to his chart, he worked very hard for all that he achieved.

Be sure to remember that Venus is in the 5th house, and that wherever Venus is placed in the chart indicates what we like to do. Venus is also involved in the yod previously discussed and therefore plays a very important role in the chart. Since Venus is also in Capricorn, it substantiates the fact that whatever efforts Disney puts forth should bring him tangible results.

Answer to Review Question - Lesson 15

Aspects to the Ascendant & Midheaven - Walt Disney

Venus Trine the Ascendant: Disney's Venus trines his Ascendant from the 5th house; both planets are in earth signs. This earthy element, plus the Capricorn stellium and final signature of Capricorn, eliminates any possibility of laziness. With the Moon in Libra in the 1st house he is charming and, with Sagittarius on the cusp of the 4th, a good host. Friends, siblings and children mean a great deal to him as shown by Venus in the 5th which represents children. He enjoys being with them but in a disciplined, Capricornian way. Siblings are represented by the 3rd house where we find the Sun, Mercury and Uranus, confirming the fact that siblings are important here. All the words regarding talent and creativity have been confirmed many times before, so we know that they will apply.

Pluto and Neptune Conjunct the Midheaven: The orbs here exceed 6°; keep this in mind as you delineate. Whatever importance we give these aspects has to be modified by the orb in question. Some of the strength of a conjunction lessens as the width of the orb increases from 0°, despite the fact that Pluto and the Midheaven are both in Gemini. It is also a good idea to remember that a planet coming to the Midheaven from the 9th house will work differently from a planet placed in the 10th house (Neptune is in the 10th - Pluto is in the 9th). Now, with all of these admonitions in mind, let's see which of the keywords apply to Disney.

Starting first with Neptune. Glamor is meant more for the female of the species; a compelling, charismatic personality most certainly would apply here. We all know of his career in TV and motion pictures. Since he used his energies in that direction, we do not concern ourselves with photography or shipping or oil. With the rest of the chart in mind, we feel that he could have done some writing if he had wished to, but since Disney was a very successful and busy man, he probably did not find the necessary time to do so. With a Capricorn stellium in the 4th house there was a tendency to get depressed when things didn't go his way immediately. Whether he let this get him down periodically, or whether he learned to overcome it at an early age, we do not know. Any psychic inclinations would probably be disregarded with Virgo rising and Capricorn so strong in his chart, but his intuition should be very good and prove to be quite useful in many areas of his life. And after all, his production of "Fantasia" was one of his most successful pictures.

Pluto is conjunct the Midheaven from the 9th house, so all keywords have to be very carefully analyzed here before you use them. The need to go your own way and to be a leader is there, but instead of leading people Disney decided to be a leader in the application of his talents and ensuing career. In other words, he blended the idealism of the 9th house with the need to lead inherent in the conjunction to the Midheaven. Since the entire sentence regarding parental relationships relates to a 10th house Pluto, we disregard it. As to change of direction in the lifetime, Disney most certainly went through this when he switched his considerable talents to an amusement park and to television, probably never realizing that this would become an all encompassing endeavor until it became so.

Answers to Quiz Part Two

1. False
2. True
3. False
4. False
5. False
6. True
7. True
8. True
9. True
10. False
11. True
12. False
13. True
14. False
15. True
16. False
17. True
18. False
19. False
20. True
21. True

Answer to Review Question · Lesson 16

Planets in Oriental Appearance · Joan Sutherland: In Joan Sutherland's chart Venus is the planet in oriental appearance, having risen just before the Sun. Venus now assumes additional importance, not only because it is the chart ruler (Taurus rising, ruled by Venus), and because it is in an angular house which always emphasizes a planet, but also because we now realize that Venus and whatever it stands for in her chart will show some psychological factors that motivate her. Venus stands for values, affection, love in its purest connotation, artistic talents and the social urges. In the 7th house, we realize that whatever she does will be motivated by a partner or by the public. In her case, it's both. Joan is, of course, a very public person, devoting her life to her career as an opera singer, but interestingly enough, she never sings anywhere without her conductor-husband, Richard Bonynge in charge, whether it is a concert, opera, or recording session.

Pre-Natal Eclipse Point · Sutherland and Disney: Joan Sutherland's pre-natal eclipse point is at 1 Aquarius 22. It falls in her 9th house, conjunct the Midheaven, confirming that a career is important to her; especially one in which she can travel the world. This lunar eclipse in Aquarius also marks the uniqueness of her profession.

Walt Disney's pre-natal solar eclipse point is at 18° Scorpio, in his 2nd house.

The Vertex · Disney: Walt Disney's 4th house cusp is 24° Sagittarius. Find that as the M.C. in the Table of Houses. (In Koch, on page 137). His natal latitude of 41°N53', when subtracted from 90° becomes 48°N07'. Go down to 48°N on page 137. Look in the Ascendant column and you will see 16° ♓ 23'. This is Disney's vertex point. It falls in his 6th house.

Lesson 17 · Calculations of the Parts of Fortune and Spirit.

The Parts of Fortune and Spirit for Walt Disney, Hermann Hesse and Farrah Fawcett.

Part of Fortune ⊗	Walt Disney	Hermann Hesse	Farrah Fawcett
Ascendant	5^S 24° 53'	8^S 21° 20'	3^S 5° 26'
+ Moon	6^S 9° 07'	11^S 28° 16'	3^S 4° 39'
	11^S 33° 60'	19^S 49° 36'	6^S 9° 65'
− Sun	8^S 12° 26'	3^S 10° 52'	10^S 13° 11'
	3^S 21° 34'	16^S 38° 44'	7^S 26° 54'
		17^S 8° 44'*	
		5^S 8° 44'	
	21° ♋ 34'	8° ♍ 44'	26° ♍ 54'

Part of Spirit ⊕			
Ascendant	5^S 24° 53'	8^S 21° 20'	3^S 5° 26'
+ Sun	8^S 12° 26'	3^S 10° 52'	10^S 13° 11'
	13^S 36° 79'	11^S 31° 72'	13^S 18° 37'
− Moon	6^S 9° 07'	11^S 28° 16'	3^S 4° 39'
	7^S 27° 72'	0^S 3° 56'	10^S 13° 58'
	7^S 28° 12'		
	28° ♍ 12'	3° ♈ 56'	13° ♒ 58'

*There are only 12 signs of the zodiac, therefore we subtract 12 from 17 to find the correct sign.

Answers to Review Questions · Lesson 18

The Fixed Stars · Sutherland and Fawcett: In Joan Sutherland's chart the Fixed Star ACRUX is conjunct her Venus. It is now at 11° ♏ 29'; when she was born in 1926, it was at approximately 10°♏45', and was most certainly in orb. We don't know whether Sutherland has any occult or religious leanings, but we can confirm that the Femme Fatale image applies, maybe not in its sexual implication, but certainly as a most statuesque and intriguing personality to whom the public is strongly attracted.

For Farrah Fawcett the Fixed Star MARKAB is conjunct her Midheaven. She was born in 1947 when Markab was at approximately 22° ♓ 41', within orb. We know that she has received honors and riches, or in today's terms - she's famous! We do not know how much sorrow she has suffered or may yet suffer, but the rest of her chart will give some indication as to how she would handle any sorrows that may come her way. You may note that we did not use the Fixed Stars ALDEBARAN or ANTARES conjunct her North and South Nodes of the Moon. We have found that Fixed Stars seem most potent when they are conjunct a planet, the Ascendant, or the Midheaven, and not very important when conjunct one of the Nodes, the other house cusps, Arabic Points or other points. But, please do not take our word for this; try it out for yourself.

Critical Degrees · Hermann Hesse: In Hesse's chart, only one planet is truly on a critical degree—Venus, at 26° ♋ 12'. The nodes are on the critical degree for mutable signs, but we do not consider the Nodes to be planets. Some astrologers include the Nodes in critical degrees, in chart patterns, in configurations, and so on. We do not. Here again, we urge you to try this for yourself and use whatever seems to work best for you.

Venus is not one of the strongest planets in Hesse's chart. It is not angular, nor dignified or exalted. It has no squares to challenge it into action, and no oppositions or conjunctions. Yet, Venus rules Hesse's 5th house of creativity as well as his 10th house of career, status and ego. Where does it gain its strength to utilize the trines to the Moon and Saturn and the sextile to Pluto? Because we know that Hesse used Venus in all his work, his writings, his poetry, his painting, and even his love of nature and gardening. One answer, of couse, lies in the yod (Jupiter/Venus/Pluto), but the additional emphasis of sensitivity created by the critical degree also helped. It gives us the confirmation we always look for in astrological delineation.

Meet The Authors

Marion March and Joan McEvers are the co-founders of Aquarius Workshops Inc., a non-profit corporation, in the San Fernando Valley of Los Angeles. They organized Aquarius Workshops to promote a positive approach to Astrology through research, teaching, lecturing and practice, to promote a correct legal status for legitimate astrological practice, and to establish high professional standards of competence. That this organization has attained a respected national reputation is indicated through its members all over the United States, and internationally. Their quarterly publication, "Aspects", is widely recognized for the wealth of astrological information contained in each issue.

Both Marion and Joan have achieved a national reputation as teachers and lecturers. Many have come to know them through their lectures and workshops at such national conventions as the American Federation of Astrologers, the International Society for Astrological Research, and the annual Southwestern Astrology Conference. Both remain active as teachers, continuing to lecture and teach to overflow classes. Joan McEvers recently moved to Coeur D'Alene, Idaho near the Spokane, Washington area. The response she received here has been as great and as welcome as that which she experienced in Los Angeles .

Both Joan and Marion started their serious study of Astrology in 1965. Marion's first teacher was one of Los Angeles' better known teachers - Kiyo. It was in 1969 that Marion and Joan first met while taking an intermediate course in Astrology with Ruth Hale Oliver. Later, both studied together with other fine teachers. It was during this time that they decided to pool their resources and their notes. Together they formulated a very successful teaching outline, which was quickly adopted by the professional teachers of Aquarius Workshops, and ultimately resulted in the writing and publication of this series of books. Their basic philosophy "A Positive Approach to Astrology", is incorporated in the motto of Aquarius Workshops and in these books. Since their first publication, many teachers of astrology around the world have adopted them as their official text for beginning courses in astrology.

MARION MARCH was born on February 10, 1923, in Nurenberg, Germany. Until the outbreak of the Second World War she lived in Ascona, Switzerland, moving to the United States in the summer of 1941. After a brief stage and film career in the mid 1940's she later returned to Switzerland in 1947 where she worked for the Foreign Service and met her husband, Nico. They were married in 1948 and shortly thereafter returned to this country. Here they raised two children, who are now grown; Michele is a pediatric nurse practitioner, now married with 2 children and living in Monte Carlo and Nick is working in the field of Oceanography and under-water studies. Coming from a respected family of European bankers on her father's side and publishers on her mother's side, Marion's early life provided her with a rich exposure to many of the world's top writers, artists and musicians. Her father's interest in Eastern philosophies led them both to the Vedanta center. Marion and Nico are very active in all cultural happenings in Los Angeles and do quite a bit of traveling "so we don't forget all of our foreign languages" as Marion jokingly says; in fact she does a lot of European lecturing now.

JOAN McEVERS was born 2/7/25 and raised in Chicago, Illinois. She majored in art and attended the Art Institute in Chicago for nearly four years. Her first job was for Vogue Wright Art Studio as a spot illustrator, lay-out and paste-up artist and model. Joan moved to the Los Angeles area in November, 1948, where she continued her professional career in the field of sales. It was in Los Angeles that she met her husband, Dean, and raised their four children. In 1977 they moved their family to Coeur D'Alene, Idaho, where Joan now has a busy astrological practice as a consultant and teacher, and has organized a group known as Astrology Now. A daughter, Bridget in high school and a son, Daren in college keep her busy. Two older sons, Woody and Brent are businessmen; Woody in Palm Springs, Brent in Thousand Oaks, California.

Both authors are professional members and supporters of the American Federation of Astrologers, and both have taken a very active role in supporting efforts to legalize the practice of astrology. Through their efforts in Aquarius Workshops they have brought to the Los Angeles astrological community many of the world's leading experts and teachers for lectures and workshops. Both were born with their Sun in Aquarius, which accounts in part for the name of the professional organization that they have founded and developed.

It is with great pride that Astro Computing Services presents this series of textbooks for the beginning and intermediate students of astrology everywhere. The dedication and the devotion of these two fine teachers continues to move Astrology to the point of far greater public acceptance and understanding that it so rightly deserves.

We calculate... You delineate!